BABY
BOOMERS

PAUL C. LIGHT

BABY BOOMERS

W · W · NORTON & COMPANY

NEW YORK · LONDON

First published as a Norton paperback 1990

The text of this book is composed in Janson Alternate, with display type set in Bembo and Benguiat. Composition and manufacturing by the Haddon Craftsmen.

Library of Congress Cataloging in Publication Data

Light, Paul Charles.
  Baby boomers / Paul Charles Light.
    p. cm.
    Includes index.
1. Baby boom generation—United States.   2. United States—Social conditions—
1980-   3. United States—Economic conditions—1981-   4. United States—
Politics and government—1981-   I. Title. HN59.2.L54   1988
305.2′4—dc19   87—25653

ISBN 0-393-30639-9

W. W. Norton & Company, Inc., 500 Fifth Avenue, New York, N.Y. 10110
W. W. Norton & Company Ltd., 37 Great Russell Street, London WC1B 3NU

2 3 4 5 6 7 8 9 0

To Mark Joseph Light,
the first baby boomer I ever met,
and my dearest friend still.

Contents

Introduction

A T SEVENTY-FIVE MILLION STRONG, the baby boomers packed the maternity wards as infants, the classrooms as children, and the campuses, employment lines, and mortgage markets as young adults. Born between 1946 and 1964, they are members of one of the largest generations in U.S. history. To the extent seventy-five million people think alike, they define the contemporary culture. To the extent they buy alike, they shape the economy. To the extent they are both preceded and followed by much smaller generations, they stand out in sharp contrast to those around them. It has been that way for the past four decades, and it's likely to stay that way for the next six.

Yet, the baby boomers have not quite decided whether they are members of a distinctive generation, bound together by history and demography, or merely a collection of small groups and individuals who just happen to share the same birthday.

On the one hand, the baby boomers belong to one of the most diverse generations in history. Some baby boomers are rich, others poor. Some are black, others white. Not all went to college—some served in Vietnam instead, some went straight to work. Nor did all baby boomers get good jobs—some are still caught in the American underclass of the unemployed, others are stranded in dead-end jobs, trapped behind other baby boomers. Though it has become fashionable to warn of impending conflict between the young and the old over Social Security and taxes, it is far more likely that the baby boomers will divide against themselves in an intragenerational war between the haves and the have-nots. To the extent these divisions come to the surface in the future, the baby boom will be a generation divided against itself.

On the other hand, the baby boomers have much in common. They grew up as the first standardized generation, drawn together by the history around them, the intimacy of television, and the crowding that came from the sheer onslaught of other baby boomers. They shared the great economic expectations of the 1950s and the fears that came with Sputnik and the dawn of the nuclear era. They shared the hopes of John F. Kennedy's New Frontier and Lyndon Johnson's Great Society, and the disillusionment that came with the assassinations, Vietnam, Watergate, and the resignations. To the extent these memories remain fresh, the baby boom will be a generation united.

So which is the real baby boom? The generation divided or the generation united? At times, the baby boomers show glimpses of unity and a deep sense of social commitment. At times, they show great apathy and disengagement. The baby boomers remain the unseen players in a twenty-year political and social version of "Waiting for Godot."

One place to start a book about the baby boom's future is with the baby boom's past and present. Even before *Time* named the generation "Man of the Year" in 1965, the baby boomers were an easy target for caricature. Even to today, they are better known by the tiny number of yuppies than by the much larger number of blue-collar workers and moderate-income families. Chapter One debunks the caricatures by asking some basic questions about the real baby boomers. Where did the baby boomers come from? How have they differed from people who came both before and after, and why? What was so special about their childhoods anyway?

Chapter Two continues the search for the real baby boomers by addressing the growing worry about intergenerational warfare. Because of their size, the baby boomers have been locked in a perpetual buyer's labor pool and seller's housing market: they make less but are paying more. Compared to their parents at the same stage of life, the baby boomers are in financial trouble. That does not mean, however, that the baby boomers are competing with their parents or grandparents. Are there real economic problems within the baby boom? Absolutely. Do the baby boomers want to solve those problems by cutting Social Security and Medicare for their parents and grandparents? Absolutely not.

Baby boomers themselves are not alike. The younger baby boomers are different from their older siblings; women are different from men; those who completed a year or more of college are different from those who did not; the rich are different from the poor and disappearing middle class; and those who served in Vietnam are very different from those who protested. Such diversity can be a source of great generational pride. But as Chapter Three suggests, it can also be a source of great polarization. Indeed, the greatest gaps exist within the baby boom, not between the baby boomers and their parents and grandparents. The baby boom's gender gap, for example, is unparalleled by other generations, and will likely widen in the future.

Nevertheless, the baby boomers do share some common ground. They grew up in the standardized kitchens and houses that came with the building codes of the 1940s, studied the standarized curricula that came with the drive for universal access to education of the 1950s, and lived with the standardized fear that came with atomic bomb drills and the Vietnam War in the 1960s. They were battered by the nonstop advertising that catered to the material joys of owning rather than the status of keeping up with the Joneses, and the nonstop crowding that created a deep need for privacy and individual distinction. There is no doubt that the baby boomers shared a unique childhood and adolescence which marks them even today. Chapter Four analyzes those early memories in an effort to understand why the baby boomers remain so focused on the short term.

The question is whether the baby boom's past makes any difference today. Chapter Five provides a first answer in a portrait of the baby boom's separation from political and social traditions. Not only have the baby boomers abandoned the traditional meanings of marriage, parenthood, and work, they have even become very different consumers from their elders. They don't buy products on the basis of habit or brand-name loyalty. Nor do they automatically pick politicians from the party slate. This separation reflects more than a distaste for social labels and a deep distrust of leaders and institutions, however. As Chapter Six suggests, the baby boom's separation also involves a rejection of party identification as a basis for political decisions and an abiding commitment to individualism, self-reliance, and introspection as a generational style for solving problems.

The baby boomers did not start out this way, of course. Early studies showed a generation well on its way toward a traditional attachment to politics and society. As the portrait of separation shows, however, the cumulative result of three assassinations, the Vietnam War, Watergate, two OPEC oil embargoes, two Social Security crises, and countless calls for political and social reform is a generation with little interest in the national community. Perhaps the baby boomers ask "what have you done for me lately" because they don't believe their leaders and institutions can be trusted for much longer.

So what is a political party or candidate to do? If they want to reconnect the generation to the national community and build in them a commitment to the long term, the first step is to understand that the baby boomers retain much of their earlier liberalism, albeit tempered by age and experience. The second step is to acknowledge that the baby boomers do not talk in traditional "liberal" or "conservative" terms. Rather, as Chapter Seven concludes, the baby boomers appear to think about politics in three dimensions: *a search for personal opportunity and space,* which emerges from their crowding and poor economic performance, *a search for safety*, which emerges from their fears of crime and nuclear war, and a renewed *search for meaning*, which emerges from a growing frustration with self-interest. To the extent that future campaigns focus on issues in these three dimensions, the baby boomers may begin to bring their formidable concern with performance to bear on political issues that affect their long-term needs.

There is not much a party or candidate can do if the baby boomers do not have the forbearance to invest in a long-term agenda. Yet, forbearance is exactly what the baby boomers will need most to make it through the next two decades. Every generation has its golden days of peak earning power and political influence. Every generation also has its days of crisis and bad luck. Unfortunately for the baby boomers, the days of crisis may well overlap with the golden days. Many will soon find themselves locked into frustrating job plateaus with no promotions in sight. Many will also find themselves stuck with the bills for national infrastructure renewal and the budget debt. As Chapter Eight suggests, even if the parties and candidates stay with their short-term sales pitch, the baby boomers need to adopt a "what-will-you-do-for-all-of-us-tomorrow" approach to politics. That is the only way to solve the problems the baby boomers face.

By 2016, of course, all of these questions about the baby boomers will have been answered. America will know whether the baby boomers ever made a difference. By 2016, for example, the baby boomers will have cast perhaps 700 million votes. The question is whether those votes will add up to anything more than a series of short-term, image elections. Eventually, the baby boomers may be held accountable by their own children and grandchildren for what they did or did not do with their great potential. Indeed, as Chapter Nine concludes, the election of 2016 may be the first election in history that will be more a referendum on a generation than on a party or candidate.

Acknowledgments

Thus book could not have been written without the help of many friends, some baby boomers, some not. Rudy Bauer, Gary Bryner, Sharon Caudle, Linda Fisher, Rich Greenough, Robert Katzmann, Celinda Lake, Burdette Loomis, G. Calvin Mackenzie, Gerry McCauley, Katie Nelson, Carole Neves, David O'Brien, Stephen Wayne, and James Wolf, all enriched this book with their insights. My editors at Norton, Linda Healey, Donald Fusting, and Marjorie Brassil also added immensely to the book. None of these individuals bears any responsibility for the mistakes and misunderstandings in this book, of course, but they all deserve my thanks.

Further, I could not have written this book without the training I received at Macalester College and the University of Michigan where I had the opportunity to learn about political and social behavior from some of the finest scholars in the United States, people like Charles Green, Hans Wendt, Joseph Veroff, John Kingdon, Jack Walker, Elizabeth Douvan, Gregory Markus, Warren Miller, and Arthur Miller. It was an education that hopefully suited me well in this project.

Finally, my wife and friend, Sharon Pamepinto has my deepest gratitude for her patience as an editor. The book could not have been written without her.

BABY BOOMERS

1

The Real Baby Boomers

THIS BOOK is about the real baby boomers—not just the young, urban professionals; not just their grim, ruthless, upwardly mobile peers; not just their dual-income, childless neighbors. It is not that the yuppies, grumpies, and dinks don't exist. It is just that they are such a small part of a very large generation.

The fact is that the baby boom is both big and wide, covering seventy-five million children born over a span from 1946 to 1964. It includes some who came of political age with Sputnik and the civil rights movement, others who grew up with Vietnam and Earth Day, and still others who awoke with Watergate and the OPEC oil embargo. Some were on the front-lines of the 1960s both here and in Vietnam, some merely watched on television, and still others have yet to rent the video cassette.

Unfortunately, diversity is the enemy of simplicity, making the baby boom an easy target for caricature. As a result, the baby boomers have always been known by a handful of stereotypes—hippies in the 1960s, yuppies in the 1980s. Ask the average American to define the baby boom of today, and he or she will likely think of yuppies or grumpies on Wall Street, or dinks in the suburbs, long before remembering the real people just down the street.

Each caricature describes a slightly different version of the same white, affluent baby boomer. Grumpies are aggressive consumers willing to give up personal service for a lower price; dinks are basically yuppies who marry and commute. Though the majority of baby boomers make less than $30,000 per year, the generation has always been known by this small band of high-income shoppers because it is easier to know a small group of highly visible consumers than a large number of diverse individuals.

That is how it was in 1965 when *Time* named the entire baby boom "Man of the Year," focusing almost exclusively on the future yuppies: "Cushioned by unprecedented affluence and the welfare state, he has a sense of economic security unmatched in history. Granted an ever-lengthening adolescence and lifespan, he no longer feels the cold pressures of hunger and mortality that drove Mozart to compose an entire canon before death at 35."

The problem with *Time*'s portrait is not that most baby boomers were poor. The 1950s and early 1960s were years of exceptional economic growth. It's just that *Time* missed the baby boomers who were passed over. There was no mention of black baby boomers in America's ghettos. Nor any mention of the 200,000 or so baby boomers already in Vietnam. And by naming the generation "Man of the Year," *Time* ignored baby-boom women, who just happened to be in the generation's majority.

Twenty years later, *Time* still stayed with the yuppie stereotype in wishing the entire baby boom a happy 40th birthday: "From the first, the Baby Boomers were accustomed to instant gratification. Hopping from one instant fad to another—from Davy Crockett coonskin caps to Hula-Hoops—they moved as a single mass, conditioned to think alike and do alike. Trendiness became a generation hallmark: from pot to yoga to jogging, they embraced the In thing of the moment and then quickly chucked it for another." What a way to say happy birthday, especially to the 25 million baby boomers who were born after Davy Crocket left the air, and the 25 million who never had the money to jump from fad to fad in the first place.

It is not that the caricatures are entirely wrong—there are plenty of white, affluent baby boomers. In fact, the element of truth is what makes a caricature seductive. The problem is that the upscale baby boomers often obscure the rest of the generation, hiding the millions of blue-collars, single parents, minorities, and poor, thereby creating a false image of baby-boom economic prosperity and political conservatism.

According to *American Demographics*, for example, only four million baby boomers qualify as yuppies, formally defined as 25-to-39-year-olds who live in metropolitan areas, work in professional or managerial occupations, and earn at least $30,000 if living alone and $40,000 if married or living with someone else—a grand 5 percent of all baby boomers. Even adding the baby boomers who try to look and buy like yuppies—the "would be's" as advertisers call them—roughly 60 million baby boomers do not fit this picture. Thus, there are four baby boomers at or below the poverty line for every yuppie far above it.

Indeed, the biggest numbers are at the lower end of the income spectrum. And even here, caricatures abound. The baby boomers at the very low end of the earnings curve, for example, are sometimes called the yuffies—young, urban failures who make less than $10,000 a year. "Like it or not," says one report, "they are a major part of the larger baby boomer universe that everyone is going out of their way to reach." In 1985, four out of ten baby boomers made less than $10,000 a year, making them roughly eight times as numerous as the yuppies.

Baby boomers just above the yuffies on the income ladder are often called the "new collars" or the new middle class. "You have a picture in your mind of guy in his early 30s," political consultant Ralph Whitehead, Jr., says of these lower- and middle-class baby boomers, "running shoes, work pants, a Miami Dolphins T-shirt, a handlebar mustache, and a baseball cap." And what they lack in taste, they make up for in numbers—according to Whitehead, 25 million baby boomers meet the two main new-collar demographic criteria: (1) at least a year in college, and (2) incomes above

$20,000 but below $40,000. "You tell a new collar voter about $600 toilet seats at the Defense Department and he'll want to fire the people involved," Whitehead jokes. "You tell a yuppie about one and he'll want to know what colors they come in."

The "news," as Whitehead sometimes calls them, are liberal on social issues, but conservative on taxes and national defense. "They aren't so much the young people in the baby-boom generation who put on the show we call the Sixties," he says. "They're the people who were at home watching it on television. But they were picking up its influence and acting on [it] at a later time, maybe several years later. What you see is the slow but steady penetration of Sixties values into the new collars."[1] They are more like Renko, the sensitive, redneck policeman from *Hill Street Blues*, than Rambo.

Obviously, a generation that contains yuppies, grumpies, dinks, yuffies, and new collars all at the same time can hardly be called a monolith. Yet, if these baby boomers are not all alike, they are not always different either. They all happen to share a common birthdate (1946–1964), some common history (civil rights, Vietnam, Watergate, Carter, and Reagan), some common ideas (tolerance, a rejection of social and political traditions), and some important differences (income, education, race).

The only way to know whether and how these shared experiences will affect their political and social future is to start with simple questions about when the baby boomers were born and why; what makes them different from their parents and children, and whether those differences are temporary or enduring; and what makes their history so powerful as a source of generational identity.

Demographers were clearly surprised by the baby boom. Even as the first baby boomers were being born in 1946, most population forecasters were predicting a continued decline in fertility. Most expected a slight rise in births as families made up for lost time following the war, but with a quick return to the Depression-era baby bust. None were prepared for the twenty-year surge that was the baby boom. The Population Reference Bureau, a Washington, D.C., research institute, describes it this way: "Simply put, the baby boom was a 'disturbance' which emanated from a decade-and-a-half-long fertility splurge on the part of American couples. This post–World War II phenomenon upset what had been a century-long decline in the U.S. fertility rate,"[2] a decline which resumed at the end of the baby boom in the mid-1960s. Though demographers quibble over the relative merits of using fertility rates or total births as a way to define the baby boom, most nevertheless agree on the 1946–1964 birthdate. Whereas the fertility rate had averaged roughly 2.1 births per woman in the 1930s, it peaked at 3.7 in the late 1950s, and fell to 1.8 by the mid-1970s.

The demographers also agree on the underlying social engine that kept the baby boom going long past the normal post-war increase. Louise Russell, a senior fellow at the Brookings Institution, a Washington think tank, sums up the simple facts as follows: "More women married than ever before. More women who married had children. They had their children earlier. And some had more children."[3] Thus did a relatively small generation beget a very large one. It is particularly important, however, to recognize that most baby boomers did not grow up in large families. Though there was some increase in the number of women who had three or four children, the number who had five actually fell during the twenty-year period. Much of the boom came from women who would have remained childless in other times.

Indeed, the key to understanding the birth of the baby boom is the remarkable social homogeneity of the era.[4] The baby boom was the product of standardized fertility. It was as if every American couple had taken an oath at marriage to love, honor, and obey the national average of two kids per family. Members of the baby boom were more likely than those in the generation before it to grow up in roughly the same sized family—two married natural parents, one or two brothers or sisters. According to demographer Charles Westoff, the baby boom involved a "movement away from spinsterhood, childless marriage and the one-child family, and a bunching together of births at early ages."[5]

The statistics prove the point. The number of women having at least two children increased by half between the 1930s and 1950s, resulting in a demographic wedge of 75 million children. It was a sea of babies, with one wave of four million babies after another every year for a decade. With the maternity wards filled to capacity, many baby boomers spent their first days of life neatly tucked away in hospital hallways, operating suites, even boiler rooms—one crib after another lined up in a seemingly endless line of babies.

Some argue that this deluge was the simple product of post-war euphoria, of passions rekindled in the wake of a fifteen-year struggle against economic depression and world war, of new families formed in a more hopeful time. Others believe the boom merely paralleled a decade of remarkable economic performance with cars and children rolling off assembly lines in unprecedented numbers. Still others point to the social climate of the 1950s: keeping up with the Joneses involved having the "right" number of kids, too.

By itself, World War II cannot explain a twenty-year fertility boom. However, it can explain its beginning. And what the war may have started, social conformity continued. The baby boom was born during a period of profoundly pro-child social values. As sociologist William Simon argues, "those who didn't want children were an embarrassed and embattled minority. It was almost evidence of a physical or mental deficiency."

Yet, if having children was the be-all and end-all of womanhood, why did most families stop at two or three? Why not keep going? Demographers are not sure. Though the baby boom came during a period of remarkable economic expansion, sociologist Frank Bean believes that "social and cultural conditions during the era supported having families, while at the same time increasing the cost of having large families. If economic prosperity made marriage and family formation easier, rising labor-force participation among married women of childbearing ages in the absence of changes in traditional sex-role attitudes made having large families harder."[6]

In short, couples were pushed toward a magic number of kids, encouraged to have at least one, rewarded for two, congratulated for three, but exhausted and financially pressed at four or more. Hence, the homogenized, two-child family which so characterized the start of the baby boom. By the 1960s, however, divorce was increasing rapidly—altering the life course for the youngest baby boomers—and the "normal" family was in decline.

Ultimately, the baby boom may be best understood as part of a much larger historical cycle of fertility boom and bust. The baby boom's parents were part of a baby bust which occurred during the 1930s, and the baby boom's children are part of a bust which is now underway in the 1980s and 1990s. According to this theory of birth and fortune, the current baby-bust generation may eventually produce a new baby boom, just in the nick of time to save their grandparents' retirement in the 2020s.

At least that is what demographer/economist Richard Easterlin predicts. According to Easterlin, small generations follow large in a predictable pattern. Simply put, small generations can afford children, while large generations cannot. Small generations create labor shortages, and can command higher wages and more opportunities. Small generations may even be happier. According to Easterlin, smaller generations have fewer suicides and lower crime rates. In contrast, large generations create labor surpluses, and must accept lower wages and fewer promotions. Large generations face more competition, longer lines, and more frustration. No wonder they do not want children.

In this cycle, political optimism might follow cynicism, too. Small generations face a lifelong seller's market. Perhaps that is why Reagan is so popular among the baby busters. They are living his "Morning in America." Indeed, they may also be moving back toward earlier marriages, larger families, and fewer divorces. As Easterlin predicts, "crime rates among the young are not likely to continue to rise as they have. Reports of alienation among the young are likely to decline, so that the general improvement in the circumstances of the young will contribute to a happier economic and social environment over the next 20 years, just as in the last 20 years it has contributed to a deterioration and the feeling of social malaise—that things are going to hell."[7] Thus does the baby boom move through life as the middle of a generational sandwich —a less successful baby boom with two well-healed baby busts on either side.

Before investing in baby futures, however, it is important to remember that Easterlin's theory remains unproven. To date, baby-bust fertility has not moved up as Easterlin's model predicts. First, changing social values may have affected the baby bust just as much as the baby boom. Second, a decade of economic uncertainty may have blunted the baby bust's optimism. Baby bust or not, young couples may be reluctant to invest in families. Third, the baby boom is so large that its economic frustrations may spill over onto its younger siblings. The longer the baby boom waits for promotions, the longer it stays in entry-level jobs, and the longer the baby bust must wait to move either in or up.

Thus, Easterlin may have the right model but the wrong society. Perhaps women in a social vacuum would respond to subconscious generational instincts, if such instincts truly exist. However, America is not a social vacuum. It is a complex society with a variety of incentives for having and not having children. If the 1950s provided ample encouragement for childbearing, the 1960s provided ample reinforcement for family planning and a decline in unwanted pregnancies.

More important, the 1960s also provided the needed birth-control technologies—technologies which continue to be available and widely used in the present. Unplanned births dropped in the 1960s and remained low as women gained control of their own fertility. Indeed, according to most research, it was the drop in unwanted births that signalled the end of the baby boom. Couples got serious about not having babies. After hitting its high in the late 1950s, the fertility rate began a plunge which continues today. In absolute numbers, of course, the baby boomers will have a large number of babies. But in terms of fertility rates, they are below the numbers needed even to replace themselves. They are not only at zero population growth—they are below it.

These demographic facts translate into the most basic difference between the baby boom and the generations which came both before and after: the baby boom is big and the others are not. As Landon Jones, editor of *Money*, writes of the 1960s, "There was a generation gap, all right. But it was not between the young and old. It was between the many and the few. It was between the large generation of the boom, painfully swollen with its numbers and trying to find its place in the world, and the small generation in power which was just as firmly resisting it. The real struggle of the young was not with parents but with a society that could not accommodate them."[8]

Size is not the only difference between the generations, however. The baby boomers have a perception of themselves as being very different from other generations—a perception that has existed from childhood, in part because children naturally want to be different from their parents. According to one typical 1960s study, college students were twice as likely as their parents to say there was a generation gap, and to define it in more permanent terms. When asked to define the gap, for example, students concentrated on values and tolerance, while their parents talked about immaturity and age. When asked about differences within their own families, students talked again about values, while their parents focused on personal habits and interpersonal styles. The authors of the study concluded, "It is as if the parents were saying, 'Yes, there are differences between the generations, but these are not intrinsic; they are simply due to differences in life status and maturity.' The students, by contrast, are saying 'The contrasts we see are in values and basic orientations to life. There are differences; and they are important.' "[9]

More important, the perceptions are based on very real differences in attitudes. They may love their parents, but when it comes time to talk about politics, marriage, drugs, or sex, the baby boomers respectfully disagree. From questions on the government's role in creating jobs, religion in the schools, war and peace, political trust, and race, to questions on AIDS, homosexuality, drugs, pornography, and women's rights, the baby boomers maintain their distance from their parents and grandparents.

The generation gaps are most pronounced on basic issues of lifestyles and social roles. The baby boom appears to be living by a set of what pollster Daniel Yankelovitch calls "new rules"—if not by no rules at all. For example, an August 1986, CBS News/ *New York Times* Poll found a generation gap on the cocaine crisis. Those under 44 years of age were much less likely than those over 45 to say that drug abuse reflects a fundamental breakdown in social morals, and were more likely to blame the drug problem on individual users instead of on society. These younger Americans were almost twice as likely to say that alcohol abuse was a more serious problem than drug abuse. Further, asked if testing workers for illegal drugs would be an invasion of privacy, over half of the under-44 age group said that it would, compared to 32 percent of the older respondents.[10]

A May 1986, *Washington Post*/ABC News Poll found similar differences in attitudes regarding gender roles. The baby boomers were twice as likely as those over 40 years old to approve of men and women living together without being married (61 percent versus 30 percent), and 25 percent more likely to approve of a woman calling a man for a date (84 percent versus 59 percent).[11] Other surveys have demonstrated similar differences on acceptance of sexual freedom and homosexuality. Only time will tell, of course, if these liberal sexual attitudes will survive the AIDS crisis. At least for the time being, the baby boomers no longer practice everything they once preached.[12]

Generational disagreements on social values show themselves

in many ways, and eventually they also manifest themselves in politics. Supreme Court nominee Douglas Ginsberg may well be remembered as the first political victim of the baby-boom lifestyle. Just 41 years old when nominated for the Supreme Court by President Reagan, Ginsberg had been selected in a hurried effort to find a strong conservative who could be confirmed in the wake of Judge Robert Bork's Senate defeat.

However, in the search for ideological purity, the Reagan administration forgot to check Ginsberg's social vitae. What was perfectly normal social behavior for a baby boomer was not automatically acceptable for a Supreme Court nominee. Ginsberg had supported Robert Kennedy in the 1968 Democratic presidential primaries and had dropped out of Cornell for a time to run a computer dating service. After receiving his law degree, he clerked for Thurgood Marshall, the black liberal Supreme Court justice.

Ginsberg had also been married twice, the first time to an anti-nuclear activist, the second to an obstetrician who had performed at least two abortions as part of her medical training. Both wives had kept their maiden names; Ginsberg's two daughters, one from each marriage, had been given their mother's last name; one was even given her mother's full name. Avant-garde even for the baby boom.

Even with his liberal social credentials, Ginsberg might have survived but for the most normal of all college activities: he had tried marijuana, first in the 1960s and again as a Harvard Law School professor in the 1970s. It hardly mattered that a large number of his baby-boom peers had also tried marijuana. For a candidate being advertised as tough on crime and a strict believer in the rule of law, Ginsberg's past was scandalous. Older Americans were shocked. His nomination lasted all of nine days.

Ginsberg's story will be repeated many times over the coming decade. As the baby boom begins to take its place at the highest levels of government, marijuana use will become a standard ques-

tion and likely a standard answer. Unless the baby boom wishes
to restrict its leaders to those who never touched the stuff, the
generation will continue to recruit many politicians who, at least
once, "just said yes" to marijuana.

Other differences between the baby boom and its parents are
revealed in survey interviews. The baby boomers are much more
willing than their parents to take positions on issues, whether they
know something or not. Older Americans are much more comfortable simply saying that they don't know. The difference is
based in part on the baby boom's greater education and on its
self-confidence. Three other gaps also deserve brief comment here
as part of this first cut at a baby-boom portrait.

First, compared to their parents, the baby boomers have less
party loyalty. If the parents tried to pass down a sense of the
family's party loyalty, they failed miserably. Some argue that the
parents simply didn't care, that memories of the Great Depression
and the New Deal had faded to the point where no one really
worried what their children thought about Democrats or Republicans. Party politics was hardly the topic of nightly debate in the
quiet of the 1950s and early 1960s. Others suggest that the parents
simply didn't know what to teach, that they were in the midst of
their own crisis of party identification. Still others believe that the
parents were too tired, that "quality time" was in short supply
even in the 1960s.

Second, compared to their parents, the baby boomers have less
use for the terms "liberal" and "conservative." The baby boomers
do not use the terms as often as their parents once did for defining political issues. Nor do they automatically link "liberal" with
Democrats and "conservative" with Republicans. The baby boomers appear quite willing to apply the terms to contradictory issues
and politicians alike, supporting civil rights on one hand and
capital punishment on the other, former senator Gary Hart in the
1984 primaries and Reagan in the general election.

Third, the baby boomers appear to be much more tolerant of

social diversity than their parents. The tolerance is reflected in the changing American family. Baby-boom families are smaller, more likely to have a single parent, more likely to experience a divorce when children are young, and more likely to have two working parents. The demographic norms of the 1950s are dead. Joseph Plummer, director of research at Young and Rubicam, a New York advertising agency, notes that by the mid-1970s, "the world was no longer comprised of moms and dads, with three kids, a high-school education, and three-quarters of a dog. That picture was an anachronism."

These family differences in social and political values reflect generation gaps of past and present, but not necessarily of the future. As baby boomers replace their parents as the elder generation different gaps will appear. It is part of the natural life cycle of generations. The gap to watch in coming years will be between the baby boomers and their baby-bust children. While the baby boomers remain uncommitted to a single party or candidate, the next generation is being organized into a potent Republican voting block. What they lack in size when compared to the baby boom, they may more than make up for in passion.

Surveys of high-school seniors and college freshmen chronicle the change across these two generations. In the clearest split between the 1960s and 1980s, students of today are more concerned with making money than with developing a meaningful philosophy of life. The number who place money as their top priority has grown 30 percent over the past two decades, while the search for meaning has dropped 40 percent. However, anti-abortion activist Phyllis Schlafly will search in vain for evidence of a return to traditional family values. Despite greater opposition to abortion and marijuana, recent college freshmen have been even more liberal than their baby-boom elders on gender equality. They are more likely to believe in equal pay for equal work and to agree that a job gives a wife more of a chance to develop herself as a person. They are more likely to say they would vote for a qualified black or woman for president. They are firm supporters of equal opportunity.

Some of these social and political gaps will last over time as the baby boomers cling to the remnants of the 1960s and early 1970s. Other gaps will fade with aging memories. Still others will evaporate with passage into new life roles or the rise of new issues, like AIDS (free love is easier to champion as a college student than as the parent of a teenage son or daughter). The challenge is to figure out where the gaps come from: are they due to a unique generational perspective or are they only from a temporary pause along the life cycle?

Consider the conundrum in sorting out the differences between younger and older corporate executives. According to a 1986 *Business Week* survey, the two generations of corporate captains are very different indeed: "Younger managers generally don't subscribe to a code of loyalty. Neither do they demand it from employees. . . . Lacking memories of a depression, young corporate climbers boast unusual optimism and unquestioning faith in corporate capitalism—to the point that many of them seem brash. . . . Instead of being fearful of change, these fast-trackers seem to thrive on it."

In contrast, older managers are much more cautious: "Born of the Depression and World War II, the old guard was preoccupied with security. In exchange for that security, they took a pledge of loyalty to the corporation. They accepted with equanimity corporate control of their destiny." Adding up the list of differences, *Business Week* concluded that the older generation is more cautious, insecure, resistant to change, loyal, comfortable in bureaucracies, people-oriented, willing to put in a good day's work, and searching for 25-year security, while the workaholic younger generation is more eager to take risks, optimistic, willing to job-hop, more comfortable with numbers, and searching for autonomy and instant gratification.[13] (Some of these differences may have disappeared in the wake of the 1987 stock-market crash. That is just the kind of historical event that may mark an age group for life.)

The problem with any such comparison is that some of the differences between the two age groups are transitory and likely to disappear with time, while others may be generational, fixed in the baby-boom consciousness by their unique passage through history. Thus, younger managers might be different because (a) they can afford to take risks early in their life cycle, (b) because their parents are still alive to provide support and confidence, (c) because they grew up in an era of much greater financial security, or (d) because they are marked by a distinctive generational identity that puts the good of the individual over the good of the corporation.

Together, these four explanations provide very different angles on baby-boom attitudes and behavior, separating what is temporary from what is more permanent. The baby boomers will not be young and brash for long, but will always be marked by their personal and social histories. Thus, the baby boomers' social and political values may be different because of their place in the life cycle, their place within their own families, their place in history, or their sense of a shared generational experience.

The first explanation for what has made the baby boom different involves a person's position in the life cycle. No matter whether people were born in 1920, 1940, 1960, or 1980, the survivors will eventually pass through similar stages of the life cycle—childhood, adolescence, adulthood, and retirement—usually once, and only once, and at roughly the same age. This passage through the life cycle means that all generations will share experiences, although at different points in time. Sooner or later, and whether they want to or not, many baby boomers will become grandparents, with all that means for growing concerns about care giving, family, and dying. Time works its will on all generations.

However, age is no longer the hard and fast predictor of what people think and do as it once was. Age markers have blurred considerably over the past two decades as people delay marriage and childbearing, retire early and start new careers, and even start second and third families. Yet, the rough boundaries of youth and adulthood remain, creating different public-policy priorities and political positions across generations. As the baby boomers move through their childbearing years, education issues may receive greater emphasis. Thirty years from now, however, baby boomers will be far more concerned with retirement. Thus, value differences based on position in the life cycle may be the most temporary of all.

The second explanation for baby-boom differences rests on a person's place within his or her own family. Every baby boomer is someone's son or daughter. An individual can be a member of a distinctive social generation while remaining a caring son or daughter, father or mother. Indeed, for all the social differences between young and old as generations, the baby boomers still retain their family ties.

Studies of three- and four-generation families, for example, show remarkable solidarity between grandparents, parents, and grandchildren. In one recent study comparing three generations of women, baby boomers were often more willing than their mothers to provide help to their ailing grandparents.[14] Contrary to the yuppie caricature, these women were not willing to abandon their care-giving responsibilities. Indeed, they were more likely than their mothers to disagree with the notion that adult children "should not be expected to do household tasks for their parents," and more likely to believe that "it is all right for older people to take financial help from grown children." They were clearly willing to provide more help than their grandparents wanted. While over half of the grandmothers in the study said professional services "can usually take the place of family care," only 16 percent of the granddaughters agreed.

There is no doubt that these family members share a commitment to care giving across generations. That commitment to caring exists even given substantial family differences on social issues.

Whereas almost half of the grandmothers said "sons in a family should be given more encouragement than daughters to go to college," only 10 percent of their daughters and granddaughters agreed. Whereas 21 percent of the grandmothers said a "working father should not have to spend as much time bringing up children as a working mother does," only 3 percent of the granddaughters agreed.

There was evidence of intergenerational solidarity, too. All three generations agreed that young women should have careers, and that having a paying job makes a woman feel better about herself as a person. However, as the baby boomers move from being children to being parents and finally grandparents, some views may change. Parents may be more protective of children, no matter what they promised themselves in adolescence. Grandparents do not want to impose on grandchildren, no matter what they may have thought when they were young. Thus, differences based on positions within a family may change with the natural ebb and flow of life.

The third explanation for what makes the baby boom different from other generations is mere location in history. People under 40 could not have lived through the Great Depression or World War II. People under 20 could not have experienced the civil rights movement or Vietnam. To the extent that they could have participated in protests, they would have been in strollers. That is not to say they do not have attitudes about Vietnam or civil rights. However, they could not have received a draft number; they could not have felt the sting of tear gas or billy clubs; they could not have marched on the 1968 Democratic convention in Chicago; they did not hear Martin Luther King, Jr.; they did not join the freedom marches. Everything they experience of the events of the 1960s is in reruns.

Even those present at a given time in history do not always experience events the same way. Because they have not been "innoculated" against history through experience or education, young people may be more vulnerable to the impact of events than their parents would be. As sociologists Lillian Troll and Vern Bengston argue, "All people living at the same time do not necessarily share the same history. Crucial events have impacted them at different points in their life and thus affected them differently."[15] The Vietnam War is a prime example. Children born in the early 1960s might have lived through the Vietnam era, but the war could only have been an abstract threat to them—unless, of course, an older brother or relative was somehow involved. For adolescents, however, especially black males, the war represented a more immediate menace: they were more likely to be drafted and to be sent into heavy combat.

The impact of history may also depend on intervening events. Draft numbers, for example, explain at least some differences in how some baby boomers felt about Vietnam. Baby boomers with low draft lottery numbers must have felt a more personal threat than those with safe draws. Yet, as at least one study suggests, those with the safest numbers may have opposed the war more than those in the mid-range because they felt guilty about their good fortune compared to those who were certain to serve.[16]

This is not to argue that children were immune to the impact of Vietnam. Everyone shared in the war to some extent. All anyone needed was a television. Witnessing the war in living color, the youngest baby boomers had few intellectual defenses against the onslaught of vivid imagery. Research at the time showed that even young children had some awareness of what was going on in Southeast Asia. Ultimately, however, a war that must have seemed like so much chaos to children had to be a palpable threat to those about to serve. The photos of the dead in *Life* could only exist as a distant image to children, but were hard reminders of what might be in store for those en route to Southeast Asia.

The final explanation for what has made the baby boom a different generation involves a person's possible membership in a social movement. Such generations are based on much more than shared birthdates; they reflect a shared sense of time, a shared feeling for an era. German sociologist Karl Mannheim called such a shared feeling a zeitgeist—a spirit of the times.[17] During relatively quiet moments in history, there may be no zeitgeist at all—nothing but a sense of boredom or normalcy. During particularly volatile periods in time, however, a zeitgeist may arise, engulfing those in the midst of the crisis. And because young people have fewer ways of explaining away events, they are most likely to be caught up in the spirit of the times. Children raised during war or economic depression, for example, often carry the lessons more deeply than their parents.

Thus, the year in which a child or adolescent first notices the world can sometimes be a powerful guide to their beliefs and future behavior. Baby boomers who first experienced the world around them at the height of the Vietnam War are very different from those who awoke during Watergate or the "Morning in America" eras. As pollster Patrick Caddell notes, "People now under 25 look like they have more in common with people of 45 than they do with people who are between 25 and 40, and thank God there are so few of them. That's for all of you who never liked your younger brothers and sisters—now you understand why."

Just because an age group grows up at the same time does not mean it will become a social generation, however. Not every one will share the zeitgeist. Moreover, just because a zeitgeist existed in the 1960s does not mean it perseveres today. People and times change. Vietnam protestors, for example, have changed between the 1960s and 1980s. According to political scientist M. Kent Jennings, public opinion surveys of the protestors show both continuity and change. On some attitudes, there has been "absolute continuity," meaning no change, across the two eras. The protestors are still liberal on social issues, holding the 1960s line on abortion and women's rights. For other attitudes, there has been what Jennings calls "relative continuity," meaning a softening of position but continued distance from other generations. The protestors have become more conservative on economic issues, but they still remain more liberal than other members of their own generation. In turn, the baby boom as a whole remains more liberal than older and younger generations alike.[18] The zeitgeist may be fading with time, but it still exists at some level of political consciousness, and such differences may last a lifetime.

The differences that mark the baby boom are a result of its social and political history. The baby boomers carry the imprint of two distinct crises. One that covered less than a decade from civil rights to Vietnam resulted in a clear separation of the baby boomers from traditional politics. The other crisis spanned the better part of this century and resulted in a new definition of American families. Though all Americans were touched by these two crises, there is considerable evidence to suggest that the baby boomers reacted more intensely because they were younger and therefore more impressionable when the crises hit.

The causes of the political crisis were clear. It began in the summer of 1965, which may have been the breaking point for most Americans. Like a stock market collapse, party loyalty had begun dropping in late winter and continued until it hit a low in October. For older Americans, the collapse of party loyalty reflected concerns about civil rights. According to University of Michigan scholar Phillip Converse, "For liberals, the period was laced with an astonishing sequence of acquittals and quashed indictments by southern juries and judges in a spate of civil rights murders. For conservatives, it was a period in which the federal courts and the Johnson Administration lost no opportunity to demonstrate a national resolve to enforce without delay the comparatively 'radical' Civil Rights Act passed in July of 1964."[19]

There were 38 separate "events" the summer of 1965—from murders in Selma, Alabama, to riots in Watts—that left a mark on the 15 to 20 million baby boomers who were adolescents at the time. They not only saw what was happening to their parents, they also saw the stark pictures of racism on television. They saw the school children marching in Birmingham and the ghettos burning in a dozen cities. Whatever the singular impact of civil rights, there is no doubt that these older baby boomers made their

first contacts with politics during a period of profound controversy. As David Boaz, of the Cato Institute, summarizes the baby
boom's political resume, the average baby boomer "was 11 during
the Cuban missile crisis, when his classmates huddled in the hall
during air-raid drills and learned of the imminent threat of nuclear
war. He was 14 when the bombing of North Vietnam began, 18
and trying to avoid the draft when the number of U.S. troops in
Vietnam peaked, 23 when President Nixon resigned in disgrace,
and 29 when inflation hit double digits under President Carter."

It was one crisis after another. Vietnam followed Selma; Watergate followed Cambodia; Iran followed OPEC; Beruit followed
Abscam. But of the crises, surely none had as great a catalytic
impact on the baby boomers as Vietnam.

As the *Washington Post*'s Myra MacPherson writes of the period: "Vietnam tore away any remaining myths or innocence the
generation possessed about war and warriors." Twenty-seven million baby-boom men came of draft age in the 1960s and 1970s.
Even though only a third were drafted, and less than a tenth went
to Vietnam, according to McPherson, "the war was to divide
them, sear them, wound them, and would ultimately leave lasting
scars. Some of those scars are raw and visible—such as the thousands of physically and psychologically maimed veterans. Other
scars are indistinct and blurred, such as the quiet guilts of many
who dodged the war and painfully acknowledge more than a
decade later their feelings about the other men who went in their
places."[20]

Even as Vietnam ended, other crises arose to take its place.
According to Converse's analysis, a second, milder political crisis
began in 1972 with the Watergate scandals. Looking back, it all
seems barely possible: a president forced to resign after secret
White House tapes revealed his involvement in a second-rate
cover-up of a third-rate burglary of a vastly undersupported oppo-
nent; a vice-president forced to resign after his indictment for
taking bribes when he was governor; a deep network of dirty
tricks and illegal campaign contributions; a clandestine White

House team called "the plumbers" created to plug security leaks about the Vietnam War; a secret war in Cambodia; a cast of characters that included names like Vesco, Hunt, Liddy, Ehrlichman, Haldeman, and Dean; a new president who took office with the words "our long national nightmare is over." Only by remembering the 1960s can such events be seen as mild.

According to Converse, this second crisis affected all Americans. However, because of their age and lack of past experience, it hit the younger baby boomers hardest. Indeed, the two crises may have created very different reasons for the baby boom's political separation. The older baby boomers may have lost interest because of a *dis*illusionment based on the failure of a dream, the younger baby boomers may have started out with *no* illusions at all. After listening to tales of disappointment from older siblings, the younger baby boomers would have expected the system to act pretty much as it did.

The political crisis nested in the midst of a much longer crisis of the American family. With riots in the cities and a war heating up in Southeast Asia, many baby boomers found that their families were collapsing, too. Though divorce is sometimes seen as a unique baby-boom phenomenon, the wave began in the late 1950s, when many baby boomers were still small children, and represented the death of the "breadwinner" society in which the baby boomer's parents and grandparents had been raised.

Before the 1950s, children were raised to obey strict social rules regarding family and work. According to sociologist Kingsley Davis, the breadwinner system was an anomaly of the industrial revolution at the turn of the century. In the new division of labor, "Wives did, on a full-time basis, what they had always done on a part-time basis—they tended to duties concerned with the house, children, and husband—and, as a result, they lost their role in economic production. Single women, not burdened with children, always participated substantially in the labor market."[21] Married women in this system were not allowed to work, no matter what the financial need of the family.

Life in the breadwinner system was hardly easy. According to a study of fifty years of change in Muncie, Indiana, the baby boom's grandparents settled for "the most modest goals, a more cautious development of resources, and a less ambitious occupational career, lagging behind the succeeding generations year by year from early marriage onward."[22] Their lives were spent "at the mercy of an unplanned economy and limited occupational opportunities." They rarely changed jobs and rarely moved up. Luxuries waited until after their children left home, if then. According to the research, "unprotected by life insurance over most of their careers and prevented from saving for retirement because of the Great Depression, the people of this generation launched children into marriage later and over a longer period of time and, altogether, spent a longer time in childbearing, child rearing, and leave taking."[23]

In this world of limited choices, the baby boom's grandmothers had only one chance to succeed in life: they had to marry the right man. Husbands controlled all of the economic power; divorce was difficult if not impossible. As Davis argues, "the system could not operate without strong normative controls. The husband's obligation to support his family, even after his death had to be enforced by law and public opinion; illegitimate sexual relations and reproduction had to be condemned, divorce had to be punished, and marriage had to be encouraged by making the lot of the spinster a pitiful one."[24] The system had to ensure that husbands and wives stayed together.

By the end of World War II, the breadwinner system was unravelling. Some women who had gone to work during World War II simply did not go home. Whereas only 3 percent of white, married women were in the labor force in 1890, 15 percent were working by 1950, and just over 30 percent by 1960. When the kids were in diapers, their mothers still stayed home. Once the kids hit grade school, 40 percent of their mothers went to work. By the 1980s, over half of all married women were working, but unlike their mothers, almost half with young children were working, too.

It should be clear, however, that the baby boom's mothers made the major break with the breadwinner system. It may be common-place to talk about gallant baby-boom women struggling to balance corporate jobs and family á la Diane Keaton in the 1988 film *Baby Boom*, but many of the struggles were fought and won by their mothers.

Eventually, the system collapsed under the weight of its own rules. By the 1950s, there was just enough divorce to suggest that women needed economic alternatives. By the early 1960s, "the exploding divorce rate struck at the heart of the nineteenth-century sex-role system," Davis writes. "If a young wife could not count on her husband remaining married to her, she could not count on his economic support either. Divorce thus broke the central bargain of marriage by which a woman traded her services as a wife and mother for the financial support of the husband." For a woman, the "best hedge against the disaster of divorce was to earn her own money, by outside employment."[25]

Divorce was not the only suspect in the death of the breadwinner system. Increasing delays in marriage during the 1960s and 1970s meant women had more time to get into the work habit. Decreasing fertility during the same period meant women had fewer children to occupy their time and interest. Perhaps most important, increasing longevity meant that women had to plan for longer lives and a greater probability of being alone and in poverty in old age. Davis and colleague Pietronella van den Oever paint a sobering comparison of a woman's life in 1900 and 1980. "Assuming that she married at age 22, even as late as 1900 she could expect to live only until age 64. True, she would be widowed by age 60, but the chances were that she would die before her last child left home."

Today, a baby-boom woman can expect to live to almost 80. Yet, as the study shows, she will stop having children earlier. "Assuming that the last child will leave home at age 18, the mother will still have 32.5 more years to live free from caring for children." As Davis and van den Oever ask, "What is she to do during this period, which comprises more than half of her lifetime after marriage? Some of it she can spend with her husband. He will survive until she is 69. That is long enough, but at 69 she still has an expected 16 years of life remaining, which is 43 percent of what is now her post-child lifetime."

For baby-boom women, however, the chances are better than fifty-fifty that the marriage will not survive anyway. "On average," according to Davis and van den Oever, "the wife will have become a widow or divorcee by the time she is 44 years old. If she does not remarry, she will retain that status for 36 years." Even if she does remarry at 45, "she will still have another 35 years to live. A part of these would be spent with her second husband, but his age would be older than hers by a wider margin than in the first marriage, and the marriage would be more susceptible to divorce or widowhood. She would stand an even chance of being divorced or widowed a second time within 11 years, when she would still have more than 26 years of life remaining."[26]

Ultimately, these two crises of political and social life were intensified by the 1960s—by the sheer size of the generation and its inevitable social and economic crowding, by a culture of standardized homes, entertainment, and nuclear fear, which reinforced standardized generational emotions, and by the deeply felt sadness following the death of President John F. Kennedy. History and demography came together at the most sensitive moment in the baby boom's life cycle, just as the generation was making the transition from the carefree world of childhood to the already confusing period of adolescence and young adulthood. Other generations were surely affected, too, but none with the lasting impact and shared zeitgeist of the baby boom. It was a life-cycle, historical, and generational effect with lasting impacts on the baby boom's ties within its own families.

These early crises were compounded by the remarkably poor economic performance of the 1970s and early 1980s. Three recessions, double-digit inflation, double-digit unemployment, 20 percent mortgage rates, a price and wage freeze, the collapse of the manufacturing sector, two oil embargoes, a 600 percent jump in the price of gold, and a 300 percent rise in the cost of Pampers, all contributed to a clear sense of baby-boom economic anxiety. With consumer prices up 170 percent between 1972 and 1987, it should come as no surprise that the savings rate would tumble by almost half.

At least for now, most baby boomers are trailing what was once the normal economic growth curve. Home ownership is down, real earnings are down, promotions are less frequent. The baby boomers can barely pay their bills on time, let alone put away a little money for the future. The question is whether current economic history is creating a new baby-boom zeitgeist, one based on economic survival, not tolerance, on bitterness, not compassion.

2
Intergenerational
War or Peace?

THERE HAS BEEN a lot of talk about intergenerational warfare lately. Some argue that the baby boomers are so frustrated with their poor economic performance and so jealous of their parents and grandparents that they are about to rebel. The baby boom is certainly big enough to impose its will on older generations, but is it self-centered enough to demand an intergenerational accounting? The answer depends on whether the baby boomers think in the short term or the long term.

Looking at the short-term balance sheet, the baby boomers should be starting to wonder what went wrong. How ironic that the baby boomers would do so poorly. Two-thirds voted for Reagan. Twice. It is not that Reagan started the economic decline. Quite the contrary. It was well underway in the mid-1970s. Rather, given almost 50 million baby-boom votes, one might think Reagan would have done something about their lagging performance.

Instead, under Reagan the baby boomers' real income has declined, their housing ownership has lagged, their savings rate is nil, and their promotion prospects are lousy. And, as far as the advertising industry goes, the baby boom is no longer number one on the marketing charts. It is just the kind of thing to turn the baby boomers bitter. Didn't their parents do better when they were young? Didn't the economy owe the baby boom a fast start, too?

The good news from 1972 to 1987 was that median incomes went up 153 percent. The bad news was that inflation went up 170 percent, creating a net loss of 17 percent. Moreover, baby boomers faced increases in cost of living far beyond 153 percent. The average price of a new house went up almost $83,000 or 294 percent. The average monthly mortgage payment jumped from $152 to $581 or 282 percent. Average federal taxes only went up 175 percent, but Social Security levies increased from $468 to $2,018 or 331 percent, and state and local taxes jumped 520 percent. No wonder the average baby boomer carried between $6,000 and $7,000 in personal debt in 1986. And that does not include mortgages.

The hyper-inflation economy hit the baby boomers across the board. According to *Money* magazine, the average cost of the bestselling car, for example, went from $3,700 for a '72 Impala to $11,800 for an '87 Celebrity. Baby boomers who stayed with the old wheels still felt the increase: a quart of oil increased from $0.85 to $2.50. Indeed, only two items on *Money*'s list of ups and downs actually went down: a Zenith 19-inch color TV (down 3.8 percent) and a Texas Instruments calculator (down a whopping 1,407 percent).

Though inflation affected all Americans, it seemed to take aim at the baby boom. Take the costs of having a child as an example. During the 1972-1987 period, the cost of Ultra Pampers almost quadrupled from just under $1 to $3.75, the cost of OshKosh B'gosh denim overalls more than tripled from $5.95 to $19.29, and a pair of white baby socks rose from $0.85 to $2.50, all while the hospital costs of having a baby in the first place surged 233 percent and the price of tuition at Bennington College jumped 254 percent. Even the cost of admission to Disneyland increased—an adult ticket went from $5.95 to $20.00. Luckily, the cost of birth control pills increased from $1.65 a month to $13.82, or 738 percent, otherwise, some would say, the baby boomers might have given up on children altogether.

During the same period, Social Security benefits for the elderly increased 205 percent. Lest anyone conclude that the increase was excessive, however, the average monthly benefit for a married couple went from $272 in 1972 to $832 in 1987—enough to keep many elderly above the poverty line, but hardly excessive.

The difficulty in comparing generations is that the baby boomers still have plenty of economic life to live. It may be a little early to demand an economic accounting. Every generation has its good times and bad times. The baby boom's grandparents, for example, suffered through a deep recession following World War I and then the Great Depression. Thus, the baby boom's current economic performance prompts four questions: Are the baby boomers doing worse than their parents or grandparents? Is it possible to make any meaningful intergenerational comparisons? Are the baby boomers starting to feel bitter toward the elderly? And most important, is America on the verge of some great intergenerational war between young and old?

Obviously, some baby boomers did very well during the 1970s and early 1980s. That is why advertisers created the yuppie caricature. However, most baby boomers do not own a BMW or a vacation home on the shore. Many do not have a private pension or an IRA. And, following the stock market crash, even the yuppies may be in some jeopardy.[1]

Looking across the entire generation, according to Richard Michel, a senior economist at Washington's Urban Institute, the average baby boomer in 1987 was likely to be part of "a young married couple earning $25,000 a year total, trying to raise one kid, postponing a second one and wondering how to buy a first house—or, if they're in a house, wondering how they can afford higher education for their kids. The bulk of them aren't doing as

well as their parents, though it's hard to convince people that
something is amiss."

Indeed, on virtually every available economic indicator, the
baby boom is lagging behind past generations, paying a premium
because of its size and its poor historical timing. Not only is the
baby boom destined by size to be in a perpetual buyer's labor
market, it entered the workforce at the beginning of a fifteen-year
period of sustained inflation and slow growth. As it now stands,
according to economist Frank Levy, "You go up to somebody,
let's say 30 years old, and you say, tell me about what life was like
when you were growing up, and then you say, okay, suppose that
your life depended on living the same way. Could you swing three
kids, a single-family house and put away something for retirement
on just one person's earnings? And what are they going to do?
They're going to laugh at you."

Yet, they might also say Levy is crazy for asking the question
that way. The breadwinner system is no longer relevant to most
baby-boom women. Many would not leave the labor force even
given the chance. Do baby-boom women want to exist on their
husband's earnings? Do they wish to rely on their husband's savings for retirement? Not with the divorce rate at 60 percent they
don't! Nevertheless, Michel and Levy's economic facts are clear.
Compared to their parents, the baby boomers had higher unemployment and crime rates as teenagers, fewer good jobs and higher
mortgage rates as young adults, fewer promotions today and a
federal debt crisis in the future. The problem, as Michel acknowledges, is just that the baby boomers do not know they are doing
poorly.

Much of the poor performance rests on economic crowding.
Big generations have big trouble. The baby boomers have been
competing against each other for the good jobs, lower starting
wages, less credit, and limited promotions. Starting from lower
entry-level wages, the baby boomers have never quite caught up.[2]
Being born into the baby boom was certainly an economic mistake. As economic reporter Robert Kuttner says, "Those people

are going to be competing with each other for breadwinner jobs for 40 or 50 years. Now, that's not a glitch. I mean, the whole Great Depression was only 10 years. So the ability of an awful lot of people to live at the standard of living that they think they deserve to live at is going to be out of phase for some time to come." No wonder corporate personnel recruiters are happy these days. As one headhunter puts it, "the corporate officers are pretty happy with the new crops. Because there is so much competition between them and everyone realizes they have to stay on the ball, it leads to increased productivity. It never hurts to run a little scared."

Unfortunately, what is good for corporate productivity may be bad for baby-boom mental health. At least that is what Richard Easterlin argues: not only is a generation's size a predictor of divorce—members of small generations have less marital stress—and illegimate births—members of small generations can afford to get married before the baby is born—it is a barometer of personal adjustment. "The young man or woman who has difficulty getting a 'decent' job or securing a desired promotion is likely to feel increasingly frustrated and doubt his or her ability. The reaction may take the form of resentment toward others—to blame, say, one's employer, 'politicians,' or society generally." In turn, "a damaged self-image may result from failure to come up to society's and one's own expectations," even leading to higher crime and suicide rates as "people blame society for their failure to live up to expectations and react against it, sometimes criminally."[3] No wonder Easterlin celebrates the "lucky babies of the 1970s."

Fortunately, it's not that bad. The baby boom is having some trouble, but it is hardly on the verge of a new crime wave or self-destruction. Not only does Easterlin's model oversimplify baby-boom social decisions, it is based on little more than speculative evidence. Indeed, according to James Q. Wilson and Richard Hernstein, the baby boom's crime rate involves much more than size. It also reflects "a protracted period of great prosperity, a lessened use of sanctions for crime, and a shift in the dominant values from self-control to self-expression." Indeed, in an exhaustive analysis of crime, they conclude that it "is hopeless to try to disentangle these social forces or to assign exact numerical weights to each." Rather, each of these forces fueled the other—baby-boom spending created a youth market, which in turn gave rise to the ethos of self-expression, which in turn led to a belief in the perfectibility of human nature and encouraged social permissiveness.[4]

Despite more sophisticated evidence to the contrary, Easterlin continues to link high divorce and low fertility to the baby boom's size. If we could just get the economy going, he argues, the baby boomers would stay with their marriages and have more children. In the current crowded economy, the only way for baby boomers to improve their standard of living, Easterlin says, is to accept "an awful lot of sacrifice. They're putting off getting married, they're putting off having kids, and more women are having to work."

Some Democrats buy the argument. Geoffrey Faux, director of a new Democratic think tank called the Economic Policy Institute, says, "If you ask this guy whether he's better off than his father, he'll look around his living room and see the color TV and the VCR and say yes. But when you point out that he doesn't have as many children as his father did, and what's more, his wife has to work, he isn't so sure."

If that is the Democrats' definition of the ideal family—dad at work, mom at home with the kids—the party is in deep trouble. In fact, there is little hard evidence to prove that poor economic performance creates a delay in either marriage or childbearing. Greater education for women is a better culprit—one the Democrats would presumably wish to support. Access to education means women stay in school longer, and start their careers before marriage. To assume that the 1950 model is the standard by which to measure current families is to deny the collapse of the breadwinner system.

Nevertheless, the question of economic fortunes remains: are the baby boomers trailing their parents and grandparents, and how far are they behind? The answer involves comparing the three generations at the same point in the life cycle—whether young adulthood, middle age, or retirement—even if that means comparing them at different points in time. It is inappropriate to compare the baby boomers as young workers to their parents in mid-career or their grandparents in retirement, if only because each will be at a different point on the life-long earnings curve. Any generational comparison must be made at the same point in respective "life time"—the baby boomers as young adults in the 1980s versus their parents as young adults in the 1950s.

Such comparisons, however, are limited by the simple fact that the baby boomers have yet to reach middle age or retirement. The only basis for a comparison with their parents and grandparents is to look at how well each generation did at the beginning of life. Thus far at least, the baby boomers have not done as well as their parents. In a report commissioned by the Joint Economic Committee of Congress, Levy and Michel argue that "the young middle class (principally the baby boomers) has experienced a dramatic decline in its ability to pursue the conventional American dream: a home, financial security and education for their children." According to the authors, the American economy entered a quiet depression in the mid-1970s, at a point when many baby boomers were either still in their first jobs or about to start. Because the depression was characterized by a series of small events —an oil embargo here, a recession there, two Social Security tax hikes, steady inflation—no one noticed the massive cumulative impact on baby-boom incomes and purchasing power.

The baby boomers had very little armor against the onslaught of bad economic performance, as Levy and Michel conclude, "People who had already attained the middle-class dream found they had certain protections. One was the protection of job seniority. . . . Another was a fixed-payment mortgage which kept their housing costs under control, particularly since mortgage payments stayed constant in the face of inflation. But for people who had not yet attained the middle-class standard (or who had lost the standard and were trying to regain it), the standard looked increasing out of reach."[5] The adjustable rate mortgage (ARM) was the best many baby boomers could get, leaving them always vulnerable to the vicissitudes of inflation.

Much of the good news seems to be on the parents' side of the comparison. From 1950 to 1960, for example, the average 25-year-old man gained 118 percent in income. In contrast, from 1974 to 1984, the average 25-year-old man gained just 16 percent, and most of the increase was absorbed by spiralling costs of the kind outlined at the beginning of this chapter. For baby-boom families headed by 25- to 34-year-olds, for example, the 1970s brought a 54 percent jump in utility costs and a 65 percent rise in gasoline prices. It is no surprise that consumption by baby-boom families declined by $1,000 per year over the 1974-1984 period.[6] After subtracting increases in rent and mortgage costs, young families had six percent less discretionary income at the end of the ten years than at the beginning. There was little room for the kinds of luxuries so typically linked to the yuppies.

Levy and Michel report, "A young family in 1981 spent 14 percent less on furniture, 30 percent less on clothes, 15 percent less on personal care and 38 percent less on charitable contributions than a similar young family in 1973. And contrary to popular belief, the average young family in 1981 spent only $47 more per year on food outside the home."[7] The figures refute those who argue that the baby boomers' savings rate is evidence of instant gratification. "The savings and debt figures are not to be trivialized," Levy and Michel conclude. "The less a young family is able to save, the more it must postpone its entrance into the housing market. The greater its debt, the less its ability to qualify for mortgage loans given the affordability guidelines used by financial institutions."[8]

In a recent effort to control mortgage-loan defaults, the federal government has tightened those eligibility rules even further, raising the amount needed for down payments and the minimum incomes needed to qualify. It is now much tougher to get past the loan officers in either the federal government or the private sector. The result is that housing has become more difficult to get, especially for young families. A recent study by the Joint Center for Housing Studies found that "homeownership rates among younger households declined again in 1985, and are now well below the 1980 level. Unless young adults achieve substantial income growth or unless the cost of homeownership declines to more traditional levels, many more young families than in the past will find themselves unable to purchase a home."[9]

One reason for the lower figures is that housing costs have increased faster than rental costs. Some younger home-buyers decided not to enter the market, at least for the time being. Another reason is the baby boom's own social history. Delayed marriage and high divorce rates are hardly the ingredients of stable homeownership. Divorce usually results in the division of assets, not the purchase of new homes. What was once a home usually becomes two apartments. As such, divorce is the great self-inflicted crisis in the baby-boom housing fortunes.

Still another reason for the lower homeownership rate is that much of the new housing stock, as it is called, consists of new homes designed for "trade-up" buyers—that is, people who already own homes and want something bigger. With higher down-payment and income eligibility thresholds, the old housing is not automatically available to younger buyers. Hence, there is more housing available for rental, keeping rents down somewhat. A final reason for the lower homeownership among the baby boomers is that the net cost of owning a house increased dramatically in the 1970s. In 1978, the average mortgage payment was 22 percent of family income. By 1985, it was up to 36 percent, and has only recently begun to fall back.

The housing problem is particularly acute for the younger baby boomers. They may have gotten into the market too late. Those who could afford the downpayments in the late 1970s faced much higher interest rates. "These people were born five years too late to get the maximum income and the maximum house for their money," University of California economist Kenneth Rosen says. "The first wave pushed up all the prices and took the jobs." But even the older baby boomers have had their trouble. The home-ownership rate among people aged 30 to 34 dropped five percent between 1981 and 1986—from 59 to 54 percent. The rate fell four percent among people aged 25 to 29, too—from 42 to 39 percent. The figures may seem small, but they represent millions of potential homeowners.

Not everyone believes the baby boomers are behind. "They are coping," *Money* editor Landon Jones says, "but they're getting it all, too. And they're getting the houses, and they're getting the VCRs, and they're living near their parents. They're just moaning about it a lot." Another version of the yuppie caricature, also not exactly accurate. According to his own magazine, the average price of an existing house jumped from $27,000 in 1972 to $87,000 in 1987, or 222 percent, exceeding inflation by a half and driving potential baby-boom buyers out of the market. Furthermore, at least in 1986, according to the housing data, several million baby boomers had no choice but to live near their parents. Many were still living in their parents' homes, waiting to get enough money together to strike out on their own.

Like Jones, Brookings economist Louise Russell does not believe the baby boomers are behind either. Using data only up to 1980, she writes that "the baby boom has not had a harder time economically than other generations." Still, she says, there have been rough spots, particularly higher unemployment rates as the generation entered the labor force in record numbers in the late 1960s and early 1970s. "Established relationships have failed to hold for this generation," she continues, "and it has had to adjust to the end (whether temporary or permanent remains to be seen) of the steady growth in educational expenditures, in earnings, and in many other aspects of life, which had come to be accepted as an economic birthright."

Despite this lower economic growth, Russell still concludes

that "on balance, the baby boom has done better than earlier generations."[10] Because more baby boomers went to college and because college graduates earn more money, the baby boom has a slightly larger gross income than previous generations. However, as individuals, the baby boomers who went to college are earning less than members of previous generations who went to college. This certainly was not what many expected. Having grown up in a period of remarkable, indeed unprecedented economic growth, many baby boomers may have expected an easier time.

The question is whether the poor performance is a sign of intergenerational inequity. If the baby boom is doing poorly, and the elderly are doing well, perhaps society should step in to redress the imbalance. Author Phillip Longman would say yes, even if that means taking from the old to give to the young. He blames the elderly, in part, for the baby boom's housing shortage. The elderly have been much too slow in putting their houses up for sale, he argues, pushing prices beyond the baby boom's grasp.

According to Longman, the elderly should get out of the way, even if it means giving up their independence. After all, Longman writes, past generations of elderly "have often found it more convenient to move to an apartment after their children leave than to try and keep up a large, empty house."[11] Longman concludes, "Life often presents us with opportunities to enrich ourselves at the expense of latecomers. Often the transaction is inadvertent as, for example, when generations of Ethiopians overgrazed their land through ignorance of ecology, gaining more food for themselves but leaving their children and grandchildren to starve. . . . America's current housing policies will certainly not cost future Americans their food and succor. But, unless reformed, they will cost us the wealth that we need to buy houses to live in."[12] The "us-versus-them" rhetoric is unmistakable. Why not just move everyone out at age 70?

Taken to this extreme, the search for intergenerational equity becomes yet another caricature. In the abstract, most Americans support the notion of equal opportunity and fairness. They do not believe that one generation should benefit at the expense of another. However, that does not mean Americans believe society should establish priorities based on a generational balance sheet, that it should force the elderly to sell their houses early. Nor do most believe government should make it easier to make substandard housing. Unlike Longman, who worries that baby boomers no longer have "the option of buying a new, no-frills, unfinished 'starter house' of the size and kind that Levitt made famous, for in most towns across America such houses had already been declared illegal to build,"[13] most Americans remember enough about Levittowns to know that some housing regulation is needed.

Perhaps Longman should read Joseph Goulden's description of Levitt's golden days of starter housing. "Levitt used asphalt tile for the floors, even in the living room and dining area (*area*, not room), and explained that the traditional hardwood floor was not available because of shortages. Since most of his buyers had never owned a home, why should they know enough to object?" According to Goulden, the goal of these post-war builders was to see how little house they could sell for how much money. "What they offered, all too often," Goulden wrote, "was two bedrooms atop a concrete slab, containing little more space than one would find in a two-bedroom apartment." In these new, no-frills, unfinished starter homes, "Builders substituted linoleum for tile in bathrooms, pine for oak, plywood for pine; they used one coat of paint, rather than three. Floors were splintery, knotty horrors; tops and bottoms of doors were left unsealed and unpainted." Lawns disappeared with the first hard rain.[14]

Ultimately, sour grapes is not the way to find either political support or meaningful solutions to what is a very real baby boomer housing problem. No one likes a whiner. Consider Michel's description of the baby boom's recent housing crisis as an example of how *not* to win political backing: "They've settled for a smaller initial house. They've not taken for granted things that were taken as central to the American single-family home in the seventies. Many new houses don't have garages or a second bathroom; they're smaller in square footage, and a lot of people settled for one-bedroom condos—and are now finding themselves in the position of not being able to trade up, as their parents did." Settled for condos? Only one bathroom? Is Michel speaking for the baby boomers or the yuppies? It is doubtful that Congress will ever pass a "Second Bathroom Addition Act," and it is hard to find sympathy for baby boomers without garages. The generation may need help getting started, but not because it has to wait longer to trade up to a better neighborhood.

Further, a generational balance sheet cannot capture the advantages of growing up in the baby boom. Take the generation's educational achievement as one example. Only the most myopic economist would reduce the baby boom's education to a simple earnings equation. The fact that so many baby boomers were able to complete high school and go to college is an achievement shared by no other generation either past or present. The baby boomers have a greater appreciation for things not economic, a sense of aesthetic value beyond paycheck-to-paycheck survival. Whether that education always means more income is not the question. Indeed, perhaps this high level of education is why the baby boomers have not yet noticed their poor economic performance. Perhaps their search for a meaningful philosophy of life, which so dominated their thinking as high-school seniors and college freshmen, still takes precedence.

Perhaps the baby boomers also realize that their educational good fortune was the product of great sacrifice by their parents. As former Social Security commissioner Robert Ball argues in refuting the intergenerational equity lobby, "We owe much of what we are to the past. We all stand on the shoulders of generations that came before. They built the schools and established the ideals of an educated society. They wrote the books, developed the scientific ways of thinking, passed on ethical and spiritual values, discovered our country, developed it, won its freedom, held it together, cleared its forests, built its railroads and factories and invented new technology."[15] Just as the parents did well in the 1950s, so did the children. Indeed, the first decades of baby-boom life were rich with educational and social opportunities.

The greatest problem with these intergenerational accountings lies in comparing generations based on one or two decades of economic performance, especially since most Americans now live through seven or eight. It is one thing to compare young adults in the 1980s to their parents in the 1950s to show how the economy has changed, quite another to use such a limited snapshot to conclude that the eldery are soaking the young. Afterall, compared to their parents, the baby boomers are at the very beginning of the life-long earnings curve. Who knows what will happen in coming years?

Imagine, for example, what a similar comparison would have shown fifty years ago. The 25-year-old males who did so well in the 1950s and who created a standard against which to measure the baby boom's much poorer performance today, actually started life in a much more frightening economic climate. They were only four years old when the Great Depression hit, and faced a reasonable probability that one of their parents, most likely their father, would die before their eighteenth birthday. Unlike the baby boomers, only half made it through high school, and few went on to college.

Many served in World War II or Korea, and some died. Those who stayed home suffered through housing shortages and food rationing that would make Phillip Longman shudder. After the world war, most married quickly and most had children almost immediately, with all that means for lost freedom and privacy. (Indeed, surveys repeatedly show that the presence of even one child cuts into marital satisfaction.[16]) Nevertheless, even as their wages doubled during the 1950s, they set aside something every month for each child's future education.

Following the 1950s, they witnessed the same social and political unrest that shaped the baby boom, and at least 56,000 had a child die in Vietnam. They were hit by the same OPEC oil embargoes and stagflation that affected the baby boomers in the 1970s, and are only now entering retirement. Were these such lucky people afterall? Do one or two decades of exceptional economic performance compensate for the earlier losses? Given what they went through before turning 25, perhaps a 118 percent boost in income over the 1950s was far too little compensation. Though they had some protection against the poor economic performance of the 1970s through their job seniority and low mortgages, perhaps it was the least they had earned.

Life always presents economic rough spots. There is no doubt that the baby boomers have suffered a run of bad luck lately. And there is no doubt that the generation's size makes more bad luck likely. However, it is a little early to write off the baby boom's future. Its first four decades have been mixed fifty-fifty between good and bad. After a healthy childhood it had the bad luck to enter the labor force just about the time the Arab oil cartel figured out how to control the price of oil. That does not mean the baby boomers face a lifetime of poor performance.

What it does mean is that the baby boomers should concentrate on solvable problems, while praying for a little good luck. If size is going to be a continuing problem in the housing and labor markets—and all evidence says yes—the baby boomers should concentrate on ways to make the first home purchase easier and jobs more flexible. To date, the federal government and private mortgage companies appear to be more interested in making first home purchases tougher. If bad historical timing is going to continue, perhaps all the baby boomers can do is take solace in the fact that other generations have survived black Mondays in the stock market, too. "Baby boomers have short memories," writes economist Lester Thurow. "Some of them expect to have the same things when they walk out of college that their parents didn't have until they were 35 or 40."[17] A little patience will go a long way.

What may be particularly galling for some baby boomers is the rise of the elderly as the new media darlings. During childhood

and adolescence, the baby boomers were the most heavily mar-
keted generation in history. But, under Reagan, elderly disposable
income has gone steadily upward and the over-65 poverty rate has
dropped. Advertisers would have been blind not to notice a market composed of 60 million consumers.

The baby boomers have not quite decided what to think about
the marketing eclipse. Some gripe about the lost attention and the
need for an accounting. Others accept the so-called "maturity
market" as a good sign of the changing definition of aging in
America. "Just because they pass into the 'golden years,'" one
advertiser says about the elderly, "doesn't mean they quit living.
There are growing numbers of them who resent the implication
that old age is simply a time of leisure and rest."

The shifting focus off the baby boom and onto the maturity
market is obvious. *American Demographics* recently celebrated the
"Surprisingly Affluent Edlerly." The Ford modelling agency
now has a "Classic Women" department to meet the growing
demand for older models. Dozens of corporations now offer special discounts to attract the elderly's business, from discounts on
United and American airlines to a new "Silver Pages" phone
directory, from special discount clubs to an advertising blitz
on television. "Before, you gave discounts because the elderly
couldn't afford things," the director of Sears' "Mature Outlook"
discount club says. "Now, it is entirely different. We became
very aware that the 50-and-up market was the fastest growing
market and would continue that way well into the the next century. . . . They account for 77 percent of all financial assets controlled in the United States," the Sears' team concluded. "You
start to look at these kinds of statistics and as a mass marketer,
which is what Sears is, it became very apparent that as a company
we had to position ourselves much more strongly than before to
this new market."

Housing developers are taking aim, too, building hundreds of
new retirement villages in the past five years as trade-up housing

for older Americans in search of upscale "enclave" living. As Leisure Technology, Inc., puts it: "Older Americans are moving off the front porch, out of the rocking chair, into exciting new lives. They are starting new careers or continuing former careers but in a different fashion. This new generation of older Americans also demands a new generation of adult retirement communities —communities designed for elegant living, active recreational pursuits, diverse cultural programs and a secured environment."

None of these companies would be interested in the elderly but for the fact that the elderly have money, particularly discretionary money. As Peter Kim, a vice president at the J. Walter Thompson advertising agency, said in 1986, "Just as baby boomers were hot last year, this year it is the 49-plus market and seniors." The key term here is *discretionary*. In absolute numbers, the baby boomers have more income but they also have more nondiscretionary expenses—kids, mortgages, credit-card debts, etc. Because older Americans have fewer fixed financial obligations— they carry less than half as much personal debt as the baby boomers, for example—they have more freedom to spend. Thus, by 1986, the over-50 generation represented roughly 25 percent of all households, but 50 percent of the discretionary dollars. In contrast, the baby boom represented about 40 percent of all households, but only 30 percent of discretionary spending.[18]

These figures feed the debate about the possible imbalance between young and old in America. As former Colorado governor Richard Lamm suggested, "The generation currently running America is made up of prodigal parents. Unlike the biblical story, we have enriched ourselves at the expense of our children. We have mortgaged their future to pay for our excesses. We inherited a rich country from our parents and we have bequeathed an encumbered country to our children." Even the normally liberal *New Republic* agrees, warning the elderly in 1985 that their "demands on federal taxpayers, on working Americans, their demands on their own children and grandchildren have grown far beyond what is fair and can reasonably be provided. America's elders are burdening their heirs with debts and unfunded liabilities that have reached dangerous proportions."

This debate is less about a grand intergenerational accounting, however, and more about shared sacrifice in combatting the growing national debt and budget crisis—a debt which more than doubled during the first six years of the Reagan presidency. As with personal debt, the interest costs eventually become the great frustration. As the comptroller general of the United States said in 1986, "The $135 billion we paid last year in net interest on the federal debt did not buy us a thing—except the privilege of paying it again this year. It didn't buy a single tank or airplane, it did not pave a mile of highway or replace a single obsolete bridge, and it didn't pay the salary of a single FBI agent or air traffic controller."

All totalled, the baby boomers face a $2 to $3 trillion burden over the next four decades—roughly $40,000 a piece on top of an average $6,000-7,000 in personal debt. Even if they retire their personal debts, the baby boomers will carry the national debt throughout their lifetime as a constant reminder of the Reagan revolution, a revolution fueled by their own votes.

As Sen. David Durenberger (R-MN) argues, this debt "gets used against the young in two ways. First, it forces them to pay installments well into the future on yesterday's consumption, and next, it allows those of us in government to tell the young that we can't repair sewage systems, or take care of ground water problems, or invest in education, because the money isn't there." And yet, when congressional negotiators dared hint at a freeze on Social Security cost-of-living adjustments (COLAs) as part of a broad budget-cutting compromise in the wake of the stock market crash, elderly lobbying groups said absolutely no. One might ask which is the truly self-absorbed generation: the one which said yes to a 331 percent increase in Social Security taxes from 1972 to 1987 or the one which said no to what would have been but a 2 percent COLA freeze designed to restore confidence in the stock market in 1987?

Moreover, there is a growing concern that the elderly may be using their considerable political power to exploit the nation's children. At least that is what University of Pennsylvania scholar Samuel Preston argues. Addressing the Population Association of America in 1984, Preston concluded, "Conditions have deteriorated for children and improved dramatically for the elderly," largely because of Social Security and a new set of political priorities.[19] In 1984, for example, the federal government spent $217 billion on various programs for the elderly and $36 billion on children. However, the figures do not include the amounts spent by parents on kids—at least for now, America still relies on parents to provide for children. Yet, there is no doubt that poverty among children has been rising, while poverty among the elderly has been falling.

According to Preston, "It's no mystery that the main factor in the reduction of poverty among the elderly is the expansion of Social Security benefits. It's been calculated that 56 percent of the elderly would have been in poverty in 1978 had it not been for such income transfers." Instead, there were less than 30 percent. Looking at the federal budget in 1984, Preston calculated that children received roughly one-quarter as much support as the elderly. Though Preston did not blame the elderly per se, there was enough suspicion to go around: "Do we care about our collective future—the commonwealth—or only about our individual futures? If only our individual futures matter, then our concerns will naturally focus on ourselves as older persons and we will continue down the road we appear to be on."[20]

Perhaps the *New Republic* is right to criticize the growing list of federal welfare programs for the elderly rich. Whether they need it or not, Americans are entitled to a host of benefits by merely celebrating their sixty-fifth birthday. If elderly poverty is the problem, why is the federal government so generous with the elderly rich? Federal tax breaks are one example. The elderly poor have little need for a capital gains exclusion on their home sales or protection from federal income tax on half their Social Security benefits. They do not have homes to sell and are already protected against income tax on their Social Security through income thresholds enacted in 1983.

The taxpayers who benefit most from such "tax expenditures" are the taxpayers with deductions. In 1977, for example, when the capital gains exclusion applied only to those over 65 (it is now 55) and the ceiling on the exclusion was just $35,000 (it is now $125,000), half of all tax savings went to older Americans who were already making over $50,000 a year.[21] The recent changes could only improve the harvest. Indeed, in helping well-to-do elderly with a knotty tax problem, the federal government will give up in excess of $12 billion in revenues over the 1985–89 period, revenues that might be better used for the elderly homeless or disabled. The question is, why should 55-year-olds receive tax protection when they sell a home for up to $125,000? Such protection is of no help to a 85-year-old widow about to be forced into a nursing home.

It is not that the baby boomers are mad at their parents and grandparents. Not yet at least. Rather, they may be starting to wonder why they are bearing so much of the burden. The 1983 Social Security rescue is one example. There is no doubt that the rescue was needed. The Social Security system was in the midst of its second major crisis in five years, and checks were about to be delayed. The question is whether the baby boom paid too much for the compromise. On top of the substantial Social Security tax increase on the baby boomers, two other legislative changes suggest that the answer is yes.

The first change made some Social Security benefits subject to federal income tax. However, to protect the elderly poor, only retirees who made more than $25,000 a year single or $32,000 married were covered. It was a good way to take back some of the welfare for the rich that the *New Republic* criticized as part of the "Social Security Rip-Off" where the poor pay and the rich ride. The only catch for the baby boomers is that Congress did not index the income levels to rise with inflation over the next thirty years. As a result, virtually all of the baby boomers will be paying taxes on their Social Security benefits when they retire. No one seemed to think to ask whether they will all be able to afford it then.

The second, even more significant change pushed the baby boomer retirement age upward from 65 to 67. Starting at the turn of the next century, the retirement age will begin to increase two months each year in 2000–2005 and 2017–2022. The change was seen as a way to adjust future benefits for increasing lifespans. Since the baby boomers are going to live longer, Congress concluded, they should work longer, too. The only catch is that an increase in longevity does not necessarily mean a day-for-day increase in the quality of life. Congress may have taken away two of the best years of retirement, from 65 to 67, in exchange for two of the worst.

Even in 1983, there was increasing evidence that baby-boom longevity would not necessarily bring much of an increase in good retirement years. Writing just months before Congress acted, National Institute of Health researchers Edward Schneider and Jacob Brody concluded that, "the number of very old people is increasing rapidly, that the average period of diminished vigor will probably increase, that chronic diseases will probably occupy a larger proportion of our life span, and that the needs for medical care in later life are likely to increase substantially."[22] Indeed, as National Institute of Aging director Robert Butler warned the National Commission on Social Security Reform in mid-1982, "it appears that morbidity rates are rising and that the drop in mortality rates means a growing burden of serious sickness problems in the oldest population."

Simply put, these scholars were merely acknowledging the plain truth that medicine is an imperfect science. To date, it has been unable to reduce mortality and poor health simultaneously. People may survive diseases which would have killed them twenty years ago, but not without a loss in quality of life. The retirement age increase may have been a very unfair bargain indeed, resulting in a slow but steady compression of the generation's good years. However, instead of using *health expectancy* in place of *life expectancy* for evaluating the impact of a change in the retirement age, Congress moved ahead under the simpleminded notion that longevity and good health walk hand-in-hand.

These two changes also altered the baby boom's rate of return from their Social Security taxes. In 1980, for example, the average retiree needed only thirteen months of benefits to equal all the taxes he or she had paid into Social Security over forty years of work (the program did not begin until 1940). Adding in the equal amount that employers must pay, plus a fair rate of interest, the average retiree needed just over five years of benefits to equal past taxes and interest paid in. It was a very fine investment indeed, particularly since the life expectancy for someone turning 65 years of age in 1980 was 82—or twelve years past the point when the average retiree had recouped his or her initial Social Security investment.

In contrast, by the 2020s, it will take the average baby-boom retiree over fifteen years to get back just the taxes he or she will have paid into the system over roughly fifty years of work. The reasons are twofold. First, the baby boomers are paying a much higher tax rate today than in the 1940s—during its first decade, the total Social Security tax was 1 percent; in January 1988, it moved past 7.5 percent, and will go up again in 1990. Moreover, that tax rate is applied to an ever-larger portion of income—a portion which rises each year with inflation; up from $42,000 in 1987 to $43,500 in 1988. Second, the later retirement age means they will be paying those higher taxes longer.

When combined, the taxes and retirement age affect Social Security's hypothetical rate of return—that is, the ratio of benefits taken out to taxes paid in. As two conservative economists argue, "The baby boom which, because of its great numbers, is able to support the gains conferred on today's retirees, cannot expect anywhere near similar gains when it retires, again because of its numbers. The gains conferred on today's retirees are the result of a Social Security system, populations, and economy that were expanding and growing more rapidly in the past than can be expected in the future. The 1983 Social Security Amendments mark the beginning of the process of amortizing the start-up gains from Social Security by reducing the gains to younger generations."[23]

The lower rate of return does not mean, however, that Social Security will be a bad deal for the baby boomers. They will still get a reasonable return. Rather, it means that their rate of return will be nowhere near that of their parents and grandparents. Whereas some parents and grandparents will take out as much as 200 percent more than what they put in, most baby boomers will be lucky to get even a double-digit return—assuming, of course, that future workers will be able to pay the taxes. The fact is that the baby boomers will inherit a fully mature Social Security system in which benefits taken out more closely resemble taxes paid in. That is the way the system ought to work. As such, it is the parents and grandparents who were the truly lucky ones, having joined a very young Social Security system in which benefits could far exceed taxes paid, in large part because the baby boomers eventually would be able to absorb whatever tax increases might be needed.

The baby boom's lagging performance is clearly an important problem in and of itself. Unfortunately, it is all too often swallowed up in the intergenerational equity debate, reduced to a set of scare headlines about future catastrophes and young-versus-old.

The equity advocates even have their own lobbying group. Created by a former Senate staff member who noticed that every special interest had its own lobbying group except the baby boom, Americans for Generational Equity, or AGE, hopes intergenerational comparisons will become a tool for making national policy decisions. According to AGE, even airline discounts should be allocated by need. Why should the elderly receive cheap airline tickets or free checking, asks an AGE researcher, when "such discounts must come at least indirectly at the expense of younger customers?"[24]

Though AGE has been raising important long-term questions about baby-boom health and retirement, it has often reduced the issues to a simple "us-versus-them" calculation.[25] By emphasizing the "baby" in baby boom, AGE has shifted the discussion off the generation's real problems and onto a much less productive inter-generational track. Jack Ossofsky, president of the National Council on Aging, characterizes this strategy as, there is "no generational war, but there are warmongers."

Thus, the equity debate has its share of caricatures, too. Many elderly cannot afford even a 2 percent COLA cut, especially not with Medicare cost increases. Despite the new stereotype of the surprisingly affluent elderly, it was not until 1984 that the elderly poverty rate first fell below the national average. Even today, one out of five older Americans still live either below the poverty line or dangerously close to it. They have no way of protecting their fixed income against inflation, and live in constant fear of catastrophic illness. Like the yuppies, the maturity market is only a small part of the true population.

Further, the notion that children and the elderly have to compete against each other for scarce dollars lets defense entirely off the hook. Aging experts Eric Kingson, Barbara Hirshorn, and John Cornman argue, "the intergenerational equity approach to public policy incorporates a deep pessimism about the implications of an aging society. It presents the 20th century trend of increasing longevity of the population and the significant improvements of the past 30 years in the economic well-being of most elderly persons as if these changes are somehow signs of the failure of our society, rather than among its greatest achievements."

As for those who worry about baby-boom retirement and the growing national debt, Kingson and colleagues offer a more optimistic future, chiding the pessimists who question the ability of the future economy to meet the needs of all citizens, and the economic doubters who say "we are relatively powerless to confront some of the problems emerging in an aging society through, for example, the development of new technology and research-based knowledge." According to Kingson et al., these doom-and-gloomers "fail to recognize opportunities associated with this demographic event, including increased quality of life for today's young when they are old and the opportunity— and necessity— to use the productive abilities of future cohorts of the elderly as fully as possible."[26]

Clearly, all generations have a common stake in working together to solve the budget and debt crisis. Unfortunately, future economic growth may be impossible when much of the needed research on new technology and research-based knowledge, as Kingson and his colleagues call it, is being cut to the bone as one special interest after another enforces its demands on the political process. If the debt crisis is not soon solved, it is hard to create a hopeful scenario for the coming decades. Further, whatever Kingson and his colleagues say, there is no crime in being less than wildly optimistic about the future. Some pessimism seems warranted by recent economic performance. A 22 percent fall in stock prices is hardly the basis for enthusiasm about the coming years. Finally, the first step in developing new technologies and knowledge may be in recognizing the growing need to build a new economic base capable of supporting the baby boom and its offspring.

In the midst of all the bad economic news, however, the baby boomers remain reasonably satisfied with their current progress. Indeed, that is the biggest frustration for lobbyists like AGE. They can never generate any mail to Congress. In surveys during the 1984 campaign, for example, the baby boomers saw the economy as being much healthier and their own finances as being much stronger than older Americans.

Richard Michel argues that the baby boomers are just not yet aware of their problems, that "the changes have been gradual, and

many baby boomers don't realize what has happened." But perhaps Landon Jones is on point when he says "I'll be darned if I
can figure out why the people themselves don't know it. When
they're asked, 'How are you doing?' they do say, 'I'm doing
great.' "

When asked in a survey by the Conference Board in 1986 to
"compare your present standard of living with that of your parents
during the last few years that you were living at home," a quarter
of those under 35 actually said it was much better, 40 percent said
better, a quarter said about the same, and only a quarter said not
quite as good or worse. Though Conference Board researcher
Fabian Linden rightly says that the bottom 25 percent is "a very,
very large number, and if we had done the same survey 25 years
ago, we would have gotten a much lower percent," the figures
have been widely used as evidence of baby-boom happiness. Linden himself concludes that the idea that the baby boom "ain't got
it so good is really a fiction."

In recent financial surveys, the baby boomers have been much
more likely to say the economy is getting better, while the elderly
are more likely to say it is getting worse. In the 1984 University
of Michigan national election surveys, the baby boom was over
three times more likely than the elderly to say that their financial
condition was better or somewhat better than the previous year.[27]
An ABC News/*Money* survey two years later confirmed the continued optimism. Of those under 35, six out of ten said the economy was in good or excellent shape, compared to only a third of
the people over 65.[28] If there is any perception of a poor economy,
it exists among older Americans, perhaps explaining why they are
so reluctant to compromise on Social Security COLAs.

The baby boomers are also more likely than older Americans
to say that individuals are responsible for their own lot in life.
According to Daniel Yankelovich, the "national psychology holds
that those who play the game according to the rules (and the rules
include luck, hard work and 'good connections') are entitled to
their success, and should be able to reinvest liberally what they

get."[29] In the same vein, those who lose should not complain, even if it is not their fault. To the lasting chagrin of the lobbyists who would be king of the intergenerational movement, the baby boomers remain at intergenerational peace.

Indeed, a special January 1983 survey by the American Council of Life Insurance (ACLI) shows deep baby boomer acceptance of intergenerational responsibility. Over a third of the baby boomers interviewed said they had a great deal of responsibility to make sure their aging parents have an adequate income. Over half felt they should help guarantee that their parents have good housing. Two-thirds felt responsible for keeping their parents from being lonely. Almost three-quarters said they accepted a great deal of responsibility for ensuring that their parents got good health care. Conversely, only 15 percent felt little or no responsibility for their parents' income, and even fewer showed no willingness to help on housing, companionship, and health care.[30]

This is not intergenerational war at all. It is hardly the kind of data to give solace to those who hope to forge a political coalition based on bitterness between generations. Further, the baby boomers may not want their parents' and grandparents' help in any case. In the ACLI survey, only six percent of the baby boomers said parents should give their children a great deal of help in buying a house, and less than 20 percent said parents ought to leave their estates to their children after death. Only a third felt parents should provide a place to live for their adult children even if those children could not afford shelter. And only a third said parents should give their children a college education.[31] One cannot know, however, whether the baby boomers answered these questions as children or as parents—that is, whether their limited expectations of what a parent should do for a child is a warning sign to their own offspring.

The lack of intergenerational conflict does not mean that the baby boom will never react to its economic performance. There are already signs of increasing worry. There appears to be a growing sense of fear that the bills are due. After two Social Security

crises, three tax reforms, and repeated promises of balanced budgets, the public may finally sense that it is time to wake up, that the
"Morning in America" is over.

At least those are the findings of a team of *Washington Post*
reporters led by David Broder and Haynes Johnson. According
to their interviews with baby boomers and older Americans alike,
voters were on the "cusp" by 1986. They still liked Reaganomics
and the end of double-digit inflation, but, according to Broder,
they "were very much aware of and ready to verbalize their sense
of concern about the economic challenges that they could see on
the horizon and their feeling that those challenges, if not addressed, might come down on them and their communities and
their families in a way that would be as tough to deal with as the
inflation had been at the end of the 1970s." What struck Broder
most was "that these problems were linked in their minds as being
symptoms of a kind of national excess for which they were very
ready and willing to take some of the responsibility themselves."

This growing concern is particularly clear when the baby
boomers compare their current performance against their high-
school expectations. In 1986, for example, the CBS News/*New
York Times* Poll asked Americans whether they felt they had a
better life than their parents, and whether they had accomplished
more than they had expected when they had been in high school.
Comparing their lives to their parents, 72 percent of the 30- to
39-year-olds said they had done better than their parents, while
only 10 percent said worse.

However, when asked to think back to high school, one-third
said they had accomplished less than they had once expected, a
third said about as much, and just under a third said more. The
figures suggest a gap between expectations and reality. When
asked whether they were better off financially than they expected
to be by their age, 27 percent of the baby boomers said they were
worse off, with a third better off, and a third about the same.[32]

Three other surveys confirm the baby boom's increasing
awareness that something is wrong, not because parents are rip-

ping off children, but because life just is not working out quite as planned. First, a 1984 Harris Poll showed surprising levels of doubt about the baby boom's generational success, and a rare glimpse of possible intergenerational conflict. Almost 75 percent of the baby boomers said they felt the generation faces "more competition from others their same age for jobs, promotions, and the chance to get ahead because there are so many of them." Another 36 percent said the generation "often finds itself blocked by an older generation which won't yield control and tends to play off these young people against each other." Two-thirds said the baby boomers "had to wait much longer to be able to buy a new house or apartment," and a third said the baby boomers "had not had as good a chance to get things out of life as their parents." Finally, and perhaps most troubling, 40 percent felt that "the people who hold the real political power by and large have kept younger people from the Baby Boom generation from playing a more important role in politics and government in this country."[33]

Second, a 1986 Roper Poll suggests that the baby boom is beginning to think the American dream is slipping away. Almost half of the baby boomers said the American dream is harder to reach now than it was a generation ago, compared to just one in five who said that it was easier. Only two percent of the baby boomers said they had reached the American dream—defined by most Americans generally as "freedom of choice in how to live one's life," owning a home, and sending one's children to college. No wonder: the majority of baby boomers say they would need about $70,000 a year to achieve that dream. Not that older Americans feel much better. Only 16 percent of the over-65 group said they had attained the dream.[34] But at least they see it as being somewhat less expensive. Most said it would cost them about $40,000 a year.

Third, a 1985 survey by Market Facts, Inc., suggests that people under 35 may be slightly more willing to take risks than those over 55, but only if they can achieve their prime investment objective of not losing money.[35] The short-term economic climate may be just uncertain enough to keep the generation from taking personal financial gambles. Perhaps Levy is right after all. Perhaps the baby boomers are starting to ask "Is there something wrong with me? Is something wrong with my job? What the heck's going on here?"

If these figures do not show a growing conflict between generations, they do suggest a future battle between baby boomers, rich and poor. Some baby boomers are doing fine, many are not, but none see the problem as being the elderly. The baby boomers are divided across a number of lines, creating great potential for political and social polarization—not between young and old, but between men and women, upper class and under class, black and white—all within the baby boom.

3

A Generation Divided

ALL BABY BOOMERS were not born identical. Some were born male, others female. Some were born black, others white. Some were born rich, some poor, but most were born in the middle. These divisions have yet to surface as intragenerational conflicts, but they exist nonetheless.

Most of the divisions are just below the surface. Take a magazine like *Quality* as one example. If ever a magazine was designed for yuppies, it was *Quality*. But in order to stretch its subscription base, *Quality* billed itself as a magazine for everyone, rich and poor alike. Launched in 1987, the premier issue claimed that quality was a "democratic value," something to be found in hot dogs and caviar alike. "*Quality* will not dictate or seek to impose identical standards on everyone," the publisher wrote. "Instead *Quality* will articulate the best alternatives and help you decide for yourself what serves you best." All baby boomers were welcome.

However, if the lead issue was any indication, baby boomers may have wanted *Quality* but only the yuppies could afford it. Why else did Cartier, Audi, Volvo, BMW, Chivas Regal, Topsiders, Lands' End, and Fidelity Mutual Funds buy space? Why else did the editors pick articles on Apple's new computer for tots and a piece entitled "Joyce Carol Oates Test-Drives the Ferrari

Testarossa" for the first issue? Why did they do a taste-test comparing virtually every brand of strawberry jam on the market—from Silver Palate Strawberry Field Preserves to Grafton Goodjam, Les Fins Gourmet Confiture, Soleillou Preserves, Staud's of Vienna Preserves, and Nelson of Aintree—without the slightest mention of Welch's Squeeze-Bottle Strawberry Jam? Why did the advice column lead with a question on whether replacing the original movement of an antique watch affects its value, and follow with the always pressing baby-boom need for help on how to commission an original painting or sculpture?

Quality was a slick, elegant magazine, an example of the excellence it celebrated. However, it remained very much a yuppie product, designed to tap a small segment of the baby boom. Perhaps that is why the magazine is temporarily on the Time/Life shelf. Its production costs were high, its initial subscription base slim.

More important, by first portraying itself as a magazine for everyone and then delivering a "yuppies-only" message, *Quality* offered a not-so-subtle confirmation of the baby boom's mixed economic success. Whatever the publisher said about hot dogs and strawberry jam, this was not a magazine for an about-to-be divorced baby-boom woman facing an approximately 73 percent cut in her disposable income, nor for an urban high-school dropout trapped in poverty.

The problem for anyone trying to tap the baby boom as a generation is that there is no such thing as a standard-issue baby boomer. The generation—like other generations—appears to be divided most by age, gender, education, economic class. One division important and particular to the baby boom is service in Vietnam. Vietnam vets are different from Vietnam protestors.

Too many who set out to solicit to baby boomers overlook the age division. Baby boomers born at the very front end of the generation in 1946 are different from the baby boomers born at the very back in 1964. After all, they are almost twenty years apart.

Not only are the oldest baby boomers at a different point in their life cycle, they have a very different social and political history than the younger group. They are old enough to remember atomic-bomb drills and the freedom marches, and most have very clear recollections of President Kennedy's assassination. They are more likely to already have both children and mortgages, and many have second marriages.

In contrast, the youngest baby boomers are only now beginning their first careers, and may still be a year or two from first marriages. They are more likely to remember MIA bracelets and Earth Day than bomb shelters and civil rights. Their memories of the Kennedy assassination are about Bobby not John. They are less likely to have either children or mortgages, and some are still living at home.

Given their respective positions in both history and the life cycle, it is best to talk about two baby booms: the old wave, born from 1946 to 1954, and the new wave, born from 1955 to 1964. The two halves experienced a different social and political history and continue to experience a different economic reality. Like the firstborns in a family, the old wave has received the lion's share of economic and social benefits. Like the later-borns in a family, the new wave has taken whatever is left. Further, the simple differences in age may explain a host of political data. Because they are at a different point in the life cycle, the older baby boomers have more experience with politics and society. Consider the following differences that emerged from data collected by the University of Michigan's Center for Political Studies in 1984:

• Younger baby boomers were 12 percent less likely to watch network news every day, perhaps because they were less settled down. They were almost 10 percent less likely to be very interested in the 1984 campaign, in part because they had less at stake, and were less likely to know their congressional candidates, in part because candidates may have trouble finding them as they move.

• Younger baby boomers also were less confident about their ability to influence government. Sixty-five percent said that a person should not vote if they don't care about the outcome of an election, compared to just 53 percent of the older baby boomers. They were also more likely to say that people like them did not have a say about what government does.

• Contrary to those who see younger baby boomers as a bulwark of Republicanism, they were less likely than their older peers to approve of Reagan's handling of his job as president, less likely to approve of his foreign policy, his economic policy, or his efforts to balance the budget. They were also less likely to say there was anything they liked about the Republican party.

Moreover, the fact that the old wave grew up in the 1950s and early 1960s may explain why they still support Johnson's Great Society, and why their younger siblings are much less enthusiastic about it. A 1986 CBS/*New York Times* Poll found that 47 percent of the older baby boomers said government programs created in the 1960s to try to improve the condition of poor people in this country had generally made things better. Only 17 percent said the programs had made things worse. In contrast, not only was the new wave 14 percent less likely to say the programs had made things better, 41 percent said the programs had had no impact.[1]

Perhaps the old wave can afford to be generous. They have higher incomes, lower mortgage rates, and lower personal debts than their younger siblings, in part because they are further ahead in the life cycle—and therefore further along in their careers and higher on the earnings curve—and in part because they paid less of an economic penalty for being in the baby boom than their younger siblings. According to University of Kentucky economist Mark Berger, college-educated baby boomers born after 1957 may earn as much as 10 percent less over their lifetime than those born before that year. "If you were born after 1957," Berger says, "you may be in the same-size group as those born in 1953, but you've got all those people in front of you who already entered the work force, so things look a little worse."

Housing is one example. As Cheryl Russell, editor of *American Demographics*, wrote: "If you could buy before housing prices and interest rates went sky high, you will be better off your entire life than the ones who bought after the inflation in housing prices." Jean van der Tak, a senior demographer at the Population Reference Bureau, clearly agrees, "The leading edge of the baby boom has had it pretty good. They came along first, they got the jobs first and they bought their houses in the early 1970s before inflation soared. Now, they're sitting pretty, relative to those born after them, who had to buy homes in the late 1970s and early 1980s, when prices escalated and it took two incomes to buy a house."

Both waves of the boom have had their share of housing trouble, according to the Joint Center for Housing Studies. However, the data suggest that the new wave has had the worst of it. When the older baby boomers were in their early twenties, for example, they had a 23 percent homeownership rate. When the younger baby boomers were the same age, they were at 19 percent. By the time the older baby boomers passed 30, they had a 44 percent rate. By the time the first of the younger baby boomers reached the same milestone, they were four percent behind, at 40 percent.[2] Those younger baby-boom homeowners are likely to be paying more in monthly mortgage and interest, too.

In the American "first come, first serve" economy, the older baby boomers have always done just a little better than their younger siblings. They got a headstart. As such, generations may be subject to the same kinds of birth-order effects that social psychologists find in families. Just as firstborns in a family get nurtured first, firstborns in a generation get educated and employed first. And that constitutes an advantage that translates into future income and spending power. According to University of Michigan scholars Robert Zajonc and Gregory Markus, these kinds of birth-order effects involve a "confluence" theory of family resources: "It's called confluence theory because the intellectual development of a family is like a river with inputs of each family member flowing into it," Zajonc says.

The key problem for later-borns is the dwindling attention they get, whether from parents, schools, or the economy. "As families get larger, children's intellectual development suffers, and the effect is accentuated by birth order—the more older siblings a person has," Zajonc argues, "the lower his or her intellectual level because of the decrease within the family intellectual environment."[3] While parents can concentrate all of their energies and expectations on their firstborn, they must divide their attention as other children arrive. That may be why more firstborns are listed in *Who's Who*, and why more are National Merit scholars, eminent scientists, Nobel laureates, and American presidents.[4]

That may also explain why the front end of the baby boom did better on their college entrance exams (SATs) in the 1960s than the later-borns did in the mid-1970s. In 1947, Landon Jones reports, "nearly one out of every two babies born that year was the first child in its family. When those same babies took the verbal and mathematics SATs eighteen years later in 1965, they averaged 484.5. In subsequent years, the scores dropped, as did the proportion of firstborn children taking the test." By the mid-1950s, the number of firstborns had dropped to 30 percent. And, according to Jones, "when those 1955 babies took their SATs in high school in 1973, the average score had dwindled over 20 points to 463." Thus, the new wave may have suffered a double deficit: not only were they mostly later-borns in their own families, they were later-borns within society.

Being a firstborn is not all wonderful, however. They have problems, too. Although they have the advantage of being first served, they may also suffer from being the focus of so much parental attention. According to Zajonc and Markus, because firstborns may monopolize their mothers' attention, later-born siblings may have to find affection elsewhere. "Later-born children may, therefore, become less dependent than the firstborn because when young they learn to seek support from a greater variety of social sources, including other siblings." In short, later-borns may be more socially outgoing. In contrast, as political scientist Stanley Renshon suggests, "firstborn children are less autonomous and have less well-developed feelings of personal effectiveness in politics."

Birth order is not the only difference between the two waves of the baby boom, however. Younger and older baby boomers were raised under different child-rearing philosophies. According to psychologist Susie Orbach, the post-war period was an emotional rollercoaster for all children, "a world with few enduring values, little consistency and a paucity of control."[5] Parents were clearly confused by the flood of advice on how to rear children, and that confusion affected all baby boomers.

Even here, the older baby boomers may have gotten the lucky breaks, growing up in a somewhat more nurturing period than their younger siblings. At least that is what psychologists Elinor Waters and Vaughn Crandall found after documenting the child-rearing differences in remarkably detailed observations of mothers and their baby-boom children. According to their research, mothers were more babying and protective of their young children in 1950 than in 1960. They offered more help to their children whether they needed it or not, and sheltered them from "potential psychological and physical frustrations and dangers."[6]

These mothers also showed more open affection toward their children and used approval more often than punishment. They gave their children more freedom than mothers in 1940, but were always nearby. This combination of nurturance and freedom may have given these first baby boomers a sense of protected individualism, a feeling that they could explore the limits of life without fear.

By the mid-1950s, however, the pendulum was swinging back. James Dean's "Rebel without a Cause" was a hit, and a juvenile delinquency scare was on. Parents were under pressure to get tough with their kids. "What [the growing delinquency panic] often represented," writes historian James Gilbert, "was a vaguely formulated but gnawing sense of social disintegration—symbolized in the misbehavior of youth. Certainly youth had changed, and so had official response to delinquency. But the issue always stood knee deep in symbolism, making it unclear whether delinquency as crime increased significantly during this period or if juvenile behavior was more closely scrutinized and labeled criminal or if both or neither are true. The point is that a large portion of the public thought there was a delinquency crime wave, and they clamored to understand how and why this was happening."[7] One frequent answer was that parents were too lenient with their young children.

Even Dr. Benjamin Spock was convinced of this. In revising his best-selling book *Baby and Child Care* in 1957, he switched to a stricter philosophy. "If you are an older reader of this book," he wrote in the new introduction, "you'll see that a lot has been added and changed, especially about discipline, spoiling and the parents' part. When I was writing the first edition, between 1943 and 1946, the attitude of people toward infant feeding, toilet training, and general child management was still strict and inflexible. Since that time a great change in attitude has occurred, and nowadays there seems to be more chance of a conscientious parent's getting into trouble with permissiveness than with strictness. So I have tried to give a more balanced view."[8]

Mothers only took part of his advice. As Waters and Crandall report, mothers did get tougher. They showed less direct affection and approval. However, these mothers imposed even fewer restrictions on their children than in the 1950s, and were more ambiguous in placing limits on behavior. These young baby boomers had more freedom than their older siblings. If the early 1950s was the period when mothers displayed the most nurturance and affection toward their children, Waters and Crandall report that, "By 1960, the mothers studied were more similar to the 1940 sample and displayed less babying, protectiveness, affection, and approval than the 1950 mothers." Perhaps it was because so many women were returning to the workforce in the early 1960s, and had less time to think about "child management," as Spock called it. Perhaps it was force of habit from the 1950s. Whatever the

reason, this combination of less nurturance and even more freedom may have given these new-wave baby boomers a sense of
lonely individualism, a feeling that they had no choice but to
explore the boundaries of life.

Further, also because of an accident of birth order, the older
and younger baby boomers caught the rising tide of divorce at
different points in their life cycles. Thus, whereas 80 percent of
the old wave made it to age 18 without experiencing their parents'
divorce, only 50 percent of the new wave were so lucky. By the
time the younger baby boomers were three years old, 10 percent
were already in broken homes. In fact, the odds of parents staying
together actually fell faster while the new-wave children were
under ten than over.[9] By the 1960s, the time-honored notion of
"staying together for the children" was past. Most marriages were
breaking up sooner rather than later. For the old wave, divorce
was an adolescent affair. For the new wave, divorce was as much
a part of childhood as Oreos and milk.

Perhaps these differences due to birth order explain why the
older baby boomers entered college so ready to explore philosophies of life, while their younger siblings were more interested in
just getting through the day. The new wave entered adulthood
with very few illusions about life. Parents did not stay together,
did not seem to care, and children were not sheltered. Kids learned
early and often that the world was an uncertain place. That uncertainty marks the younger baby boomers today, perhaps explaining
why the younger baby boomers are more likely than their older
siblings to say they are worried about the chances of the United
States getting into either a nuclear or conventional war, and why
they feel that material success is all that matters.

In describing his "lost generation," David Leavitt writes about
the new-wave baby boomers. "We have always been the tail end
—of the Sixties, of the Baby Boom. We hit our stride in an age
of burned-out, restless, ironic disillusion. . . . Born too late and too
early, we are partially what came before us and partially what
followed." Yet, despite their different histories, Leavitt offers a

final portrait of the new wave which sounds surprisingly appropriate for the old wave, too. "Rather than move, we burrow," he writes. "We are interested in stability, neatness, entrenchment. We want to stay in one place and stay in one piece, establish careers, establish credit. We want good apartments, fulfilling jobs, nice boy/girl friends. We want American Express Gold Cards."[10]

Though their early years may differ, all baby boomers may share the same political and social volatility. The confusion of history, and breakdown of traditional families, may have come early in life or somewhat later, but it came nonetheless.

A significant division among baby boomers that appears to be growing is a gender gap over political issues, whether that gap reflects a Republican problem with women or a Democratic problem with men, whether on nuclear power or nuclear weapons, freedom of choice on abortion or equal pay for equal work, environmental protection or economic policy. And that gap on issues has increasingly appeared as a gap in elections. As political scientist Ethel Klein notes, "The long-awaited women's vote arrived in 1980 and persisted through 1984 because Republicans campaigned precisely on those issues on which men and women have most clearly parted company."[11]

It may seem surprising that a generation known for its social liberalism would have a gender gap at all. One reason is that the baby boom's gender gap is often hidden by two much more familiar gaps—the generation gap between younger and older Americans of both genders, and another between younger and older women.

There is no question that the baby boomers, as a generation, are more supportive of women's rights than their parents and grandparents. Perhaps because younger Americans are more likely to be in two-earner families, for example, they are less likely than older Americans to say that the first workers to be laid off should be women whose husbands have jobs, or to say that male and female workers ought not be given the same benefits and pay.

There is also a gap between younger and older women. As noted earlier in this book, the baby boom's grandmothers are still attached to the breadwinner system, and are much less likely to think that girls should be given the same educational and employment opportunities as boys. Because they were raised in a much more conservative social era, and because they were given limited access to education and its liberalizing effects, older women are often in rough agreement with older men on women's issues. Many still follow their husbands' leads in the voting booth. Women over 60 remain almost three times as likely as women under 20 to answer "don't know" in response to survey questions.[12]

To acknowledge these two *inter*generational gaps is not to deny the baby boom's own *intra*generational division. Indeed, looking back over recent elections, baby-boom men and women have shown the largest voting gaps of any age group. In 1980, the baby-boom gender gap hit a 10 percent margin as baby-boom women expressed their worries about peace and unemployment by voting more for Carter, while baby-boom men showed greater concern about inflation and America's position in the world by voting more for Reagan. Reagan's vocal support for increased defense spending and a "get-tough" approach toward the Soviets crystallized women's continuing concerns about war, while his rhetoric about inflation and restoring United States prestige cemented men's continuing worries about strength and leadership. The election involved a set of issues which brought the gender gap to the surface.

Just four years later, however, the baby-boom gender gap had dropped by eight percent. Baby-boom men and women voted two to one for Reagan—66 percent of the men and 64 percent of the women—and split their votes exactly the same—50/50—for congressional candidates. A small margin given Reagan's record on issues of some concern to women. The invasion of Grenada, a continuing arms build-up, Star Wars, and the death of 240 Marines in Beirut did not seem to matter. Nor did the nomination of

Rep. Geraldine Ferraro (D-NY) as Walter Mondale's running mate.

But that does not mean the baby-boom gender gap has closed, Klein argues. "The Democrats apparently felt that the Ferraro nomination in and of itself would suffice to crystallize the women's vote. After the nomination, according to Democratic pollster Dotty Lynch, the Mondale strategists focused on issues of deficits and a strong defense in order to garner support among white male ethnics."

Another problem was that the Democrats did not mount a credible campaign. "It was foreordained that the Democrats would lose the 1984 campaign," according to Klein. "The economy had improved, the nation was at peace, and Ronald Reagan was an extremely popular president."[13] Further, 1984 presented few gender-based issues to the voters, proving as Klein suggests, that "the women's vote cannot be captured simply by nominating women candidates. It is an issue-vote and can be triggered only by policy discussions that incorporate women's perspectives. By not focusing on the substantive concerns of women, the Democrats made it easier for the Republican message to draw off women's votes."[14]

For still another thing, even had Mondale presented a more aggressive women's platform, baby-boom women did not believe he would deliver. Whatever their approval of Geraldine Ferraro as Mondale's running mate, most baby-boom women questioned Mondale's leadership. On a list of sixteen personal qualities, for example, baby-boom women rated Reagan higher than Mondale on ten. They liked Reagan's decency, intelligence, morality, kindness, inspiration, knowledge, and strength most of all. They rated Mondale slightly higher on five qualities. They particularly liked his fairness and his being in touch with ordinary people. Baby-boom women gave Mondale and Reagan equal marks on compassion. Even if they agreed with Mondale's policy stands—and it is clear that they did—baby-boom women doubted Mondale's ability to follow-through in the White House. His personal negatives simply eclipsed his policy positives. Baby-boom women did not consider him to be a credible leader.

Thus, even though the gender gap did not show up in the 1984 vote, it still existed on the issues. The splits still held on environmental protection, the Equal Rights Amendment, the nuclear freeze, fairness, and programs for the poor, splits which translated into differences on party identification—38 percent of the baby-boom women said they were Democrats compared to 27 percent of the baby-boom men.

Ultimately, some elections and candidates bring the baby-boom gender differences to the surface, others do not. That does not mean the gap is a temporary disturbance. Indeed, the gap is based on baby-boom gender differences that are here to stay.

First, many baby-boom women continue to believe that there are two American economies—one for men which is supported by aggressive federal policies, and another for women supported by no one but themselves. And their economic performance tends to confirm those suspicions. Women continue to average 60 to 70 percent less in income than men. Some of the poor performance reflects the concentration of women in poorly paid occupations. Some involves traditional discrimination in women's benefits and pay. Some comes from a staggering divorce penalty. Whereas on average women get a three-quarter cut in income following divorce, men see a 40 percent boost.

In 1984, baby-boom women were less likely than men to say their income had gone up over the preceding year.[15] Little wonder then that they were also more likely than men to say they had used their savings or borrowed money to make ends meet, and were less likely to see much hope that their finances would improve over the next year. Little wonder that only 40 percent of baby-boom women said the economy had gotten better over the preceding year, compared to 56 percent of baby-boom men, or that only 16 percent of baby-boom women said that federal economic policy had made their lives better, compared to 28 percent of baby-boom men.[16]

Second, according to a detailed analysis across all age groups by the Women's Vote Project in Washington, "women look and think about politics differently than men." After examining dozens of specific issues, the project concluded that "the most consistent and long-standing difference between men and women overall is on 'peace' issues—issues involving threats to life."[17] On political trade-offs across issues, women put more emphasis on safety and social welfare than men. If men and women make different political trade-offs, the breadth of the gender gap in any specific election will vary with the rise and fall of issues on the campaign agenda —an election which brings war and peace to the surface may produce a large baby-boom gap; an election dominated by personality may not.

Those kinds of trade-offs were brought to the surface in 1980, but were muted by Reagan's control of the campaign agenda in 1984. In 1980, according to Celinda Lake, former political director of the Women's Campaign Fund, the campaign agenda revolved around a set of gender-issue packages. "Men saw a trade-off between our economic/budgetary situation and our social welfare system which women did not. Men tended to see reducing inflation, reducing government services, providing a tax cut, having minorities help themselves, and having each person get ahead on his/her own as part of the same set of choices." For men in 1980, America could have it all—budget and tax cuts were perfectly compatible with promises of a balanced budget by 1984. For women in 1980, America had to make choices—choices about economic/budgetary issues had to be kept separate from social welfare lest children and families suffer. America could either have a defense increase or a social safety net.[18]

Third, baby-boom men and women may have different underlying social values. As the Women's Vote Project reported, in both the 1980 and 1984 elections, "women were more egalitarian and less individualist than men, and saw differently the trade-offs between supporting individualism and supporting equal opportunity. Women saw limits on individualism as an inevitable result of offering everyone an equal opportunity. Men saw no relationship between the two."[19] In short, women tend to emphasize family and community networks, men the pursuit of individual glory and achievement. Joanne Howes of the Women's Vote Project team argues, "women think about issues different from men. The idea of competitiveness, winners versus losers, turns them off. Community and unity are more appealing."

Moreover, women appear to be much more concerned than men about safety as a political value. Nuclear power is one example. The fact that roughly half as many women as men favor building more nuclear power plants does not mean women are somehow naive about America's energy needs. Quite the contrary. In past surveys, women have been just as likely as men to say that past and predicted energy shortages are serious. Further, when asked in the 1970s to rank the benefits of nuclear power, women were actually more likely than men to see the economic benefits of more nuclear power plants.

However, women also were much more likely than men to see nuclear power as a threat to public health and safety, whether because of radioactive leaks, potential accidents, sabotage, waste disposal, or Chernobyl-type meltdowns. In one 1970s survey, two-thirds of the women saw explosions as a significant threat from operating more nuclear plants, compared to just over 40 percent of the men. The survey's analysis concluded, "Women appear to be no less convinced than men of the need for additional energy, and no less concerned about economic growth. Women will accept nuclear power as a means to these goals when they are provided with convincing evidence of its safety."[20]

Finally, women may communicate in what Carol Gilligan calls a "different voice." According to Gilligan, women are more nurturing and compassionate than men by their very nature. Using a battery of tests designed to elicit psychological imagery, Gilligan reports that men are more likely to use violent symbols in fantasies of intimate relationships. Further, "men and women may perceive danger in different social situations and construe danger in different ways."[21] Men may be threatened more by intimacy in relationships than by achievement, while women may see more danger in competitive success. Because of these inherent gender differences, women may seek safety in social networks, while men may strike out on their own. Though Gilligan's research is only suggestive, her theory fits well with what the Women's Vote Project found for issue packages: men tend to pursue individualism in the voting booth, too.

Some of these differences reflect baby-boom childhood socialization. Baby-boom girls and boys received very different messages about life. Susie Orbach believes, for example, that baby-boom girls were more confused by the changes in the child-rearing philosophies that came in the 1950s and 1960s. "Part of what characterized homemaking at this time was a denial that it might not satisfy all women," Orbach writes. "Women whose discontent came to the surface were pathologized. Not accepting one's place meant a trip to the general practitioner or psychiatrist for Valium, or therapy to adjust better." With nowhere to turn for self-confirmation, mothers focused on their children's or husband's success.

But, whereas boys were clearly told to be like their fathers, baby-boom girls were given a mixed message from their mothers. They were told both to "Be like me" and "Don't be like me."[22] As baby-boom women have worked through the conflict, they may have arranged social and political issues accordingly, focusing more on careers as a channel for their achievement motivation, building upon their mothers' initial forays into the labor force.[23] The fact is that many baby-boom women are torn between work and family. According to Ethel Klein, "Women's daily experiences, options, and responsibilities differ dramatically from those of their great grandmothers. The meaning of womanhood has fundamentally changed over the last three generations, a transformation that has allowed women to hope for a future based on sex equality, a wish seldom voiced by women of past generations." However, with change came problems: "Because women's work roles were merely added on to their family responsibilities, the sexual division of labor was not truly altered. As a consequence, women suffered from the burden of dual careers, at home and in the work force."[24] And the pressure will not abate any time soon.

Ultimately, those who view 1984 as the end of the baby-boom gender gap in politics are mistaken. The gap exists because of fundamental economic and social differences between baby-boom men and women, differences that will likely remain into the future. Those who take comfort in polls showing that women still like traditional courtesies should take note, too. As Rena Bartos, senior vice president at J. Walter Thompson says, "Every career woman I know values and appreciates courtesies. We all do. But if you were forced to make a choice between someone opening a door and being blocked from the executive suite, you know what choice women would make." Style does not replace substance.

Nevertheless, some tactics for reaching women voters work better than others. According to the *National Journal*, candidates are wise to use women's voices in their commercials. Lake suggests that, since women are more likely than men to keep their televisions on as background noise, when they hear a woman talk, they are more likely to listen. Candidates are also well advised to put children and families in the picture to acknowledge that the world consists of more than just white males. The key here is to show normal women, not super-achievers. Finally, candidates are more successful with women when they speak in that "different voice." Looking at particularly effective ads, Lake concludes that "the language is very inclusive. You can't say 'Vote for me because I'll be good for you.' You've got to say 'us,' or 'your family.' "[25]

The baby boom is the most educated generation in American history, unequalled at least for now by any generation before or after. Only six percent of the baby boomers' grandparents completed college. A majority never finished high school. In contrast, almost 90 percent of the baby boomers finished high school, and 22 percent graduated from college. Despite this remarkable educa-

tional achievement, the baby boom remains divided by its degree
of education. The baby boomers may have shared a nearly universal high-school education, but there is a clear division between
those who went to college and those who went straight to work
or marriage.

Education has long been recognized as a potent predictor of
a person's political attitudes, no less so within the baby boom. In
fact, looking at the 1984 election data, it would be a challenge to
find any issue on which education does *not* create a statistically
significant division between the half of the baby boom which
completed at least one or more years of college and the half which
did not, despite the fact that all baby boomers voted in roughly the
same percentages for Reagan.

Education is clearly linked to economic achievement, too. In
1984, for example, those baby boomers who did not go to college
were much more likely to face personal economic distress,
whether in finding work, having to borrow money, or using up
scarce savings, and were three times as likely as those with a
college degree to conclude that it had become much harder to find
work. Those who went to college were almost twice as likely as
those who did not to say that the economy had gotten much better
over the preceding year.[26] These concerns never came to the
surface in 1984, however, in part because the election focused
more on personality, in part because the economy was not then
in trouble. In such an election, ties tend to go to the incumbent,
especially if the public does not see a credible challenger.

If and when the economy returns as an election issue, differences in the baby boomer's educations will show. In very general
terms, baby boomers who did not go to college tend to be more
conservative on defense, more conservative on social issues, and
more liberal on government intervention in the economy. The
college-educated tend to be more liberal on defense, much more
liberal on social issues, and of a mixed mind on government intervention in the economy. In 1984, for example, they favored reduced defense spending and a more cooperative posture with the

Soviets, and were less likely than their high-school grad peers to support prayer in schools. They still supported equality for women and freedom of choice on abortion, but became more conservative on economic issues, where they showed more support for cuts in social spending and less government intervention on jobs. They supported greater government help for minorities, but only for those truly in need.[27]

These differences existed almost from the first day of baby-boom college classes. However, it is important to recognize that a year of college is not the *sine qua non* of baby-boom social liberalism. In 1968, for example, Daniel Yankelovich found significant differences between three groups of baby boomers: the high-school grads, who did not go to college, versus the "practicals" and the "forerunners," who did go to college. Among the college students, 60 percent interviewed by Yankelovich said that college was mainly a practical matter, that an education was a ticket to better jobs, higher income, and more prestige in society. The other 40 percent of the college students said they were not much concerned with the practical benefits of school. Rather, according to Yankelovich, they saw college as "something more intangible, perhaps the opportunity to change things rather than make out well within the existing system."

When compared to their peers, the forerunners were more liberal than the practicals, who were in turn more liberal than the high-school grads who had stayed at home. Almost half of the high-school grads described themselves as hawks on the Vietnam War, while over two-thirds of the forerunners said they were doves. While all three groups said they felt sympathy for the troops mired in Vietnam, the forerunners were far more likely to express disgust with the government in Washington and a feeling of helplessness in winning any change. The high-school grads were more likely to say that containing the communists in Southeast Asia and "defending our honor" were values worth fighting for—figures which contradict those who have said that all baby boomers opposed the war for the same reason.

Further, 75 percent of the high-school grads said that living the good Christian life was a personal goal, compared to only 36 percent of the forerunners and just over 50 percent of the practicals. It is not surprising that the high-school grads expressed greater support for Alabama governor George Wallace in the 1968 campaign.

Despite the different attitudes on Vietnam created by the gap in education, there were important areas of agreement between these same groups—agreement that may provide at least a common memory for bridging the education gap today. According to the same survey, all three groups supported withdrawal from Vietnam, albeit for very different reasons. All three groups agreed that America should get its own house in order before policing the rest of the world. All three agreed that there was too much emphasis on nationalism and not enough on the "brotherhood of man." All three agreed with the statement that "war solves nothing but only creates a situation of hate and mistrust which breeds more war." All three agreed that they would welcome more emphasis in Washington on combating poverty. All three admired Sen. Edward Kennedy (D-MA) as a possible presidential candidate. Finally, a majority of all three agreed that there was a large generation gap in America at the time.

These differences in education remain a powerful predictor of baby-boom values. In 1984, for example, the high-school grads were more likely than college grads to say that poor people worked just as hard as those who were more successful, that hard work did not always lead to success, and that trying to reach a goal was sometimes just not good enough. The high schoolers were also less likely to say that the poor had only themselves to blame for their failures. For these baby boomers, hard work was still the main way to get ahead, not a guarantee, but the only way.[28] As such, the high-school grads were more forgiving toward those who do not make it in life, more willing to blame the "system" for economic distress.

That may be one reason why these baby boomers are both

more cynical toward governmental institutions and more doubtful about their own potential influence. They are twice as likely as the baby boomers who went to college to say that government does not care about the opinions of people like them, and much more likely to conclude that politics is sometimes too complicated to understand. They are also more likely to say that people ought not vote in an election if they don't care who wins.

Overall, the high-school grads pay little attention to politics, in part because they do not understand some of the issues, in part because they do not have the time and energy. Not surprisingly, their turnout in elections trails that of the more-educated baby boomers. Not only are they less likely to care which party wins an election, they are less likely to identify with either the Democratic or Republican party at even the most minimal level—17 percent are unwilling to express even the slightest leaning toward one party or the other.

Yet, if these baby boomers vote at a lesser clip, they vote enough to count. Whether they will continue to vote in the same directions as their more-educated peers depends in large measure on whether future elections present issues they can understand and react to.

The education gap also creates clear income disparities between baby-boom economic classes. In turn, those income differences may create political conflict. There is a growing concern that the middle class is disappearing, that the poor are now stuck in a permanent underclass, that the rich are cornering economic resources that once provided upward mobility for the lower and middle classes. If true, the baby boom may soon be divided into a very small number of "haves" versus a very large number of "have-nots."

While the number of Americans living in poverty went up from 11.4 percent in 1979 to 14.4 in 1984, the amount of personal wealth controlled by the top 1 percent of households jumped by 25 percent.[29] Moreover, according to the Census Bureau, by 1986, the top fifth of American families—those earning more than $48,000 a year—took 43 percent of all family income, a post-war high, while the bottom fifth took only 4.7 percent, a twenty-five-year low. By 1990, according to the Conference Board, one-third of all personal income will be pulled in by households with $50,-000 or more in income, compared to a quarter today.

Robert Kuttner was among the first to sound the warning about a declining middle class. "There is a good deal of evidence," he wrote in 1983, "that job opportunities in the United States are polarizing, and that, as a result, the country's future as a middle-class society is in jeopardy. What the decline of the middle class would mean to the country can only be guessed at, but it presumably would be unwelcome to the millions of parents who hope that their children can move up the economic ladder; to American business, which needs a middle class to consume its products; and to everyone who is concerned about fairness and social harmony."[30]

According to economist David Gordon, "The most important story about the U.S. economy in the 1980s is the economic warfare that the wealthy and powerful have been waging against the vast majority of Americans. Largely unnoticed, an opulent few have already won so many decisive battles that we are witnessing a new and significant polarization of America by class."

Unfortunately, it may take years for economists to figure out just what is going on. For now, the numbers give a slight edge to those who see the beginning of a long-term shift in class structure. "The middle class still cuts itself a large slice of the American pie," Harvard economist David Bloom notes, "but the country has moved in the direction of becoming a nation of haves and have-nots, with less in between." Even the *Wall Street Journal*, the self-labeled "Journal of the American Dream," may agree. A 1986 article proclaimed "U.S. Rich and Poor Increase in Numbers; Middle Loses Ground."

In a system in which a one percent shift in class composition involves millions of workers moving up or down, what may seem like a trivial number to one economist may be a harbinger of crisis to another. After all, some argue, the ice age began with just a chilly day. Most of the debate focuses on what some see as the flattening of the traditional bell-shaped, or one-humped, earnings curve. Some see the rise of a bi-polar, or two-humped, earnings curve, with a small number of very rich on one end and a huge number of poor at the other. It is the gulf between the two that creates the greatest concern. At the minimum, the recent figures signal a reversal in past movement toward a greater earnings equilibrium between the upper and lower third.

However, because trends often take years to show up on the broad economic curves, what may appear as but a tiny blip to conservatives may be taken as the ice age by liberals. According to Democratic economist Geoffrey Faux, "These numbers are very slow to move, really glacial. So when you do get a change, you better pay attention." But as economists Sar Levitan and Peter Carlson suggest, "As with any rich set of economic data, it does not require much ingenuity to find some numbers to support the favorite hypotheses or preconceived notions of the analysts. . . . While some individuals and communities, and society at large, may benefit from the transformations, it is of little comfort to the steelworkers in Lackawanna that their place in the American middle class will be filled by unionized retail clerks in San Francisco or middle-management personnel in Houston."[31] Nevertheless, their article is titled "Middle-Class Shrinkage? Not to worry—it's largely a statistical illusion."

In the final analysis, however, if the baby boomers believe, rightly or wrongly, that the middle class is disappearing, that the American dream is now out of reach, then the debate over the figures and econometric models will seem irrelevant. Perceptions are the key. If baby boomers at the bottom sense a widening gulf between expectation and reality, if magazines like *Quality* continue to showcase a baby-boom dream far beyond reach, perhaps the class war will become a reality. Though some still argue that downward mobility is "laughable," as Conference Board researcher Fabian Linden puts it, there is just enough evidence that the lower and middle classes are falling backward to keep the debate burning in the media.

In summarizing the shopping news, for example, Barbara Ehrenreich writes, "Korvettes is gone, Gimbels is closing. Sears, Roebuck & Company and J.C. Penny are anxiously trying to reposition themselves as more 'upscale' to survive in an ever more deeply segmented market." She concludes, "whether one looks at food, clothing or furnishings, two cultures are emerging: natural fiber vs. synthetic blends; hand-crafted wood cabinets vs. mass-produced maple; David's Cookies vs. Mister Donuts."[32]

Consider the comments of three marketing executives as a hint of what is to come. General Electric's Paul Van Orden says, "We do see more of a bimodal distribution. It gives GE an increasing opportunity at the upper end of the scale." Bloomingdale's Mary Joan Glynn says, "In the 1970s it became apparent that the profitable markets would be at the top and the bottom of the scale, because of restrictions on the middle of the market." Pillsbury's Lane Cardwell says, "It's a trend that's been in place for years—it's irreversible, it's good for us." That may be why Pillsbury is so high on its two fast-food interests—Burger King for the low income and Bennigan's for the upscale—and why Whirlpool now offers two lines of appliances—the old Whirlpool standard for the low income and the newly acquired Kitchenaid for the upscale.

As go department stores, so goes the middle class? For Ehrenreich, the evidence is irrefutable: "No one, however humble, denies that there has been a profound change in the class contours of American society. No matter how you slice up the population —whether you compare the top fifth to the bottom fifth, or the top 40 percent to the poorest 40 percent—and no matter whether you look at individual earnings or household earnings, the have-nots are getting by on less and the haves are doing better than ever."[33]

Even those who are maintaining their position within the middle class may be in trouble. "Despite a life of work," Democratic consultant Stanley Greenberg argues, this "new middle class lives from paycheck to paycheck, and its children live with declining opportunities. Though it embodies the proper virtues, the new middle class sees itself as politically marginal, in the 'wrong category,' overlooked by parties, politicians, and government."[34]

Greenberg's detailed interviews in the key primary states of Iowa and New Hampshire show a growing bitterness among the remaining middle class, a belief that the middle class is under siege. "Despite the hard work, the middle class eats 'hot dogs to make the mortgage payments,' " he quotes from his respondents. "The new middle class has 'enough to get by,' to 'just go along and try to save a little bit.' " They want to be able to turn to government, he says, "for college loans, for elderly housing and social security, for decent schooling, for school lunches and day care, for veterans' benefits, for special education. The government, many believe, should be there when 'you find yourself in a situation.' " Yet, these members of the new middle class feel a deep cynicism toward the federal government, a sense that the bureaucrats will let them down when they need help most.

No matter how frustrated they get, to date, the class polarization has yet to spill over into politics. One reason is that the people most likely to feel besieged are also the people least likely to care about politics. They are also the least likely to feel that their participation counts for much, or to care which party wins. Yet, if the Rev. Jesse Jackson's success in his 1984 and 1988 presidential campaigns is any guide, the have-nots can be mobilized. Jackson's message clearly tapped the latent frustrations among America's less fortunate. For the time being, however, it is not clear whether anyone but Jackson can bring these voters to the polls, or whether Jackson can build a coalition composed of both the have-nots and the besieged middle class.

Among all the baby-boom splits, none may be felt more intensely than the one caused by Vietnam. On one side are the baby boomers who served in the armed forces between the formation of the American Military Assistance Command on February 6, 1962, and the departure of the last American troops on March 29, 1973. On the other side are the baby boomers who served in the protests to stop the war. Almost fifteen years after the fall of Saigon, the two remain far apart politically. As former Secretary of the Navy, and Vietnam veteran James Webb, suggests, "the real problem began in the 1960s with the debates about the war itself and continues because of our inability as a nation to assimilate that divisive experience."

Those who protested the war still retain some of their sharp liberalism from the 1960s. Protest involved far more than showing up for a rally. Along with the blue jeans and tie-dyed shirts, protest involved a distinctive lifestyle and outlook. From legalization of marijuana to equal rights for women and minorities, from opposition to the war in Vietnam to support for the war on poverty, the protest movement involved a package of ideas; one did not join for a day. As political scientists M. Kent Jennings and Richard Niemi argue, protestors have kept active politically, suggesting an "enduring cleavage organized around a set of unique historical experiences," even if some of their issues have been blunted by their passage through the life cycle.[35]

Trace elements of the 1960s and early 1970s appear on a number of attitudes, including support for the rights of the accused, help for minorities, and government intervention in the economy. The protestors have softened with time, but remain relatively liberal. The only issue on which there has been no retreat by the protestors is women's rights. In 1973, 91 percent of the Vietnam protestors supported equality for women. In 1982, the number was essentially unchanged, offering solid evidence of what Jennings call "absolute continuity." In fact, if anyone changed on women's rights during the 1970s, it was the non-protestors. They became more liberal over time, moving from 77 percent in support of equality for woman in 1973 to 84 percent in 1982, finally catching up to their once radical peers.[36]

In contrast, Vietnam veterans have been more difficult to place on the political spectrum. "Vietnam was a swirling, ever-changing place that in itself defies a simple common shared experience," Myra MacPherson writes. "Veterans who saw heavy combat and those who saw little do not speak the same language. Nor do those who went in 1964, when the country was moving through the long twilight of cold war containment, have much of a bond with the reluctant draftee who went to a hot and futile war in 1970."[37]

Jennings and Niemi's findings support this conclusion. Even though vets moved through history at the same time as the protestors, they were not marked in "politically distinguishable ways or with different outcomes that would set them apart from other members of their generation," Jennings and Niemi concluded in 1981. "By contrast, the protestors responded to the political-historical environment in a singular fashion," one that once carried a great potential for mobilization.[38]

However, veterans may eventually come together as a voting block as they find it now acceptable to both acknowledge their service in Vietnam and to talk about their personal reactions. Both were once taboo. As vets find that others shared their experiences, they may find some common ground. They may find, for example, that no matter where they served, they shared a bizarre experience.

"What would be the worst set of social, economic, and political, and psychological conditions you could create for the returnee?" Vietnam vet John Wilson asked in congressional testimony in 1980. His answer deserves full reading:

First, you would send a young man fresh out of high school to an unpopular, controversial guerrilla war far away from home. Expose him to intensely stressful events, some so horrible that it would be impossible to really talk about them later to anyone else except fellow "survivors." To ensure maximal stress, you would create a one-year tour of duty during which the combatant flies to and from the war zone singly, without a cohesive, intact, and emotionally supportive unit with high morale. You would also create the one-year rotation to instill a "survivor mentality" which would undercut the process of ideological commitment to winning the war and seeing it as a noble cause. Then at DEROS [Date of Expected Return from Overseas Service] you would rapidly remove the combatant and singly return him to his front porch without an opportunity to sort out the meaning of the experiences with the men in his unit. No homecoming welcome or victory parades. Ah, but yet, since you are demonic enough, you make sure that the veteran is stigmatized and portrayed to the public as a "drug-crazed psychopathic killer." By virtue of clever selection by the Selective Service system, the veteran would be unable to easily reenter the mainstream of society because he is under-educated and lacks marketable job skills. Further, since the war itself was difficult, you would want to make sure that there were no supportive systems in society for him, especially among health professionals at VA hospitals, who would find his nightmares and residual war-related anxieties unintelligible. Finally, you would want to establish a GI Bill [of post-service education and housing benefits] with inadequate benefits to pay for education and job training, coupled with an economy of high inflation and unemployment. Last, but not least, you would want him to feel isolated, stigmatized, unappreciated, and exploited for volunteering to serve his country. Tragically, of course, this scenario is not fictitious: it was the homecoming for most Vietnam veterans.[39]

This shared experience may create common vet problems long into the future, which in turn might mobilize vets politically. If a recent report in the *New England Journal of Medicine* is correct, Vietnam vets may face statistically higher odds of drug and alcohol dependency, depression, and marital stress than their peers.[40] Vets may also face statistically higher odds of suicide and death from motor vehicle accidents. The most likely explanation, according to the authors of the study, "is that military service during the Vietnam War caused an increase in subsequent deaths," whether because of post-traumatic stress disorder—that is, the delayed effects of having served in heavy combat—or some other unknown factor.

According to the statistics, the higher suicide and accident rates are not restricted just to those who actually served; men born from 1950 to 1952 who were merely eligible for the draft through unlucky lottery numbers had a 13 percent higher probability of suicide over the 1974–83 period. According to the authors of the statistical analysis, the data hold a clear message for future presidents: "before sending young men to war, especially one in which they may have experiences similar to those of Vietnam veterans, those who make the decision should weigh all the costs. The casualties of forced military service may not be limited to those that are counted on the battlefield."

Whatever the cause, Vietnam vets have begun to get together through veterans organizations. Vietnam Veterans of America, the Veterans of Foreign Wars, and the American Legion have all reported upswings in their Vietnam era membership, perhaps reflecting the national healing following the opening of the Vietnam memorial in Washington, D.C.

That does not mean that Vietnam vets are about to become average legionnaires. In fact, Vietnam-era veterans are likely to be very different from World War II and Korean vets. Surveys of Vietnam vets show a clear generation gap in attitudes toward both the Veterans Administration (VA) and veterans benefits programs. Vietnam vets are significantly more likely than older vets to say the VA is unresponsive, and are less likely to say they are satisfied with either VA medical treatment or benefits. Whereas 91 percent of older vets told the Harris Poll in 1983 that they were very satisfied with VA home loans, only 54 percent of the Vietnam vets agreed. Whereas 73 percent of the older vets said they were very satisfied with vocational rehabilitation, only 33 percent of the Vietnam vets concurred.[41] Nor are Vietnam vets confident that the VA cares about the twin Vietnam-era problems of Agent Orange, the dioxin-based herbicide used to defoliate millions of acres of Southeast Asia during the war, or post-traumatic stress disorder.

In dealing with the huge Veterans Administration bureaucracy, the Vietnam vets are starting to sound much like the protestors once did. They are less trusting of the VA than older vets and more frustrated with the red tape and the lack of openness. Like the protestors, they do not trust any big organization. Like the protestors, they are becoming more aggressive in demanding change. Now that the vets have finally been welcomed home, some may yet forge an alliance with the protestors.

Not only are these five baby-boom splits significant by themselves, they interact with each other in breaking the generation into literally dozens of possible political subunits. When combined, the divisions by age (new wave versus old wave), gender (male versus female), education (high-school graduate versus some college versus college grad), class (lower versus middle versus upper), and participation in Vietnam (protestor versus veteran) create many different baby booms, each with some potential for political polarization.

Moreover, these divisions hardly exhaust the potential for baby-boom polarization. Consider four other sources of baby-boom political conflict that will continue to exist in the future.

The first source involves marital status. Married baby boomers appear to be very different politically from the unmarried, creating what voting expert Martin Plissner calls a marriage gap. "Married people are more likely to own real property and to worry about protecting it," Plissner argues. "They are more likely to have, or expect, children and, if so, to take a benign view of authority and a dim view of social disorder. They are more likely, in other words, to respond to the conservative values which Republicans, and Reagan especially, talk about a lot."

The second source centers on employment. Especially among baby-boom women, the political views of those who work may be very different from those who don't. In 1984, for example, 62 percent of single, working, baby-boom women voted for Reagan, compared to 69 percent of married, working women, and 59 percent of married, nonworking women. "All this indicates that the GOP problem with women will not just fade away and that it will probably get worse," one analyst concludes. "As they age and settle down, these younger women will still be shaped by the memories of their early personal, professional, and political experiences—as they replace a more conservative generation of women from which Reagan and the Republicans have drawn significant support."[42]

The third source is geographic region. Southern baby boomers may differ in their views from northern baby boomers, adding yet another split to the political equation. "What was once the most solidly Democratic region of the country is now predominantly Republican in presidential elections," American Enterprise Institute scholar William Schneider writes. "Since 1964, the South has given majority support to the Democratic ticket only once, in 1976, and even then Jimmy Carter failed to carry white southerners."[43] Consider the following differences which emerged at the Mason-Dixon line in 1984 as evidence of the North/South split:

• Contrary to the image of the South as the land of economic opportunity and the Northeast as the "rust belt," southern baby boomers were 10 percent more likely than their northeastern peers to say that they were worse off economically, and much less likely to say that their income had matched the rise in the cost of living.

• Southern baby boomers were 10 percent more likely than their northeastern siblings to say that hard work is no guarantee of success, and were less likely to say that things were going well in the country, or that the United States position in the world had grown stronger under Reagan. They were also more likely than their northeastern peers to support equal opportunity for both women and minorities, less likely to say that Americans should worry less about equality, and less likely to agree that men were somehow more qualified for politics than women.

• Southern baby boomers were more religious than their peers in the North, Mountain States, or West. More said that religion was important in their lives, and almost half said that their religion was a source of great guidance to them.

• Despite the general reputation of the South as a bastion of conservatism, southern baby boomers were less approving than northeasterners of Reagan's handling of his job, less approving of his handling of the economy, and 10 percent more disapproving of his handling of the budget. They were also less likely than northeastern baby boomers to say that Reagan was a strong leader, hardworking, decent, compassionate, moral, or that he commanded respect. Not surprisingly, southern baby boomers liked Mondale much more and cast fewer votes for Reagan.

• Finally, southern baby boomers appeared to be more trusting of government than their northeastern brothers and sisters; more said that elections make government responsive, and more said that government pays a good deal of attention to people like them. Because fewer went to college after high school, however, southern baby boomers were less confident in their own abilities to understand government and politics—72 percent said politics was sometimes too complicated to understand, compared to 59 percent of the northeastern baby boomers.

Compared to fifteen years ago, however, southern baby boomers have grown more conservative. Even though they remain more Democratic than their northern peers, there has been a steady erosion in party support. The question for political strategists is whether the changes are coming from northern Republicans who moved south or from southern Democrats who changed their minds.

As *New York Times* polling director Barbara Farrah and political scientist Helmut Norpoth argue, from 1976 to 1986, "Republican identifiers among southern whites have almost doubled, mainly at the expense of the Democratic party. This conversion of the South is largely attributed to the young, native southerners who have increasingly moved away from the Democratic party into the Republican fold. But the conversion of the South has also been helped along and speeded up by the influx of migrants, who have made the South the fastest growing region in the country. The migrants who settle in the South happen to be white, young, well-educated and show a preference for the Republican party."[44] Merely moving South does not a Republican make. But the reasons why people might move—better paying jobs, fewer unions, a conservative political climate—make these migrants very attractive to the Republican party.

The fourth source of future conflict may be race. Baby-boom blacks have different views on politics than whites. Blacks clearly tend to fall more heavily into the lower-education and lower-income strata described above, and are disproportionately represented among Vietnam combat veterans. Yet, black political participation is much higher than white participation in the same economic situations. The data suggest, for instance, that being black and poor is very different from being white and poor. "An argument can be made that the black voter is more sophisticated than any other in American politics," I.A. Lewis and William Schneider wrote in 1983. "No other group identifies its self-interest so well or promotes it so forcefully or consistently."[45] As they point out, black turnout in elections has been rising over the past two decades, moving in exactly the opposite direction from whites.

Moreover, regardless of age, gender, education, class, or participation in Vietnam, blacks have voted Democratic in every presidential election since the mid-1960s. As political scientist Charles Franklin suggests, the shift to the Democratic party reflected a clear party realignment based on party performance. "In 1960, 27% of blacks called themselves strong Democrats, but in 1964 the figure was 52%," he writes. "Similarly, the percentage of blacks who considered themselves Republican (of any strength) dropped from 31% in 1960 to 12% in 1964. Such massive change should certainly qualify as a realignment."[46] It is a realignment which has lasted among black baby boomers in large part because their party *identification* is closely tied to party *performance*. They remember what the Democrats did for blacks and made a long-term commitment to the party.

That loyalty remains in the present, again in large part because of party performance. However, at least in the 1980s, blacks may have stayed with the Democrats less because of what their party had done for them lately and much more because of their nearly uniform disapproval of Ronald Reagan. According to a 1986 ABC News/*Washington Post* Poll, 56 percent of the blacks surveyed believed Reagan was a racist, and only 11 percent said the administration's economic policy had helped most blacks. The poll found that younger blacks were more optimistic about the future than their parents, but still shared the overwhelming disapproval of Reagan's performance as president. Consider the following differences that emerged in 1984 between black and white baby boomers as additional evidence of the potential split:

• Black baby boomers were almost three times more likely than whites to strongly disapprove of Reagan's handling of his job. That disapproval goes for Reagan's handling of the economy, foreign affairs, and the budget, too. Fifty-seven percent of black baby boomers said they strongly disapproved of Reagan's foreign policy, compared to 26 percent of whites.

• Black baby boomers were less likely than whites to say that Reagan's economic policy had affected them much, but were much more likely to say it had become more difficult to find work, more difficult to keep up with inflation, and tougher to make ends meet. If baby-boom women thought there was a separate economy for men, blacks thought there was a separate economy for whites.

• Though black baby boomers were generally more trusting toward the electoral process than whites—54 percent said elections make government responsive a good deal of the time, compared to 39 percent of whites—they were much less trusting toward government. More blacks said that government officials didn't care for their thoughts; more said that people like them did not have as much say about government policy.

• Given their opinions about Reaganomics, it is hardly surprising that almost 60 percent of black baby boomers said they were Democrats, compared to 28 percent of whites. Moreover, three percent of blacks identified with the Republicans, compared to almost 30 percent of white baby boomers.

• Though they were in general agreement with whites in

rating Reagan's intelligence and knowledge, they were much less likely to say he was fair, strong, compassionate, caring, inspiring, or kind. In addition, they were much more enthusiastic about Mondale's personal qualities. In contrast to their white peers, black baby boomers were much more polarized in the 1984 election, seeing Reagan and the Republican party in starkly negative terms, while holding Mondale and the Democratic party in high regard.

Combine marital status (married, never-married, and divorced), employment (working and not working), regional differences (North and South), and race (black and white) with the other major political divisions in the generation and the number of potential baby-boom subgroups skyrockets. And that does not include all the variations within the categories like region (Pacific, Midwest, Northeast, etc.), employment (full-time, part-time, service economy, manufacturing), or race (Hispanic or Asian).

The point is not that the baby boomers are infinitely divisible, however, but that the generation has great potential for polarization along a number of distinct social and demographic cleavages. This generation is hardly a monolith of political and social opinion. Not only is there a significant potential for polarization, some of the gaps are already exerting influence on baby-boom political choices. The future will tell whether the polarization will come to the surface, and whether candidates of the right or left will be able to exploit the divisions for short-term gain. The answers are still in doubt.

4

A Generation United

DESPITE THEIR DIFFERENCES, the baby boomers share considerable common ground. At a minimum, they share the simple fact that they are baby boomers, always to be reminded of their numbers and great potential, always to be congratulated at each major birthday. Is there any doubt that *Time* will have a 50th birthday issue in 1996?

At a minimum, the baby boomers shared a standardized childhood. From family size to school plans, from television habits to personal fears, the baby boomers were raised as anything but individuals. It was the best society could do with such a large mass of humanity.

Housing is only one example. With the post-war housing boom fully underway in the late 1940s, builders finally adopted a set of standard measures to build cheaper houses quickly. These building codes were but one part of the trend toward homogenized homes, families, and baby-boom childhoods. "Homes have to be designed for the greatest possible economy," one trade magazine concluded at the time. "This demands straight lines without many breaks in the foundation and roof. It means the elimination of dormers, almost to extinction." The growing popularity of the

Cape Cod, according to Joseph Goulden's history of these *Best Years*, reflected, "a decision by builders to demonstrate their expertise by housing a generation of Americans in a housing style reminiscent of a string of boxcars."

Though builders covered the "boxcars" with different colors of paint, appliance manufacturers felt no such need; every postwar American kitchen was the same. "In July, 1945," Goulden notes, "the American Gas Association, a trade group, persuaded the entire appliance industry to agree upon standard sizes for both kitchen cabinets and appliances, maintaining that a streamlined kitchen would not belong exclusively to the housewife who could afford custom workmanship."

Even if the baby boomers do not remember exactly the same political events, they will always remember the same kitchens. According to Goulden, "Working space would be thirty-six inches above the floor. To prevent toe stubbing, cabinets, stoves, and other fixtures would have a 'toe cove' three inches deep and four inches high. Countertops could extend 25 inches from the wall, allowing half an inch overhang from the cabinet base."[1]

These basic construction codes became part of the standard baby-boom childhood. Along with the norm of two children, two natural, married parents, a brand name appliance, and an American-made car, the standard baby-boom family and home gave the generation a sense of sameness that may have provoked the drive for individualism and tolerance of diversity that distinguishes the baby boom from its parents and grandparents today.

Moreover, just as five basic splits may divide the baby boomers, five shared experiences may unite them. They were part of a silent revolution in social values which continues even today. They were raised with great expectations about their future, whether thrust upon them in school or advertising. They witnessed history through the unifying image of television. They experienced social crowding which fueled their desire for individual distinction. And they shared the fears brought on by a new generation of cold-war weapons capable of ending their lives in a moment's notice. The question now is whether these shared experiences are enough to create a distinctive baby-boom outlook on both politics and life.

The baby boomers grew up in a very different era from that of their parents. For a moment at least, the worries of economic depression were gone. The growth continued unabated year after year. Inflation was low, employment and earnings were high. According to political scientist Ronald Inglehart, these fifteen to twenty years may have created a "silent revolution" in America —a revolution born of affluence and growth, not of civil war and class struggle.[2]

As Inglehart argues, generations raised in affluence do not feel the economic pressure of class conflict. They are free to think about other issues, like the search for a meaningful philosophy of life, for instance. During such historical interludes, Inglehart says, "a set of 'post-bourgeois' values, relating to the need for belonging and to aesthetic and intellectual needs, would be more likely to take priority." Someone caught in a depression thinks about jobs and income; someone raised in economic abundance thinks about tolerance and free expression.

As a result, "acquisitive" or material values would have little meaning for those raised during long periods of economic prosperity. They would already have it all. Instead, a post-materialist generation would emphasize social values like freedom of speech, giving the people more say in important governmental decisions, equality, environmental protection, and peace, while a generation raised in a more threatening era might emphasize a different set of ideals, like maintaining order, fighting rising prices, tax cuts, nationalism, and a strong defense.

Whereas economic insecurity creates a call to order, economic security forges a broader search for social meaning. "Post-materialists would be relatively supportive of social change, and would have a relatively high potential for unconventional and disruptive political action," Ingelhart writes. "Post-materialists have a larger amount of psychic energy available for politics, they are less supportive of the established, and, subjectively, they have less to lose from unconventional order than Materialists."[3]

However, post-materialists do not engage in activist politics just for the sake of protest. In the absence of some strong catalyst, like Vietnam or civil rights, they may take their post-material world for granted, settling into a pleasant complacency, even disengagement. "For some, this means seeking self-actualization through development of the inner self, rather than through social action," Inglehart speculates. "The human potential movement [of the mid-1970s] is an example. For those who remain politically active, this turning inward seems like a desertion of the cause; the current crop of youth has been characterized as the Me Generation, practicing a culture of narcissism."[4]

Is the baby boom a post-materialist generation? Pollster Florence Skelly says yes: "The boom generation was acculturated during a time of tremendous economic growth. During the '50s, when they were growing up, the country was very optimistic: the suburbs were emerging, 70 percent of Americans owned their own homes, people weren't stuck in cities." It was a period when the public believed they had achieved the American dream. Indeed, according to Skelly, "they *assumed* it. Kids could go to college if they wanted; they could certainly have their own rooms; they could live in owned homes; their families had two automobiles, an air conditioner, a refrigerator, you name it." At least in the beginning, baby boomers did not have to worry about economic survival. They had the luxury to wonder about the meaning of life.

In this silent revolution, the relatively good fortune of the 1950s and early 1960s created a sweeping value change in the late 1960s and 1970s. It was a change picked up by Daniel Yankelovich in fifteen years of data on public values. According to Yankelovich this change was "an endorsement of an almost open-ended pluralism—a tolerance of diversity in all aspects of life. In turn, the traditional notion of elitism was turned upside down."[5] In the new public morality, the pursuit of individual self-fulfillment became, as Yankelovich put it, the "pursuit of instant gratification and products reflecting one's uniqueness in the marketplace."

The silent revolution affected the political marketplace, too. As Cornell University political scientists Benjamin Ginsberg and Martin Shefter have argued, the forces that weakened people's attachment "to the political accomodations and policy settlements that had bound them together also increased their willingness to sit out an election, to defect to the opposition (including a third-party candidate such as George Wallace), or to seek political influence through nonelectoral channels."[6] In the crusade against Vietnam and racial discrimination, the new politics may have led the baby boomers to define itself as what Ginsberg and Shefter call "a political force in opposition to the public policies, political actors, and government institutions of the nation's postwar regime."[7]

Revolutions are not always hot, however. They are tempered by time and experience. As inflation increased in the 1970s, for example, the silent revolution had to bend. Besieged by economic reality for the first time in their lives, the baby boomers became more cost-conscious. Forced to watch increasingly tight budgets, they became bargain hunters and hard bargainers. Baby boomers, indeed all Americans, Yankelovich argues, still "want the material well-being that is regarded as part of our heritage, but we also want the new self-expressive opportunities won in the 1960s and 1970s. We recognize that to have these things we have to be more selective in our demands, more cunning or pragmatic in our pursuit of them, more flexible in our definition of success, and more accepting of diversity in other people."[8]

That does not mean the silent revolution is over. Certainly not in the consumer marketplace. According to Yankelovich's data, the baby boomers remain less likely than their parents to place as much emphasis on the age and experience of a manufacturer in making choices among products; more likely to reject traditional moral principles governing the consumer market; and less likely to care what others think when they make a purchase. Rather, the data suggest that the silent revolution has been detoured somewhat. "When you're forced to give things up *and* you're introspective," Yankelovich says, "you become strategic about what you should and shouldn't give up—about what is really important to you. Thus, boomers usually have a very well-thought-out sense of priorities." Thus, perhaps, does the search for a meaningful philosophy of life translate into a demand for natural fabrics, natural foods, and a reliable car.

The silent revolution does not appear to be over in baby-boom homes and families either. To date, the baby boomers continue their separation from traditional, social, and political roles. According to the ACLI survey, three-quarters of the baby boomers say they would like an "equal marriage" in which the husband and wife share responsibility for work, homemaking and child raising, while just one in ten say they want a "traditional marriage" in which the husband provides the income and the wife stays at home with the children. Over half of the baby boomers reject the notion that marriages are better when the husband works and the wife stays home, and six in ten believe that working women make more interesting partners in marriage.[9] Three-quarters of all baby boomers reject the notion that men are better for some jobs than women, and over half disagree that men are better suited for politics.[10]

It is this rejection of traditional social roles which may be the most important mark of the silent revolution on the baby boomers. "My generation has not followed an orderly path into adulthood," Cheryl Merser, author of *Grown-Ups,* writes, "either by our 'mood and manners' or by accepting without question the roles and values proscribed by the culture into which we were born— but then, the world into which we were born wasn't the same world that greeted us as adults. Our life cycle is unfolding differently from those of the generations who came before us. We haven't chosen careers, married, bought houses, had children and then stumbled into mid-life crises in a specific, linear order, the way our parents seems to have done with such atypical regularity."[11]

The baby boomers have also rejected traditional social labels, choosing to go through life as individuals. They are much less likely than older generations to use titles like "Mr." or "Mrs.," and much less likely to tell others what they do for a living. They want to be known for themselves, not for who they married or what they do. According to social psychologists Joseph Veroff, Elizabeth Douvan, and Richard Kulka, the two decades between the mid-1950s and mid-1970s witnessed a reduced integration of American adults into the traditional social structure. For example, detailed surveys in 1957 and 1976 showed that people were much less willing in the 1970s to talk about what they did for a living. "This reduced tie to the structural givens of the social order represents a potential psychological loss," Veroff and his colleagues write. "Knowing what a person does can reveal a good deal of information about the personal organization, essential and authentic aspects of a person . . . What a person does is related to what he is—in his core."[12]

The 1957 and 1976 surveys also show a sharp decline in social connections over the two decades. Ironically, the baby boom's greatest shared commitment may be to a lack of commitment. Baby boomers had been told they could be anything, and the rejection of traditional social roles and labels was part of the liberation. They were much less likely than their parents to belong to social organizations, whether a church, a club, or a traditional nuclear family.

The paradox, according to Veroff et al., is, "that disregard for status, which is urged as a counterthrust to formalism and status consciousness out of a desire to reduce obstacles to close interaction between people, actually *increases* distance between people by insisting that they turn inward for the derivation of meaning and self-definition, by placing the burden of definition entirely on the individual—and making it a matter of individual achievement rather than a consensual and shared reality."

If baby boomers are not allowed to ask the most basic of questions—"What do you do?" "Where do you work?" "Where did you grow up?"—they can only relate at the most intimate level. And that takes time and energy that many do not have. More important, in this new social system, in which individuals don't define themselves through social roles and labels, Veroff and his colleagues conclude that, "the individual must rediscover meaning in the spring of his individual detached self each day. Individual achievement becomes the whole story, and it urges distance from rather than connections to structure or to others."[13]

Unfortunately, if any generation ever needed social markers, it would seem to be the baby boom. Just as name tags and seating arrangements help break down the barriers at a meeting, social labels might help break down the barriers within a huge generation. Given their numbers, the baby boomers have more introductions to make, and given their separation from traditional social connections, they have fewer ways of making them. In the drive for individual distinction, the baby boomers have lost their connections with others. They have become equal all right, but only in their separateness.

This social disintegration may even explain the baby boom's lack of party loyalty. Party is just one more social label that helps define the individual. Whether or not the baby boomers behave like Democrats or Republicans, they refuse to accept those labels. The baby boomers may be husbands and wives, mothers and fathers, Democrats and Republicans, professionals and blue-collar workers *in fact*, but remain unwilling to admit it *in label*. To date, the labels remain, as Veroff, Douvan, and Kulka conclude, "objects of suspicion, as though they were different from—even contradictory to—the core self, the essential person."[14]

The rejection of tradition has its pluses, of course. Comparing the 1970s to the 1950s, Veroff et al., argue that, "there is a larger freedom to work out a legitimate life without conforming to rigid prescription or without comparing one's efforts to overidealized standards that so often demoralize. On many counts, Americans now feel better about themselves because they are more self-reliant and less dependent on social roles." However, they conclude, "the comforts of the social system are also given up when social roles lose their moral force. Although we obviously have not given up all role demands—or else we could no longer exist in a cooperative society—we have given up some easy rules that would guarantee legitimacy among those we know and among those we do not know."[15]

The fact that baby boomers want to be treated like individuals does not mean that they have no sense of generational identity. During the crises of the 1960s and early 1970s, the entire generation shared what Patrick Caddell called "a networking of grass roots, a networking of experiences, or pictures and words and music, that in fact allowed communication across the whole generation." And what was the message conveyed through this networking? According to Landon Jones in his book, *Great Expectations*, it was that the baby boomers "were born to be the best and the brightest."[16]

The baby boomers clearly shared an initial sense of having great economic expectations. The 1950s were not called "Happy Days" for nothing. Unemployment averaged 4.5 percent a year in the 1950s, and grew only slightly in the 1960s and 1970s. It was not until the first three years of the 1980s that unemployment soared to 8 percent. Inflation averaged just 2.1 percent a year in the 1950s, crept up slowly in the next decade, but more than tripled to 7.9 percent in the 1970s, and into the double-digits by 1979. It was not until the 1980s that inflation came back down to the 4 to 5 percent range. Finally, the growth in wages-minus-inflation was a whopping 27 percent over the 1950s, dropped to 18 percent in the 1960s, and actually fell to a negative 2 percent in the 1970s.[17] "Affluence and limitlessness were the presuppositions of the 1960s and 1970s," Yankelovich says. "Because we could send a man to the moon, we could afford anything."

The baby boom's great expectations were clearly shaped by

advertising. Long before they read their first book or saw their first movie, they had seen their first commercials. "In a simpler time, advertising merely called attention to the product and extolled its advantages," Christopher Lasch writes in the *Culture of Narcissm*. "Now it manufactures a product of its own: the consumer, perpetually unsatisfied, restless, anxious, and bored. Advertising serves not so much to advertise products as to promote consumption as a way of life. It 'educates' the masses into an unappeasable appetite not only for goods but for new experiences and personal fulfillment. It upholds consumption as the answer to the age-old discontents of loneliness, sickness, weariness, lack of sexual satisfaction; at the same time it creates new forms of content peculiar to the modern age. It plays seductively on the malaise of industrial civilization. Is your job boring and meaningless? Does it leave you with feelings of futility and fatigue? Is your life empty? Consumption promises to fill the aching void . . ."[18]

If this culture of self-absorption reached its height in the 1970s, however, it began with the expectations built up in the 1950s and early 1960s. The baby boomers were Madison Avenue's target. "They were the first generation of children to be isolated by Madison Avenue as an identifiable market," Jones reports. "That is the appropriate word: isolated. Marketing, and especially television, isolated their needs and wants from those of their parents. From the cradle, the baby boomers had been surrounded by products created especially for them, from Silly Putty to Slinkys to skateboards. New products, new toys, new commercials, new fads —the dictatorship of the new—was integral to the baby-boom experience. So prevalent was it that baby boomers themselves rarely realized how different it made them. They breathed it like air."[19]

Between 1950 and 1970 advertisers shifted from selling products based on either their merits or to keep up with the Joneses, to selling for the simple pleasures of ownership. "Ads did not show an escalating image of the good life," marketing experts Russell Belk and Richard Pollay conclude, "as much as they increasingly employed pleasure, luxury, and terminal materialism to sell their products and services." Looking at seventy years of magazine ads, the authors report that the number of ads showing a product and nothing else grew from 15 percent in the 1950s to almost half by the 1970s. By eliminating the distractions caused by "extraneous models" and other goods, the change "might be interpreted as a trend toward highlighting the product for its own sake rather than for its function."[20]

There were other advertising changes in the pages of *Life*, *Reader's Digest, Parade, Saturday Evening Post,* and *Better Homes and Gardens.* First, looking at the advertising pitch, the number of ads showing products as beautiful and pretty dropped from 25 percent of the total in the mid-1930s to just five percent in the 1960s, while the number showing luxury and pleasure as a product value climbed from 10 percent to 25 percent in the 1960s and to 50 percent by the 1970s. While 55 percent of the ads in the 1920s said something about the practical merits of a product, such images had fallen to just over 30 percent by the 1970s. Clearly, luxury was up, practical merits were down.

Second, looking at what Belk and Pollay called the different states of existence, the number of ads showing the value of "having" as reason enough for buying a product rose steadily during the baby-boom childhoods. "Don't you feel good owning a Chevy?" "Wouldn't you feel good just knowing that you have a Whirlpool in the kitchen?" the "having" ads would ask. During the same period, the number of ads showing the value of "being" fell. "Don't the Joneses look good in their new Ford?" "How come you don't own one?" the "being" ads would ask. By the mid-1960s, the number of "having" ads was up to half the total, while the number of "being" ads was down to 40 percent and falling. Finally, the number of ads showing "doing" was at an all-time high of 85 percent in the 1960s, up 20 points from the 1930s. "This Buick will get you there on time," these ads would promise. "It's cheap, it's reliable, and it works."[21]

In creating an image of what the baby boomers should value

in life, the advertising expectations seemed clear: products mattered not for social connections, but for the mere pleasure of ownership and performance—values which cross the baby-boom economic and social divisions even today. Of the values left from the advertising of the 1950s, 1960s, and 1970s, performance appears to matter most, whether in a Audi 5000 or a Ford Bronco pick-up. In that sense, *Quality* magazine was right. Whether it is hot dogs or caviar, the baby boomers appear to care most about taste, not name brands. Very few can afford the products advertised in *Quality*, but performance clearly matters to the bulk of the baby boomers.

The baby boom's great expectations were also forged in the classroom. Compared to children in the 1930s, baby boomers not only spent more time in school, they completed more levels of education. Though the school term had only increased by 20 days between 1920 and 1950, the baby boomers had a much better attendance record, spending roughly 160 days in school each year, or 40 days more than their parents and grandparents. The time apparently paid off. In the 1920s, less than 20 percent of the school-age population graduated from high school. By the 1970s, the figure had climbed past 75 percent.

It is important to note that not all baby boomers benefited equally from these "golden days" of education. As education researchers David Tyack and Elisabeth Hansot argue, "Public education emerged from the Depression years united professionally, secure in public esteem, with its system of finance and governance largely intact. But also intact were the immense inequalities that had marked the system in 1929. American public education was not one system with some 130,000 local branches, but a highly decentralized collection of districts that exhibited extremes of wealth and poverty."[22]

The majority of baby boomers, however, went to school in an enlightened era in American education. As Harvard University professor Alan Binkley notes, "American schools in the 1930s were hardly worthy of the name: unheated shacks staffed by uneducated teachers and unequipped with even the most rudimentary books and equipment; schools for rural blacks that were open only a few weeks of the year; schools in poor urban areas that students and teachers alike described as 'like prisons,' places actively hostile to learning."[23] Though the 1950s did not erase the inequalities of the system they did bring more money and a national commitment to high-school education. The idea of compulsory education had taken hold in the 1930s as a way to get younger Americans out of a crippled job market, but escalated to a national passion in the 1950s. Most Americans would get a high-school degree, no matter what the cost.

Once in school, the baby boomers shared new academic freedoms. The pendulum had swung from a traditional, authoritarian teaching philosophy to a more flexible, progressive approach. Though not all teachers and school systems bought the entire package, it is fair to say that the baby boomers entered high school during an era when most teachers emphasized active learning over passive learning—that is, practical projects instead of learning by rote—cooperation instead of competition, effective living skills rather than abstract knowledge, community over individual expression, experience over facts. According to Columbia University scholar Diane Ravitch, "the new education was consistently described as democracy in action, because it substituted teacher-pupil cooperation for teacher authoritarianism, stressed socialization to the group instead of individualism, and championed an educational program that was for all children in the here-and-now rather than for the minority that was college-bound."[24]

Not only was the baby boom the first generation to be pushed through high school, it was given unprecedented encouragement to go on to college. Half of all baby boomers started college, and almost a quarter finished. According to Ravitch, "the great struggle of the nineteenth century had been the fight to establish the principle of free universal public schooling; the great struggle of the first half of the twentieth century had been to make secondary schooling universal; and the goal for the present [the 1950s] was to make higher education a right, not just a privilege for all Americans."[25] And the baby boomers were the first beneficiaries of that goal.

Ultimately, the 1950s were a period of remarkable expansion for most of America. And the lesson for the baby boomers, according to Jones, was that they had economic power. "The landscape had been paved into suburbs; thousands of new schools had been built," he writes. "Their economic power turned their casual fancies into national fads. Madison Avenue was aiming the most powerful selling medium ever invented—television—directly at them."[26]

Whatever the medium communicated, it was always intimate. Unlike radio, which forced its young listeners to create their own visuals, the images on television were vividly clear and identical; presented one-to-one, yet as a totally shared experience. "Television itself is a baby boomer, it's a baby-boom instrument," NBC chief Brandon Tartikoff says. "The baby-boom generation has never known a living environment in which there wasn't a television." By the time the average baby boomer reached age 16, he or she had watched from 12,000 to 15,000 hours of TV, or the equivalent of 24 hours a day for 15 to 20 solid months.

There can be little doubt about the baby boom's attachment even today to the TV programming of their childhoods, which explains why television programmers continue to profit from reruns of the old standards. The 1980s are best labelled the "Re Decade," writes *Washington Post* television critic Tom Shales. "People think the eighties have no texture, no style, no tone of their own. They don't. They have the texture and style and tone of all the other decades, at least those that were recorded on film or tape, because the Re Decade is everything that preceded it thrown into one big electronic revue."[27]

Nor is there any doubt that the baby boomers continue to embrace the medium. In 1981, for example, 30 percent of those under 35 years old kept their televisions on even when they were not watching, three times as often as those over 35 years old. "The impact of television on this generation so far exceeds the impact of radio, motion pictures, and vaudeville on previous generations because of the universality of TV," says Mike Dann, former CBS programming head. "It has had a profound impact on the speech patterns, the dress, and to some extent the intellectual process of any number of people growing up even in the earliest days of television."

Looking back to the 1950s and 1960s, television affected the baby boomers in three distinctive ways. First, from the very beginning, it separated them from traditional social connections, and taught them intimate lessons about being an adult without any intervention from parents or teachers. Second, it presented a world of remarkable similarity from channel to channel, a "vast wasteland" as Federal Communications Commission (FCC) chairman Newton Minnow once called it. Third, and perhaps most important, if TV violence did not create a pathological generation, it may have created a sense of fear about the world.

Television is both a crowded medium, with multiple cuts of information packed between strict time boundaries, and an intimate medium, to be watched alone even in a crowded room. Sociologist Robert Bellah and his colleagues believe that the combination fosters social separation through the sheer succession of sensations: "But television operates not only with a complete disconnectedness between successive programs. Even within a single hour or half-hour program, there is extraordinary discontinuity. Commercials regularly break whatever mood has built up with their own, often very different emotional message. Even aside from commercials, television style is singularly abrupt and jumpy, with many quick cuts to other scenes and other characters. Dialogue is reduced to clipped sentences. No one talks long enough to express anything complex. Depth of feeling, if it exists at all, has to be expressed in a word or a glance."[28]

To the extent television gave the young baby boomers this mix of fixed time boundaries and social separation simultaneously, it reinforced the generation's separation from potential societal networks. There can be little doubt that television reduced the baby boom's contact with its peers and parents, and that the generation made its first contacts with the real world through the medium. Data from the early days of television support these ideas. "Even at the age of three," scholars Wilbur Schramm, Jack Lyle, and Edwin Parker argued in 1961, "when the average viewing time is in the neighborhood of 45 minutes a day, the child spends more time on television than even on hearing stories." It also produced a drop in the amount of time spent playing either alone or with other children, and reduced the time spent in conversation and family interaction, another privation of experience.

More important, it crowded out other sources of information and pleasure. Nine out of ten baby boomers were well acquainted with TV long before they read their first newspaper. Two-thirds were active TV viewers before they saw their first movie.[29] Moreover, television was the baby boom's window on world events. For example, it eventually became the major source for their knowledge about the war in Vietnam, far more so than for their parents or teachers, and it may have eclipsed the family as a source of political information. One political scientist even maintains that television became a new social parent in the 1960s. Recall the question of why parents did not pass on their party loyalty to their children. Perhaps one answer is that TV got in the way.

Why were the baby boomers captured? Because, as Schramm and his colleagues concluded, television was "first, and always predominantly, a magic doorway into a world of fantasy, glamour, and excitement. It is an invitation to relax, to disregard one's real-life problems, to surrender oneself to the charming and handsome people, the absorbing events, that flicker on the picture tube."[30] In that regard, television was to the baby boomers what comics had been to their parents. Yet, unlike comics, television introduced the baby boomers to a very adult world. As Schramm and his coauthors continued, "a very large proportion of children's television viewing is of adult programs. The effect of this is that the old timetable for gradually exposing a child to adult ideas is gone forever. There is no use looking nostalgically back toward it—it is gone."[31]

Long before Vietnam and double-digit inflation, the question of whether the baby boom's reality would ever be able to match the fantasy world of television was asked by child psychiatrist Eugene Glynn. "These children are in a peculiar position," Glynn wrote in the mid-1950s, "experience is exhausted in advance. There is little they have not seen or done or lived through, and yet this is secondhand experience. When the experience itself comes, it is watered down, for it has already been half lived but never truly felt."[32] In one sense, the baby boom was long composed of little adults, asked to think about the big questions long before they had the capacity to find the answers.

Television also offered baby boomers very few choices for viewing across the channels. Lower and upper classes, boys and girls, blacks and whites all shared the same programs. As Minnow told an assembly of broadcasters in May 1961, "I invite you to sit down in front of your television set when your station goes on the air and stay there without a book, magazine, newspaper, profit-and-loss sheet or rating book to distract you—and keep your eyes glued to that set until the station signs off. I can assure that you will observe a vast wasteland." According to Minnow, television was little more than "a procession of game shows, violence, audience-participation shows, formula comedies about totally unbelievable families, blood and thunder, mayhem, violence, sadism, murder, Western bad men, Western good men, private eyes, gangsters, more violence, screaming, cajoling and offending. And most of all boredom."[33]

The program schedules proved his point. Examining all 2,000 prime-time programs from 1953 to 1974, journalism professors Joseph Dominick and Millard Pearce concluded that programming became more similar over time. Action adventures were increasingly popular, growing from just 10 percent of all program in 1953 to just over half by 1960. Movies were second, capturing almost 25 percent of all prime time by 1974, while situation comedies held steady at 20 percent throughout the period.[34]

What this meant was that all baby boomers saw the same programs regardless of the channel they were watching. During the 1950s and 1960s, according to Dominick and Pearce, "more and more program time was being devoted to fewer and fewer program types. In 1954, for example, three categories—action/adventure, movies, and general drama—accounted for 81 percent of prime time." By 1964, action adventures had crowded out the general drama, leaving the baby boomers with even fewer choices. As network profits went up, diversity of programming went down. The authors noted, "the more money the industry made, the more the prime-time schedules on the networks began to resemble one another."[35] Whatever the station, the baby boomers were likely to see the same shows—if not the "Munsters" then "Addams Family," if not "Bonanza" then "Gunsmoke."

Mixed into the baby boom's programming was a staggering amount of televised violence. While television showed a world of excitement and fantasy, it also showed a world of violence and risk. Take the following list from the week of October, 1961, as an example:

Twelve murders,
Sixteen major gunfights,
Twenty-one persons shot (apparently not fatally),
Twenty-one other violent incidents with guns (ranging from shooting at but missing persons, to shooting up a town),
Thirty-seven hand-to-hand fights (fifteen fist fights, fifteen incidents in which one person slugged another, an attempted murder with a pitchfork, two stranglings, a fight in the water, a case in which a woman was gagged and tied to a bed, and so forth),
One stabbing in the back with a butcher knife,
Four attempted suicides, three successful,

Four people falling or pushed over cliffs,

Two cars running over cliffs,

Two attempts made in automobiles to run over persons on the sidewalk,

A psychotic loose and raving in a flying airliner,

Two mob scenes, in one of which the mob hangs the wrong man,

A horse grinding a man under its hooves,

A great deal of miscellaneous violence, including a plane fight, a hired killer stalking his prey, two robberies, a pickpocket working, a woman killed by falling from a train, a tidal wave, an earthquake, and a guillotining.[36]

The question frequently raised is whether such scenes of violence had an impact on the baby boom. Some have argued, for example, that TV violence creates imitation and aggression in children. The evidence for that conclusion is sparse. According to Harvard scholars James Q. Wilson and Richard Hernstein, studies that try to measure very short-term effects (i.e., watching certain programs for a week or two) on behavior that is hard to observe (aggression) "are inevitably going to produce modest findings surrounded by many qualifications."[37]

After two decades of research, the most that can be concluded is that violence on the air appears to be related to a short-term sense of anxiety and potential for aggression. That conclusion is some distance from a clear cause-and-effect relationship. "Were the facts known," Wilson and Hernstein argue, "it might be the case that merely being addicted to television, regardless of its contents, so poaches the brain or predisposes viewers to immediate gratification that they become unable to work for distant goals or engage in disciplined activity. It might then make engaging in crime (not necessarily violent crime) somewhat more likely, other things being equal."[38]

Others have argued that television violence creates heightened fears about the outside world. "Compared to light viewers," Landon Jones wrote summarizing the research, "heavy television watchers live in a darkening world of anxiety. They greatly overestimate the proportion of people involved in violence, the danger of walking alone at night, and the number of criminals in society. . . . Heavy viewers are also more likely to mistrust the motives of other people and, when asked if it is all right to hit someone if you are mad at them, they answer 'almost always' in significantly higher proportions."[39]

There was certainly enough TV violence in the 1950s and 1960s to feed baby-boom fears of a violent world. According to one study, violence was especially heavy during the late 1950s when TV cowboys ruled the range. Violent programs increased steadily from 20 percent of prime time in 1953 to 41 percent in 1959. The number fell in the early 1960s, but rose back up to near 40 percent by 1967.[40]

Examining programming content from 1967 to 1969, communications expert George Gerbner discovered three trends. First, the number of acts of violence per program went down. Second, the number of programs with at least some violence stayed about the same. Third, the violence became more sophisticated and less lethal. "Mannix" was still a tough guy, but he committed fewer acts of violence per program and fewer people were killed. Little Joe was still willing to fight on "Bonanza," but he kept his gun in its holster longer.

Further, the risks of violence never abated. To the extent that the baby boomers interpreted television as something near to real life, they must have concluded that their futures were indeed risky. According to Gerbner, of the 762 leading characters in 1967–69, 516 were involved in some kind of violence, whether as victims, violents, or both: "Thus, the 'average' character's chance of being involved in some violence [was about] twice as good as his chance of not being involved." Of those involved, "more were involved as victims than as violents. Five in ten committed some violence, but six in ten suffered. Chances of suffering violence rather than escaping it were 1.5 to one." Gerbner concluded that the "overriding message is that of the risk of victimization."[41]

The figures are particularly threatening for women. In a curious inversion, as the networks cut back on violent programming in the late 1960s, women became almost exclusively objects of violence, rather than aggressive participators. The new ground rules were simple. First, women could no longer be violent themselves. Gone were the days when a scheming wife could poison or shoot her husband on "Perry Mason." Second, women could no longer be criminals. Gone were the days when a man and woman could rob a bank on "Hawaii Five-O." Third, women could no longer appear to deserve a violent end. Gone were the days when a vicious woman could be murdered by her battered spouse on "Alfred Hitchcock."

Yet, if women were written out of the aggressive roles, they still remained as random victims. With the bad women off the air, only good women could be victims—mothers, innocent bystanders, co-eds. As Gerbner noted, "the shift toward female victimization is not so much an aspect of defeat as of fear and suffering."[42]

Violence became something that could happen to anyone, and not only to women who seemed to deserve it or to those who had chosen a life of risk. Baby-boom women could not help but conclude that the chances of escaping violence were slim indeed, which may explain why they are so much more likely than men to favor more federal spending on crime today. In 1985, for example, the gap between the genders on this issue was 11 points (75 percent to 64 percent) among 20-to 29-year-olds, and 15 points (78 percent versus 63 percent) between 30- to 39-year-olds.[43]

As a result of their childhood TV viewing, the baby boomers entered adulthood with a much clearer sense of the risks of life, whether from the fantasy of television violence or from the reality of events like Vietnam. If television was a magic doorway to fantasy, it was also a frightening doorway to violence and fear. It

was a doorway that most baby boomers passed through, regardless
of their age, gender, education, or class.

Whatever the doorway, however, the baby boomers always
had a tight fit, sharing a degree of social crowding unknown to
previous generations. This crowding placed new limits on individual achievement. The sheer numbers which made expectations
so high also made individual distinction more difficult. Maternity
wards were packed; grade schools were jammed; teenage unemployment reached new highs; high schools went to split shifts.

Great expectations or not, the baby boomers could not be
handled as individuals; the generation was too big. If universal
education and new freedoms at home gave the baby boomers a
sense of self-reliance, the crowding created a lifelong commitment
to individualism. Awash in a sea of other baby boomers, the generation began a search for space and opportunity.

Sociologists, however, are of a mixed mind on the impact of
crowding. Some say it does not matter much. "Under some circumstances," Jonathan Freedman says, "crowding may have disastrous effects on rats, mice, rabbits, and other animals, but
crowding does not have generally negative effects on humans.
People who live under crowded conditions do not suffer from
being crowded."[44]

In short, crowds don't crowd people, people do. "If you get
people who are feeling aggressive for other reasons—who have
been angered at home or at work—and you put them under high-
density conditions," Freedman acknowledges, "they are likely to
be more aggressive. On the other hand, if the same people are
feeling good and cooperative, density will also intensify that."[45]
The baby boomers at Woodstock hardly saw the crowding there
as being negative.

Take city crowding as an example. A city is not a bad environment per se, says psychologist Gerda McCahan, "just a very complex one. An effect of living in the big city is that with time people

learn to insulate themselves in a psychological sense. They learn not to allow stimuli to impinge on their consciousness. They sift out things that do not concern them." Even *Psychology Today* seems to agree: "Cities Won't Drive You Crazy," the magazine headlined in 1985, especially "Not if you learn the trick: make stress a stimulus rather than a threat."[46] In the same sense, perhaps living in a large generation had the same effect on baby boomers, intensifying shared experiences, and creating greater separation.

Other sociologists say crowding matters a great deal. Animal experiments show that crowding creates what psychologist John Calhoun called "a behavioral sink" in which rats eat their young, and "even the most normal males exhibit . . . occasional signs of pathology, going berserk, attacking females, juveniles and the less active males, and showing a particular predilection—which rats do not normally display—for biting other animals on the tail." Similar results show up in studies of blue geese, rhesus monkeys, roe bucks, and male stickleback fish.

Social psychologists see different problems in human crowding. Crowded humans do not necessarily bite each other on the tail or eat their young, but neither do they generally react with warmth and kindness. Not only do experiments show that humans become more anxious and irritable under crowded conditions, and that they also lose their sense of humor and patience, but urban crowding also may undermine people's willingness to help those in distress, perhaps because of the anonymity of experience. "There are practical limitations to the Samaritan impulse in a major city," psychologist Stanley Milgram wrote of urban living in 1970. "If a citizen attended to every needy person, if he were sensitive to and acted on every altruistic impulse that was evoked in the city, he could scarcely keep his own affairs in order." For Milgram, crowding creates a host of unseemly effects in humans, too, from the "refusal to become involved in the needs of another person, even when the person desperately needs assistance, through refusal to do favors, to the simple withdrawal of courtesies."[47]

Thus, the impact of crowding involves both perceptions and reality.[48] What may seem like crowding to some may be a pleasant gathering to others. Some people feel crowded even in an empty room, others cannot stand to be alone. The impact may also depend on when and where it occurs. Being crowded in a subway is very different from being crowded at a party.

The best research to date on crowding strongly suggests that the baby boomers would have been affected by crowding in their peer groups and schools, and by their continued crowding in the housing and labor markets. Working from a carefully selected sample of Chicago households, sociologists Walter Gove, Michael Hughes, and Omer Galle, offer a very simple theory of how crowding affects human behavior. According to their research, the number of persons per room affects people's need for privacy and their sense of social overload, which in turn affects their family relationships, marital stress, and mental health.

The key is the linkage between persons per room, what Gove and his colleagues call objective crowding, and the need for privacy and sense of overload, what they call perceived crowding. The more people in a given space, the more each will be obligated to respond to the others, and the greater the loss in privacy. There are fewer places to hide, to escape. To the extent that such crowding increased during the baby-boom childhoods, the need for space and privacy would also have increased.

The Chicago data are particularly interesting on the tie between objective crowding and the need for space. More people in the same space clearly affects individual perceptions that there is too much going on. Facing the overload, people naturally withdraw, trying to get away from it all both physically and psychologically. According to the Chicago data, people who feel crowded also feel they are less able to plan even for the short-term future, and report what the researchers call a high degree of "wash-out."

Crowding also affects personal relationships. Within Chicago families, for example, higher numbers of persons per room creates

greater marital stress, irritation, a loss in self-esteem, even alienation and a greater risk of nervous breakdown. Not surprisingly,
crowding is not particularly healthy for either marriages or children. Crowding increases the number of arguments and the level
of physical violence between spouses. Parents are more likely to
say their children are a hassle, more likely to feel relief when the
kids are outside, and less likely to know their children's playmates.
The children are less likely to have a place to study or think, and
spend more time outside. In such homes, Gove and his colleagues
conclude, "children are experienced as an irritant."[49]

The question is whether there was enough crowding to affect
the baby boomers as children and young adults. Looking back to
baby-boom families, the answer is murky at best. While the number of families with only one child declined, the number with five
children also fell. What that means is that the baby boomers were
more likely than past generations to have at least one sibling, but
less likely to have three or more.

Looking back to baby-boom schools, however, the answer is
clear. The baby boom was packed together like no other generation in history. Not only were more children enrolled than ever
before, there was also a teacher shortage. "The school system faced
two particular difficulties in responding to the onslaught of children—one peculiar to the time, the other inherent in the situation," Louise Russell says. "The peculiar difficulty was that the
schools had been starved during World War II and later suffered
from further restrictions on materials, and from competition for
teachers, during the Korean War. Offsetting these initial hand-
icaps was the unparalleled prosperity of the postwar period. The
inherent difficulty was in predicting how long the baby boom
would last and how big it would be."[50] Local governments did not
want to raise taxes for new schools unless they had to.

Because the construction and hiring boom lagged behind the
fertility rate, for the bulk of the baby boom school days meant
large classes and big schools. According to Russell, "The average
size remained close to thirty-three students per teacher through

the 1950s, consistently above the twenty-five to thirty considered desirable, and began to drop only in the 1960s when enrollment growth slowed in the elementary grades."[51] The use of split-shifts in high school became commonplace in larger school districts— one high-school student body in the morning and a completely different one in the afternoon.

Split shifts were mostly a thing of the past by the 1970s. School systems had finally caught up. The number of public-school teachers peaked at 2.2 million in the mid-1970s, 30 years after the first baby boomer was born. In constant dollars, the amount of money spent per baby-boom student eventually quadrupled from the beginning of the baby-boom school years to the end. Ultimately, the youngest baby boomers were the true beneficiaries of the expansion. As a result of increasing pressure for teacher certification, the teachers were probably better in the 1970s than in the 1950s, and the schools were certainly more modern and well equipped.

However, that does not mean that the youngest baby boomers went back to the golden days of small schools and small classes. School consolidation was well under way by the mid-1950s, never to reverse. "Big schools became the rule, not the exception," Diane Ravitch writes. "In a society where bigger was considered better, small districts and small schools were described as backward and inefficient. The number of school districts shrank dramatically, from one hundred thousand at war's end [in 1945] to sixteen thousand in 1980. While total enrollment in elementary and secondary schools nearly doubled during the thirty-five year span (from 23 million to 40 million), the number of schools dropped from one hundred and eighty-five thousand to eighty-six thousand."

The average school size was 124 students in 1945, 471 in 1980, a result ordained in part by the closing of thousands of rural schools. "The trade-off, of course," Ravitch says, "was that bigness meant impersonality, bureaucratization, diminished contact between faculty and students, formalization of relationships among colleagues, a weakening of the bonds of community."[52] It was a trade-off experience from the beginning to the end of the baby-boom educational experience.

The large classes and schools certainly brought new efficiencies, but at what cost? One answer is lower academic achievement. Looking back over two decades of educational research, Gene Glass and his colleagues offer two conclusions: (1) making a small class large undermines student achievement, and (2) making a large class larger does not seem to make a difference.[53] Being in a small class of, say, fifteen or twenty is much better than being in a large class of, say, thirty or thirty-five. Being in an even larger class of, say, forty may not hurt the student that much more. The ideal class size then is a maximum around twenty to twenty-five at which grades and test scores have been shown to be consistently higher.

Another cost of large schools is lower social interaction among students. Large classes and schools limit the opportunities for student participation. There is a reason why small schools play 8-man football. Whatever the student activity—whether sports, drama, music, debate, or student government—small schools demand greater student involvement than large schools; even if students do not want to participate, they often have no choice. School plays need actors; bands need musicians.

Past research on the baby boom itself confirms the lost social learning in big schools. One study of the class of 1969 found that 42 percent of the students in small high schools participated in ten or more school activities per year, compared with 22 percent in large schools. Further, one-third of the large-school students were characterized as inactive with less than three activities per year, compared to only 10 percent in the small schools.[54] Because large classes and schools became a national response to the size of the baby boom, the generation lost an important chance during its school years to learn how to participate. Finally, because large classes did not permit individualized instruction, big-school baby boomers would have had more freedom to withdraw or escape.

There would have been fewer payoffs in working with classmates since the best way to become known in a crowd is to stand out.

Perhaps more important than their great expectations, television, and crowding, the baby boomers shared a sense of fear about nuclear war. The question for many baby boomers was not whether they could get to the head of the class tomorrow, but whether there would be any tomorrow at all. Even though these fears subsided with the press of other issues into the headlines, they remain part of the baby-boom past and present.

For the older baby boomers, the fears came close to becoming a reality in October 1962. Never had the United States come so close to launching its nuclear missiles as in the Cuban missile crisis. Confronted with clear evidence of Soviet missiles in Cuba, Kennedy had to make the United States nuclear threat credible. Each day of the crisis ratcheted up the tension, until at last the United States stood ready to launch on Saturday, October 27, confirming the public's worst nightmares that nuclear war was indeed possible. As the secretary of defense later testified to Congress, "We had a force of several hundred thousand ready to invade Cuba. . . . Khrushchev knew without any question whatsoever that he faced the full military power of the United States, including its nuclear weapons. . . . We faced that night the possibility of launching nuclear weapons . . . and that is the reason, and the only reason, why he withdrew those weapons."

As the Soviet nuclear program had advanced, the fears of a nuclear war between the two superpowers had grown. After his disastrous Vienna summit meeting with Soviet Premier Nikita Khrushchev in 1961, Kennedy warned the nation that to accept "the possibilities of nuclear war in the nuclear age without our citizens knowing what they should do and where they should go if bombs begin to fall would be a failure of responsibility." He was convinced that a national network of fallout shelters was the answer.

The result, according to author Allan Winkler, was a $200 million program "to mark and stock existing community shelter spaces in subways, tunnels, corridors and basements where 50 million Americans could stay temporarily."[55] Many buildings still have the yellow and black civil defense insignias as a reminder of those days, although the supplies are long spoiled or stolen. Kennedy encouraged private solutions, too. By 1960, the new Office of Civil and Defense Mobilization estimated that there were a million private bomb shelters nationwide, creating secret hideaways for millions of baby-boom children to play in, if nothing else.

The federal government had also spent millions on civil defense training, teaching the baby boom's parents where to run, and how to survive. The older baby boomers had had ample training, too, including countless civil defense drills at school. New Yorker Robert Musil remembers his high-school bomb drills vividly: "Each year I watched bemused as widening circles, representing atomic destruction on a map of New York crept outward from Manhattan. Only with the advent of deliverable Russian thermonuclear weapons in the mid-1950s did those circles finally reach my home. I began to worry. I particularly recall the early atomic tests on television, that showed a model house erected by the Army crumbling and disintegrating in the blast. It was with that awful knowledge—we were not safe at all—that I experienced duck-and-cover drills, and developed an early disillusionment with, even disdain for, authority. In many ways, the styles and the explosions of the 1960s were born in those dank, subterranean high-school corridors near the boiler room where we decided that our elders were indeed unreliable, perhaps even insane."[56]

Nuclear vigilance was no less important to those in the middle of the baby boom. Besides the air-raid drills and evacuation maps, Seattle school children wore dog tags with their names and addresses. "If we were blasted away," one remembered, "at least our mothers might find these durable remnants and have the comfort of knowing for sure."[57] They still remember "Bert the Turtle," star of a U.S. Civil Defense film called "Duck and Cover," and the comic book version. Twenty million copies were distributed nationwide. A seven-part nuclear survival series appropriately entitled "Survival" was shown on NBC in 1951 and drew 12 million viewers. A film narrated by Edward R. Murrow reassured its young and old viewers alike that "You can SURVIVE."[58] No one talked much about fallout. If anyone knew about nuclear winter —that is, the ice age which might follow all-out nuclear war—they were not talking either.

Author Paul Boyer argues that nuclear fear was the shaping cultural force from the mid-1940s to the mid-1960s, "Books, essays, symposia, and conferences explored the medical, psychological and ethical implications of atomic weapons," he writes. "Novels like *On the Beach, Fail Safe,* Dexter Master's *The Accident,* and Walter Miller, Jr.'s *A Canticle for Leibowitz* offered versions of the nuclear holocaust."[59] Slim Pickens' cowboy ride on a nuclear bomb in Stanley Kubrick's movie *Dr. Strangelove* remains the brilliant satire of the period.

The nuclear era did indeed create a special bomb generation, complete with a sense of mystery about the nuclear age, and an almost ritualistic language of destruction. Despite an early emphasis in the Reagan administration on a survivable nuclear war, this bomb generation believes that nuclear war can bring nothing but victims. According to author Michael Carey, this "generation had America's only formal and extended bomb-threat education in its schools, and that education—along with the lessons about the bomb from government, the media and the family—were well learned. This generation has a collection of memories, images, and words that will not disappear, even for those who profess not to be troubled."[60]

In a 1962 study of New York City school children, Sybille Escalona asked them to think about the world in ten years and how it might be different. "The universal wish for a long life or immortality, and for lots of money, was expressed by nearly all children," Escalona reports. "A great many spoke of miracle cures for fatal diseases, of better living conditions, of an end to discrimination, of better education and housing, and of more kindness in the world."[61]

It was an optimistic outlook for sure. Unfortunately, 70 percent of the children also mentioned war as part of the future. One in three viewed war as possible or even as a certainty. As one 12-year-old imagined America's future, "We may have gone to the moon. We would maybe have a new way of transportation. Maybe we will not even be here 10 years from now. Maybe there will be no such thing as a world. Maybe there will be a World War III."

As Escalona summarizes her own analysis, "the powerful impressions of troubled and wistfully hopeful children has a cumulative effect as one reads dozens and hundreds of these answers." Indeed it does. One 11-year-old wrote, "The people will be living underground, and they would have to have a lot of light or I think the children would not be very strong as they are now. But I really hope it will be a lot better than I think it will be." The shortened time horizon is clear from the responses, as well as the children's impression of a future filled with both technological promise and potential destruction.

Other studies of young baby boomers found similar fears. In 1961, a survey of 3,000 grade schoolers showed that even the youngest baby boomers worried about the fate of family and friends in the event of a nuclear war. "Many were saddened at the thought that the great progress of mankind, its culture and civilization itself were endangered," child psychologist Milton Schwebel wrote of the results. The students were also worried about "their own survival, bitter about the possible deprivation of the satisfactions of adult life, anxious about mutations and monstrosities." Yet, as Schwebel concluded, "their strongest emotions were reserved for those adults who advocated shutting the door of a shelter on strangers and neighbors and, if need be, shooting them down. They were horrified at the suggestion and demanded that if shelters were built they must be available to all people, rich or poor."[62]

It is also clear that the fears of nuclear war subsided toward the end of the 1960s. In 1959, during a period of relative world peace, 64 percent of the public had listed war as the nation's most important problem. By 1965, as Vietnam escalated, the number had dropped to 16 percent. In a perverse sort of way, Vietnam may have made people feel safer about nuclear weapons. After all, the United States stayed with conventional weaponry throughout the conflict. Part of the change also reflected the more immediate worries about civil rights and domestic unrest, part was due to an aggressive "friendly atom" campaign by the nuclear power industry, and part was from what Boyer calls the loss of immediacy.

People did not talk about nuclear war any longer in the late 1960s. And when they did, they talked in confusing terms—mutual assured destruction, and so forth. "Even the names given the various missile systems," Boyer writes, "evoked not their actual doomsday potential but reassuring associations with the heavens, classic mythology, American history, and even popular slang: Polaris, Nike-Zeuss, Poseidon, Tomahawk, Minuteman, Pershing, Davy Crockett, Hound Dog."[63] To some extent, the MX and Cruise missiles, with their mundane names, broke that pleasantry, perhaps bringing the public back to the reality of the awesome destructive power of nuclear weapons, and to a renewed emphasis in the early 1980s on arms control and disarmament.

It is difficult to say how the nuclear era affected the new wave of the baby boomers, particularly those born in the early 1960s. There was virtually no research on the issue between 1963 and 1976, perhaps due to the general complacency toward nuclear war.[64] By 1976, however, nuclear fears had cooled down considerably. Only 7 percent of a sample of male high-school seniors said they worried about nuclear war often, and only 20 percent said they believed nuclear or biological annihilation will probably be the fate of all mankind within their lifetimes. By 1982, high-school seniors were anxious again, with 31 percent worried about nuclear war often, and 35 percent predicting nuclear or biological annihilation.[65]

It is likely, of course, that contemporary fears of nuclear war vary with the headlines. Just as Reagan's rhetoric about the Soviet Union as the evil empire once heightened worries of war, perhaps the 1987 United States–Soviet agreement on intermediate nuclear weapons will have a soothing effect. That does not mean, however, that nuclear worries will no longer exist at some level, or that baby boomers and their younger siblings will no longer feel afraid of the future.

According to a recent report by an American Psychiatric Association task force, for example, children learn about nuclear war early—often before age 12—and the resulting fear shapes their outlook on life. In a survey of the high-school class of 1979, a class which included the tail end of the baby boom, 50 percent of the sample reported that advances in nuclear weaponry affected their thoughts about marriage and the future, and a majority said they were even affected in their daily thoughts and feelings. Echoing findings from almost twenty years before, the task force reported that "there were vivid expressions of terror and powerlessness, grim images of nuclear destruction, doubt about whether they will ever have a chance to grow up and an accompanying attitude of 'live for now.' Some expressed anger toward the adult generation that seemed to have so jeopardized their future."[66]

Perhaps such early experiences explain why the baby boom remains more likely to see arms control as a more important issue than the budget deficit, tax reform, or Central America, and why they think nuclear war is more likely to occur than their parents and grandparents do.[67] Even today, childhood fears linger in the baby boom's pessimism toward the distant future.

No wonder so many baby boomers have so little confidence in the future of Social Security. How can they have trust that Social Security will exist when they do not believe the world will be able to avoid a nuclear war in their lifetimes? As psychologist Lawrence Langer argues, "Living in times of catastrophe shifts the rhythm of our imaginative efforts from creating the future—the challenge of our ancestors—to fighting a rearguard action against forces which menace with annihilation. . . . To embrace the possibility of death is to admit the possibility of inappropriate life, of a precarious existence which may be snuffed out without warning, leaving the survivors oblivious to any discernible relationship between cause and effect."[68]

Such fears may help explain why the baby boom has accumulated so much debt and seems unable to save any money, or why it lives so much in the present tense. While there is plenty of convenient economic history to take the blame, these nuclear fears do put those decisions into a broader social and historical context. The baby boomers learned very young they had to live for today.

This sense of "futurelessness," as social psychologist Robert Jay Lifton calls it, may haunt the baby boom through life, and may well be the most intense of the generation's shared experiences. Their nuclear fear, the crowding, television, their great expectations and the silent revolution all provide a common set of reference points within the generation and may have also forged a short-term focus toward life with a continuing emphasis on individualism and self-reliance.

The short-term perspective may be particularly important for understanding future baby-boom political choices. As political scientists Samuel Popkin and his colleagues suggest, instead of voting on the basis of habit and social allegiance, perhaps some Americans see their votes as investments in a public good. The theory may fit the baby boom well. Elections would become little more than another marketplace in which baby boomers must find the best product. Voting would be a highly individualized choice, stripped of its traditional meaning as an exercise of civic duty, and short-term promises and performance would take on critical importance. Such a model is based on a portrait of the baby boom as separated from traditional politics and voting cues, a portrait which is presented in the next two chapters.

5

A Portrait of Separation I

THE BABY BOOM has always been a source of great political promise and puzzling electoral achievement. From the day the first baby boomer was eligible to vote, candidates have come courting: Bobby Kennedy and Eugene McCarthy in 1968, George McGovern in 1972, Jimmy Carter in 1976, John Anderson in 1980, Gary Hart in 1984, and Joseph Biden in 1988.

There has never been any doubt about the baby boom's political potential. The numbers are obvious. In 1968, with the voting age still at 21, less than one in ten eligible voters were baby boomers. By 1972, however, with the voting age lowered to 18, and many more baby boomers eligible, they represented one out of five potential voters; in 1976, one out of three; in 1984, one out of two; in 1988, almost three out of five. They are very tempting political targets.

Yet, the baby boom has always fallen short of its promise. It has been much less a kingmaker than a heartbreaker. In 1972, the year McGovern rode the youth movement to the Democratic nomination, the baby boom's turnout gap was four percent—that is, baby boomers constituted 22 percent of the eligible electorate, but only 18 percent of the final votes. In 1980, the gap was eight percent. In 1984, five percent.

Not only do they trail in voting turnout, they appear to have abandoned traditional notions of party identification and loyalty. Compared to their parents and grandparents, the baby boomers are much less likely to swear strong allegiance to a political party, and are therefore more likely to focus on short-term events and issues in picking candidates. Only 22 percent of the baby boomers strongly identify with a political party, compared to 45 percent of Americans over age 65. When asked in 1984 if they considered themselves to be Republicans, Democrats, independents, or what, four in ten baby boomers said they were political independents. Even among those who said they identified with a party, those who were weak partisans outnumbered those who were strong by a margin of almost two to one. The question is whether the parties will ever be able to count on the baby boom for anything beyond a single election.

That does not mean the baby boomers have lost their glamour. "Even the older edge of the baby boom does not match the voter turnout of other cohorts in past years as they've reached their late 30s and 40s," Democratic pollster Patrick Caddell admits. "But the baby boom is so big that even at lesser percentages the numbers are overwhelming in terms of impact. So when we talk about the potential impact, you have to understand not only what is there but what more there could be if someone could invigorate it or make it more activist in the political sector."

For now, the baby boom remains separated from the political process—not quite out, not quite in; not turned off, but not particularly passionate either—easily exploited by the latest politician who looks or talks like John Kennedy. The challenge for the parties is how to get the baby boomers engaged in the political process when they are so actively engaged in themselves.

The baby boom's lack of political commitment reflects a set of recurring themes, including the generation's abandonment of traditional social roles, and its continued estrangement from a variety of political and social institutions, both of which are subjects for this chapter. The separation also involves the baby boom's lack of strong ties to the political parties, its abiding faith in individualism and self-reliance, and its increasing distance from television, all subjects for the next chapter.

The baby boom's political separation is hardly surprising given its rejection of other traditional roles. If nothing about the baby boomers is "normal," why should politics be any different? Indeed, the baby boom's political separation was but one part of a much broader societal separation from the homogenized families of the 1950s and early 1960s.

Advertisers saw the change first, mainly because this separation made selling products to the baby boomers a much more complicated proposition. "Back in the 1940s and 1950s, American society was largely homogeneous in its values, its morality and its aspirations," Kent Mitchel, vice president of General Foods says. "It was a relatively easy task to create a selling message that appealed to huge numbers of people, and then place it in mass media and have it delivered at a remarkably low cost—and it was effective." Advertisers created a single slogan and hit it repeatedly.

By the 1980s, however, the standard family was gone, replaced by single-parent families, two-earner couples, and a much greater focus on the individual. "Two decades ago, you could be virtually certain that the product for which you were providing advertising would be for 'any housewife, aged 18–49,' " advertising executive Rena Bartos argues. "She would be the point of entry to the American household." Today there is no such thing as a single point of entry. Nor a single selling proposition. The change reflects the decline of traditional social roles. Not only are there fewer full-time housewives, but baby boomers are much less likely to accept any traditional social label.

Marriage is a first example of the baby boom's societal separation. Perhaps the greatest change in social norms between the

1950s and 1970s was the increased tolerance toward people who stayed single by choice.

Indeed, over the twenty-year span, the number of young Americans who felt neutral toward those who stayed single by choice jumped by half.[1] In 1957, for example, 46 percent of the under-30 age group and 52 percent of the 30 to 40 age group felt negative toward people who decided never to marry, saying that those who did not marry were somehow "sick," "neurotic," or "immoral." In 1976, only 22 percent of the under-30 age group and 28 percent of the 30 to 40 age group felt the same way about those who stayed single by choice.

"This loosening of the normative necessity of being someone's wife or husband in order to be a valid adult undoubtedly has had and will continue to have profound effects on other reactions to marriage," Veroff and his coauthors argue. "The number of divorced people who stay divorced and do not remarry has clearly increased. Divorce has become more than a peripheral institution. It has come to be a much more viable alternative to marriages that are not successful."[2]

The divorce rates provide further confirmation of the change in attitudes toward marriage. By the time the older baby boomers complete their marriage course in the next century, 60 percent of women who ever married will have been divorced at least once, according to an analysis by Census Bureau experts Arthur Norton and Jeanne Moorman. Already it seems clear that the younger baby boomers will end up with a slightly lower divorce rate, not because marriage has been more stable for them, but because fewer women will take the risk of getting married in the first place.[3] "A decade ago it was apparent that the first members of the baby boom to reach adulthood were deviating from past patterns of marriage and divorce," Norton and Moorman explain. "It can be argued that the oldest baby boomers were at once deviant and trend setters whose extraordinarily high divorce rates, although somewhat anomalous, also helped to establish new normative societal standards that permit a generally high rate of divorce."

"Younger couples today not only divorce more readily, but also do so earlier in their marriages," the Rand Corporation's Peter Morrison argued in 1986. "Consider married women who are now 55 years old. Not until they reached age 43, on average, did as many as 25 percent of their marriages break up; by then, their children were mostly grown. Contrast that with women who are now age 35: They reached that 25-percent level at the average age of 29. Marital disruptions thus tend to affect everybody—mothers, fathers, and children—much earlier in their lives." However, as Cheryl Russell says, today's statistics are not the anomaly, "it's the 1950s that were different. Half of first-time brides in the 1950s were teenagers. Little wonder that by the 1970s the proportion of never-married among women in their early 30s had reached rock bottom."[4]

The fact that as many as 20 percent of the baby boomers may never marry does not mean they will all be lonely. For some, living together will be the preferred alternative to marriage. Between 1980 and 1985, for example, the number of couples living together jumped from 1.6 million to 2.2 million. Five percent of all couples who were living together in 1985 were doing so without the benefit of marriage.

Nor do the marriage and divorce rates mean baby boomers who stay married are unhappy. In fact, Veroff, Douvan, and Kulka report that most Americans in 1976 saw their marriages as being happy, perhaps in part because those who were unhappy were much more likely to seek a divorce. Couples appeared to be more likely to acknowledge problems in their marriages in the 1970s than in the 1950s, but either worked things out or left the marriage altogether. It is a curious irony of the baby boom— marriages are happier, but there are fewer of them. Thus, baby boomers may value marriage less for its role in defining the individual and much more for its value as a source of happiness and interpersonal intimacy.

Parenthood is a second example of the baby boom's societal separation. The baby boom's fertility rate is still hovering at roughly half the level of the 1950s, creating fears of a birth dearth and depopulation crisis in the coming century. The panic even led *Newsweek* to proclaim a national emergency in a September 1986 cover story. It seems that "No Baby on Board" car stickers were selling very well.

Like marriage, parenthood has become another social role of choice, not obligation. Looking back to the revolution in birth control, Veroff and his colleagues argue that the baby boom undertook a "reevaluation of traditional family forms and the framing of marriage, conception, and childbirth as *choices* to be made among alternatives, options to be weighed and balanced against other possible life choices. While earlier generations took marriage and parenthood for granted as necessary parts of adulthood, such unconsidered assumptions now gave way to processes of choice, deliberation, and decision."[5]

Whereas the public once saw having children as an almost always enriching experience, the *Inner-American* concludes that the 1960s and 1970s brought a series of cultural changes which decreased the value attached to children. The number who saw being a parent as an unconditional plus dropped significantly between 1957 and 1976, and the number who saw at least some problems increased. In 1957, 54 percent of the under-30 age group saw having children as being only positive, compared to 32 percent of the same age group in 1976. And, by 1976, 70 percent of the baby boomers were neutral in their opinion of couples who remained childless by choice, compared to just 42 percent of people over 65.

Moreover, the baby boom's lower fertility rates may be the natural result of economic and social uncertainty. Having children is a significant financial commitment, made more difficult perhaps by the baby boom's recently poor economic performance. One way to illustrate the cost is to calculate how much it takes to raise a child born in 1981 as an example. Assuming that inflation stays low, economist Thomas Espenshade estimates that eighteen years of food, housing, transportation, clothing, medical care, and recreation will cost roughly $150,000 in constant dollars. Throw in four years of college room, board, and tuition, and the total tops $200,000. Assuming a much higher rate of inflation, the bill could hit $310,000.[6] Having a child clearly involves more than a cold economic calculation. Nevertheless, the baby boomers are more likely than previous generations to both understand the costs, and to make the commitment only when they are ready.

It should be no surprise then that the baby boomers have become more cautious about parenthood. At the height of the baby boom in the early 1960s, 20 percent of all births were reported as unwanted, while another 45 percent were reported as mistimed. From 1977 to 1981, in contrast, only 7 percent of births were unwanted, and 22 percent were mistimed.[7] Apparently, the baby boomers have been more effective in controlling their fertility, in part because they have better birth control, in part because they have had more social and economic incentives to be cautious, and in part because abortion has been available and acceptable.

This changing view of parenthood is not restricted just to the baby boomers, however. The baby boom's parents became less enthusiastic about having kids over the same 20-year period, too. Where the two generations appear to differ most is on their attitudes toward child rearing. "While earlier generations stressed role aspects of parenthood and drew sharp lines between the roles of parent and child," Veroff and his coauthors note, "later generations adopted the more psychological, interpersonal orientation urged by child-raising experts in which warm interpersonal interaction, empathy and caring (rather than clear differentiation of authority and power between parent and child) were seen as the medium for ensuring effective socialization."[8] These changing norms toward parent-child relationships may closely parallel baby boomer expectations about other social and political institutions. They clearly do not want to relate merely on the basis of an abstract label like father or mother, Democrat or Republican.

Again, the fertility rates do not mean the baby boomers are

unhappy as parents. Parents by choice may be more likely to want their children, and to appreciate the joys of parenting. Nor is remaining childless desired. Although large numbers of baby-boom women say children are not essential for a happy marriage, only one or two percent say that "zero" is the ideal number of children in their own lives. Indeed, data collected by Daniel Yankelovich show a striking increase over the past ten years in the number of baby boomers who believe that having a child is an experience that every woman should have.

There is at least some evidence to suggest that voluntary childlessness among the baby boomers is a response to their growing responsibilities for aging parents and grandparents. According to demographer Jane Menken, there may be a growing baby boomer uneasiness over how to deal with the kinds of pressures that exist in contemporary family life. The question, Can I have a child? may actually disguise a more difficult question, Should I have a child? "Low fertility and voluntary childlessness have sometimes been presented as evidence of selfishness, even hedonism, among young people today," Menken writes, "They may, however, be reasonable responses to the demographic changes that have altered the structure of family dependencies and led to questioning and perhaps redefining family obligations."[9]

Indeed, according to Menken's sophisticated computer analysis, never having children eliminates eighteen years of parental responsibility and wipes out any overlap in having to care for both children and aged parents simultaneously. Menken translates her figures into very human terms for the baby boomers:

First, we are the children of living parents for much longer, with all the implications of the kinds of connections that follow. The families we grew up in remain available to us well into our own middle age. Daughters can postpone childbearing and still expect that their children will grow up with lively and active grandparents. We experience the deaths of our parents at later and later ages: they are with us longer, for better or for worse, just as our own children will have us with them longer, for better or for worse. Although age 65 is an inadequate proxy for the starting point of the dependencies associated with biological aging, most of us can expect to be in a situation where our parents will depend on us in their old age, if not financially, then emotionally.[10]

For the baby boomers, such changes clearly alter the definition of what it means to be simultaneously a parent to one's own children, and a child of one's aging parents.

Work is a third example of the baby-boom societal separation. Suits and ties may have replaced blue jeans and t-shirts, but the baby boomers appear to retain much of their commitment to finding a meaningful philosophy of life, even in the workplace. Baby boomers tend to value the content of work more than their parents, and appear to look for satisfaction and challenge to a somewhat greater extent. And unlike their parents, the baby boomers spend at least some of their work time thinking about play, and rarely feel guilty during their leisure hours. For white-collar workers who like to play on the job, some computer games even offer a fake spread sheet to call to the screen in case the boss walks in unannounced.

There is at least some data which suggests that the baby boom-ers may be deriving less pleasure from work than their parents once did. In 1955, the Gallup Poll asked people whether they enjoyed their work so much that they had trouble putting it aside at the end of the day. Of the under-30 age group (the baby boom's parents), 44 percent said yes. Twenty-five years later, in 1980, Gallup asked the question again. This time, only 25 percent of the under-30 group (now the baby boomers) said yes, a drop of almost 20 points. In contrast, 45 percent of the parents said they still had trouble putting their work aside at the end of the day, showing a remarkable stability in their commitment over time. It appears that the baby boomers have less interest in the traditional meaning of work—or perhaps a much greater generational commitment to play.

That is exactly what Michael Maccoby argues in his book *Why Work?* After interviewing thousands of workers in different industries, Maccoby concludes that younger Americans represent a growing generation "defined not by age but by values that have developed in families where both parents work. These are men and women whose main goal at work is self-development. From childhood they have sharpened intellectual and interpersonal skills to succeed at work and to get along with people."[11]

By the mid-1980s, according to Maccoby's data, as many as 30 percent of younger workers looked to work for self-development, a figure which will surely grow as other workers follow suit. Among Maccoby's sample of young leaders, for example, 90 percent describe themselves as interested in self-development. As Maccoby suggests, their style will eventually trickle down.

These self-developers, as Maccoby calls them, look inward for job satisfaction, rejecting the traditional notion of hard work as a reward in itself. "They resent work that does not allow them to improve their skills and maintain their marketability," Maccoby notes. "They want to be free to respond individually to customers and clients, to be entrepreneurs instead of narrow specialists. They want to be treated as whole persons, not as role performers. Yet they are wary of being swallowed up by work. Motivated to succeed in family life as well as at a career, and to balance work with play, they continually question how much of themselves to invest in the workplace. They want to know why they are working, as opposed to expressing themselves outside of the job."[12]

This new style of work also involves changing attitudes toward money and time. Self-developers want more than just income—they want a job where they can exercise their skills and abilities, where they can "use all of themselves." According to Maccoby, self-developers also say that work shouldn't be the most important thing in their lives. "The ones with families want to keep a balance. They want 'to be happy, both professionally and personally.' Men don't want work to separate them from family; women don't want family to undermine career possibilities. A highly competent and motivated executive, age thirty-eight says:

'I work fifty hours a week. I come in early and go home late, but I leave it at the office. I am not going to push my little son off my lap because he is messing up papers from work."[13]

The baby boom's greater focus on what work can do for them, on work as a short-term commitment instead of a long-term calling, may become a source of bitterness for them. Unlike generations before it, the baby boom tends to see its working life as part of the confirmation of the individual, an approach which puts the generation at some risk as it confronts the inevitable disappointments of life. "When the trajectory of a career flattens out, and it becomes clear that one will not, after all, make it to the top," write a team of scholars, led by sociologist Robert Bellah, in *Habits of the Heart*, "then making it loses its meaning—as opposed to continuing in a calling and practicing law, carpentry, or scholarship as best one can, even if one cannot be the best. For many in middle age, the world of work then dims, and by extension so does the public world at large. For the fortunate among the career-weary, the private world of family and friends grows brighter, and a more expressive self comes to the fore."[14] Unfortunately, many baby boomers may not have a private world of family and friends to turn to in times of need.   *Thats me*

Indeed, according to Maccoby, critics of the new generation of workers may be right about the narcissism and lack of commitment. "Without a purpose beyond the self, without a larger meaning, self-development becomes an unfocused search for self-realization." For these workers, a shallow commitment to work fits with a shallow commitment to other roles. Even for those who are married, the sources of happiness appear to be very different from those in the 1950s. "Self-developers describe their marriage in terms of doing things together, traveling, sailing, going out to dinner, taking courses. Few speak of trust, caring, or deepening knowledge of each other."[15]

The conflict between self-development and the traditional definition of work appears to cut across the baby-boom classes, affecting blue collars and white collars alike. According to Barbara

Ehrenreich, the dilemma even shows up in books by and about corporate women. "The most striking thing about the literature," she writes, "is how little it has to say about the purposes, other than personal advancement, of the corporate 'game.' " In critiquing a long list of biographies, for example, Ehrenreich discovered that few seem "to have a vast and guiding vision of the corporate life, much less a Gilderesque belief in the moral purposefulness of capitalism itself. Instead, we find successful corporate women asking, 'Why am I doing what I'm doing? What's the point here?' or confiding bleakly that 'something's missing.' "[16]

The baby boom's new rules for making consumer choices is a final example of the breakdown of traditional social roles. If the 1950s were the era of consumer commitment to big brand names, the 1970s and early 1980s brought the rise of the strategic consumer, described by Yankelovich as someone who wants to "leverage resources—time, effort, and dollars—to the fullest, in an increasingly competitive economic and social climate."[17]

Strategic buying was a natural response to the inflation of the 1970s. Young and older consumers alike could less afford to be wrong in their choice of what to buy. Yet, for the baby boomers, strategic consumption also reflected a rejection of old rules. As Yankelovich's colleague Florence Skelly argues, "boomers are buying strategically. They don't buy the way people did in the 1950s: 'If Mr. Jones has a washer-drier, then I must have a washer-drier.' They're thinking it over. That's why we have a flat month [in sales], then a month with a blip of buying in it, then another flat month. . . . One of the reasons the computer business is so unpredictable is that boomers are not conformists. It's very hard to predict a buying thrust in any area, because strategic consumers know what they want, and they don't care what anybody else has."

This trend in buying shows up in virtually every corner of the consumer marketplace—from car showrooms to grocery carts, from hospital delivery rooms to drug stores. The baby boomers are more willing than most consumers to buy "no name" or generic brands, and are more suspicious of advertising in general. They see little reason for trying to stick with well-known brand names just for the sake of it. Not surprisingly, they are less likely than older Americans to believe that the length of time a company has been in business is a good indicator of its expertise and quality. Indeed, compared to older consumers, the baby boomers are almost 20 percent less likely to prefer products made by well-established businesses over those made by a new company.

The data also suggest that the baby boomers are experts in what Yankelovich calls the pragmatic method. "The strategic consumer will perform a kind of 'self-audit,' assigning priorities depending on a product/product category's expendability (i.e., Do I need it? Do I need it now?); the perception of 'right' or 'wrong' choices and their associated benefits and/or penalties; and the extent of knowledge possessed or required in order to make a purchase decision. Overall then, consumers will continue to take a more holistic approach to products, evaluating them increasingly in terms of how they 'fit' into a broader picture."[18]

Baby boomers are also more likely than older Americans to break the old rules when making a purchase—they will return a product if they don't like it, and are more likely than older consumers to ask tough questions about products and to say that performance is more important than brand name. This emphasis on performance may reflect what Yankelovich calls a belief in consumer power. "Consumers see themselves more and more as capable of influencing product mix, product quality, and product distribution via their behavior in the marketplace. Simply put, consumers appear to feel more 'in charge' of the consuming process."[19] What matters most to the baby boomers is not that a cake mix is from Duncan Hines or Betty Crocker, but that they first know the ingredients, and then that it tastes good. What matters most is not that a car is built in Detroit or Tokyo, but that they first know the facts about reliability, gas mileage, price, and power, and then that it will actually deliver the promised performance.

This rebellion against traditional buying habits also reflects the generation's cynicism towards advertising. They are just not as likely as older Americans to believe product claims. This cynicism is perhaps best reflected in the rise of "liar" advertising in the mid-1980s. The best of the ads starred Joe Isuzu as a smarmy car salesman who promised that his Isuzus would get 94 miles to the gallon, cost only $9, accelerate faster than a speeding bullet, and climb Mt. Everest. Who could resist Joe's "buy one, get one free" special? Obviously, the ads were lies. Indeed, Joe's commercials were all subtitled with the truth, including the familiar first line "He's Lying."

The commercials clearly were a not-so-subtle indictment of the advertising industry itself. As *Adweek* critic Barbara Lippert argues, the ads touched a chord among burned-out viewers. "The ad is as literal an approach as we've ever gotten on television to explicating both obvious and hidden meanings, text and subtext. We are literally reading between the lines, after years of patriotic advertising which asked us to accept the idea that symbol and reality were the same." According to the ad's creator, Jerry Della Femina, "Young people who sat by and watched Reagan get reelected are cynical as hell. They've been lied to before. They're amused by the shocking simple trust of the liar commercials."[20]

This is not to argue that the baby boomers are completely incapable of brand loyalty. As Thomas Exter, research editor of *American Demographics* suggests, "people can become brand loyal to products they purchase frequently out of inertia. After people buy a product once, the laws of probability suggests that they will buy it again. But products that people buy infrequently—such as cars or computers—can develop fiercely loyal followings even though a customer's loyalty is cashed in less often."[21] The key for baby-boom politics is to get the generation to pay as much atten-tion to picking a president as they do to buying a car or computer. At least for now, their political brand loyalty appears to be based on inertia, easily shakable by the latest scandal or newest promise.

Nor are the baby boomers incapable of commitment in mar-riage, parenthood, and work. However, the commitments are not tied to the traditional social cues of the past. The baby boomers don't marry to punch a social ticket and don't have children to pass a social test. These separations from the old meanings of marriage, parenthood, work, and buying also say a great deal about the baby boom's separation from the traditional political process. Two decades of political and economic reality seem to have twisted Kennedy's great call. Ask not what you can do for politics, the baby boomers now appear to be saying, but what politics can do for you. The answer appears to be that participation and long-term loyalty have little meaning for a generation committed to self-definition with a view of a short-term horizon.

The baby boom's shallow political commitment also reflects its estrangement from political institutions. As political consultant Lee Atwater argues, "Baby boomers are by and large anti-big government, anti-big labor unions, and anti-big institutions in general. What we as Republicans have always got to be aware of is that they're also anti-big business, and if we once again become viewed as the party that caters solely to big business, we would be in trouble with this group."

Distrust of government is not, however, unique to the baby boom. "Anti-establishment populism is the great engine of political innovation in this country," William Schneider writes. "Americans are deeply conservative about their system and their institutions. But they are deeply radical in their attitudes toward the rich and power: suspicious of how they got that way, resentful that they think they are better than everyone else. The American public instinctively distrusts concentrations of power."[22] Perhaps that is why Chrysler president Lee Iacocca and New York real estate tycoon Donald Trump may be better off outside of politics. The public might admire their entrepreneurial spirit, but might also question their empathy with the average citizen.

In the 1960s and early 1970s, of course, the public had ample reason to distrust government. "The active phase of the most recent crisis," Schneider and his colleague Seymour Martin Lipset argue, "appeared to decline as the Vietnam War ended. Protesters in the United States, and then in other developed countries, gradually returned to the normal routines of their usual occupations. The host of organizations and publications that promoted the amorphous 'movement' slowly dissolved and disappeared. The crisis of authority seemed to end, leaving in its wake major changes in social values bearing on personal behavior, sexual practices, and minority rights." Yet, in *The Confidence Gap*, Schneider and Lipset write that the alienation did not end. "Survey after survey reveals that the sharp increase in negative feelings about the performance of the major institutions of American society, which first became evident during the late 1960s, did not reverse during the 1970s and early 1980s."[23]

Americans of all ages lost faith in their institutions and leaders in the 1960s, and have yet to recover. The issue, as Caddell wrote in the late 1970s, "is not, as some have so quickly pointed out, that people have lost faith in our basic system of government or the free enterprise system. They most certainly have not. What they are losing faith in is the ability of our institutions or their leaders to be responsive or to solve their problems."[24] The government's failures on civil rights and Vietnam in the 1960s were compounded by failures on Watergate and the economy in the 1970s, and on the Iran-Contra connection and Wall Street in the 1980s.

Americans also lost faith in the political process. The public just does not believe that their political participation makes much difference in the way the government works. In 1984, for example, almost 60 percent of the public said that having elections makes little or no difference in what government does, while 85 percent said that government pays little or no attention to what people think when it decides what to do. Almost six in ten said people should not vote if they don't care about the outcomes of an election. These and other measures of civic duty show an American public in various states of disengagement from the political process. It is little wonder that turnout in national elections continues to decline. Why would people vote when they see so little return?

Among the age groups, the baby boomers are least likely to think that elections matter: just 40 percent say that elections make a great deal of difference, compared to 47 percent of those over 65 years old and almost 50 percent of those under 20 years old.[25]

That does not mean the baby boomers feel less effective as individual citizens. In fact, they feel more confident than older Americans that they can make government work for them if they so choose. However, given their high levels of education, the baby boomers may be more willing to admit that elections are blunt instruments and that politicians do not always care about the national good when they make policy.

In short, the baby boomers may be the least trusting of how the governmental system works. It may work fine on parchment paper, but it is only as good as its institutions and leaders at a given moment in time. All Americans share this basic suspicion toward government and social institutions. However, starting in the 1960s and continuing to the present, the baby boomers lead the way. Asked by the Harris Poll to rate the *leaders* of fifteen institutions in 1985, the baby boomers were the least trusting toward eight: organized religion, the military, the press, TV news, major companies, the White House, Congress, and the Executive Branch.

The baby boomers were about even with other age groups in their lack of trust in the leaders of higher education, organized labor, law firms, state government, and local government, and actually ahead in their trust of the justices on the Supreme Court.[26] Perhaps the baby boomers still remember the Court as the source of the great breakthroughs in civil rights and abortion. Perhaps they also see the Court as an institution in tune with their tolerance of diversity. Whatever the reason, the Court is the baby boom's favorite institution. Whether the Court will remain so depends, of course, on the kinds of decisions that emerge from the Reagan appointees.

Their distrust also applies to the basic *institutions themselves.* Also asked in 1985 by the Gallup Poll to rate a list of ten social and political institutions without reference to their leaders, the baby boomers emerged as the least trusting of all age groups toward eight: organized religion, the military, banks/banking, public schools, Congress, newspapers, big business, and organized labor.

The baby boomers were about even with other age groups in their lack of trust in television, and again led in their trust of the Supreme Court.[27] It is clear that merely finding a new generation of leaders will not restore baby boomer confidence.

Schneider and Lipset's analysis confirms the general Harris and Gallup findings. Looking at a staggering array of data, they conclude that older people tend to be more positive toward the military, major companies, organized religion, the executive branch, and, to a slight degree, education and Congress. In contrast, younger people were generally more positive toward the scientific community and medicine, and again roughly equal on television and organized labor. As Schneider and Lipset also argue, the baby boomers are less polarized in their dislike of both big labor and big business than older generations. Whereas older Americans tend to dislike one or the other, the baby boomers generally distrust both.[28]

Thus, the baby boom bears the clearest imprint of the 1960s and 1970s. The failures, as Schneider suggests, were failures of government, not people. "Not only was the federal government unable to manage problems like Vietnam, Watergate, inflation, and the energy crisis but it had created those problems in the first place. To the Depression generation, government meant the New Deal, the second World War, and the prosperity of the fifties; government was the solution. To the generation that came of age in the sixties and seventies, government was the problem."[29]

Perhaps that is why Gary Hart did so well among the baby boomers immediately after reentering the 1988 presidential sweepstakes. According to a *Washington Post*/ABC News poll only days after Hart announced his return to the campaign, younger voters were the most willing to forgive him for his affair with Donna Rice. Two-thirds of the under-30 age group supported his return, compared to 47 percent of those over 45 years old.[30]

According to one campaign aide, the highly negative reaction of Democratic party leaders to Hart's announcement fit the strategy perfectly. "It sets up the 'Rocky' story line, where you say to the voters, you know, 'All the elites are against me, so I hope the people will be for me.' " Hart's campaign rhetoric seemed fitting to the baby boom's rejection of brand-name politics: "If you're fed up with these media-oriented campaigns . . . then come with me. A handful of powerful people in Washington are not going to pick the next president. . . . The people of this country are going to pick the next president."

The reason candidates do well among the baby boom by running against Washington is because the baby boom has a basic distrust of politics. But, as former Mondale campaign director Robert Beckel said of Hart in late 1987, "the reason he's not electable is the thing we discovered back in the red phone days. The issues are unpredictability, unsteadiness, recklessness. You put the word 'uncertainty' in the same sentence with the word 'president' and it doesn't fit." Moreover, at least within the Democratic constituency, Hart's dalliances with adultery seemed likely to bring the baby-boom gender gap to the surface. Ultimately, Hart's strategy could not overcome his negatives. He asked the people to decide his future and they did, giving him less than one percent of the vote in the first Democratic primaries. By mid-March, he was out of the running for a second, and final, time.

The baby boomers were not always so cynical about their social and political institutions. Studies in the late 1950s and early 1960s showed a generation well on its way to a normal respect for both the president and the political system. Interviewed as young children, baby boomers often talked about the president as a benevolent leader, a kind of political father-figure, as someone to be trusted, even loved. They had inklings of what society expected from a good citizen.

According to political scientist Fred Greenstein's 1958 study of New Haven school children, not only were almost all of the children likely to know the president's name, 92 percent rated him as very good or fairly good at his job. (At that point in Eisenhower's term, only 58 percent of adults gave the president such high ratings.) As Greenstein reported, these children "are just as likely as adults to perceive high political roles as being important; they seem to be more sympathetic to individual politicals (and, in general, to politics) than are adults."[31]

To be sure, Greenstein's data also showed that older children were less trusting of politics than younger children. Eighth graders were about one-sixth as likely as fourth graders to see the president as a benevolent leader. Of course, trust tends to decline with age. As children learn more about politics, they become less enthusiastic and trusting. It is part of the natural life cycle. The pattern holds even in good times. A study of Chicago school children in the early 1960s, for example, found that second graders were *thirty* times more likely than eighth graders to say the president was the best person in the world.

It is important to note, however, the baby boom's early faith in government. In the Chicago study, for example, younger and older baby boomers alike felt that the president was at least a good person, and that he was at least as honest as most men. Both also agreed that the president worked harder than most people, and certainly knew more than most men.[32] The president's image as a benevolent leader remained intact—albeit tempered by age. If he wasn't the best person in the world to older baby boomers, he was still certainly not the worst.

Early studies also showed the baby boom's growing sense of political and social efficacy, a feeling which remains today. In a 1961 study of 12,000 baby boomers, political scientists David Easton and Jack Dennis found that half of the older baby boomers felt government cared about what people like their families thought, and thought that their families had a say about what the government did. As the authors concluded, the "fact that from a tender age children are able even to mirror adult feelings of mastery over their political environment and that this feeling gradually takes on a high positive value for increasing proportions of children has vital implications for the input of support for a democratic regime. . . . This early acquisition of the norm may operate as a potent and critical force in offsetting later adult experiences which, in a modern, rationally organized mass society, undermine the political importance of the ordinary member. But for the inculcation of this norm at an early and impressionable age, later adult political frustrations might be less easily contained; disillusionment with this norm of democracy might well find more favorable conditions for growth."[33] Perhaps this residue of efficacy kept the baby boomers from abandoning the American system altogether in the late 1960s.

Nevertheless, even in quiet times, the older the baby boomers got, the more they understood that government was hardly perfect. Eighth graders were much less likely than younger children to say that government almost never makes mistakes or to say that government would want to help them if they needed it. Older children were also more aware of government's capacity to punish —26 percent of the eighth graders in one study said government could punish anyone, compared to only half as many fourth graders.[34] What started out in children as a deep affection for the president appeared to evolve in adolescence to a much clearer sense of the individual's relationship to a complex and potentially powerful system.

Overall, these early studies showed a generation moving toward a normal attachment to politics. The youngest baby boomers were affectionate toward the president, and their older siblings remained respectful, if more skeptical. There was little reason to suspect that the generation would later disengage from politics. In foreign policy, for example, Yankelovich argues that public attitudes could be summed up as "President knows best." "Virtually throughout the Vietnam War, up to its very end, the public gave the President—whether Kennedy, Johnson, or Nixon—the benefit of the doubt. A President was presumed to possess vital information unavailable to others, and therefore to be in the best position to judge what actions were in the nation's interest."[35]

Within a span of ten years from 1963 through 1973, however, the baby boom abandoned its once hopeful outlook for a new course of political independence and separation. By the end of the 1960s, baby-boom party loyalty was almost nonexistent and trust had hit bottom. The explanation lies in a chain of events which began with the Kennedy assassination in 1963 and continued for ten years after. The era of "President knows best" ended, replaced by "President knows least."

Kennedy's death clearly left the baby boom in need of a political and social leadership which never came. There can be little doubt that the assassination left a mark on the generation. The assassination came during a particularly tense moment in the cold war, and during a particularly vulnerable moment in the baby boom's political development. Not only was the Cuban missile crisis still fresh in baby-boom memories, but the generation was entering a period when it would have made its basic life commitments to political parties and ideology.

More important perhaps, the older baby boomers had been captivated by Kennedy's youthful leadership. Most still remember exactly where they were when they first heard the news of his death. It was just after noon on Friday, November 22, 1963. Most baby boomers heard the news from their teachers, and then went home to spend the weekend watching the horror unfold on television. The images were haunting—the countless replays of the assassination, Jackie Kennedy's bloodstained dress, the flag-draped casket, the Kennedy children in mourning, the brutal murder of Lee Harvey Oswald. Similar scenes of horror were repeated throughout the rest of the decade: in Memphis and in California, at My Lai and Kent State. The cumulative impact resulted in much more than a shared memory of isolated historical events. The first Kennedy assassination was the start of a twenty-year separation from political life.

The assassination was particularly painful given the fact that baby boomers were enchanted by Kennedy and his family. "One can speculate that John Kennedy's loving and highly publicized fatherhood, his self-mocking sense of humor, his personal attractiveness, his vitality, his seeming calm and strength—all added up to everyone's favorite daddy (or movie hero)," political scientist David Sears explains. "His seemingly protective role in the nuclear confrontations of the 1960s could have made him especially important to children. Or he could have seemed the youthful David in battle against aging Goliaths."[36]

Whatever the reasons for the baby boom's affection, his assassination was devastating. Talking with a sample of almost 1,400 school children within days after the assassination, political scientist Roberta Sigel found that Kennedy was much more than some abstract symbol of the presidency to the young baby boomers.[37]

The children certainly remembered Kennedy as a political leader. According to Sigel, all of the children showed a concern for peace and a sensitivity to the cold war. "There was no doubt that even young children were aware that they were living in troubled times full of international conflicts and the dangers of war." The loss of Kennedy heightened those fears.

The children also remembered Kennedy as the friend of the children of other nations. Asked what they remembered most about the slain president, older children were particularly likely to mention his efforts on the nuclear test ban treaty and the Peace Corps.

The children also remembered Kennedy as a national healer. "They seem to have seen him as a latter-day Abraham Lincoln, an emancipator," Sigel wrote, a man bent on granting freedom and equality. Though young blacks were the most likely to remember Kennedy's leadership on civil rights, this memory of Kennedy as a champion of all races showed up among whites as well.

Finally, the children clearly remembered Kennedy as a father. "Kennedy the man, as distinct from Kennedy the President," Sigel wrote, "was liked and remembered for his kindness and courage. For most children it was the Kennedy warmth, not his competence, which stood out. They liked him for his liking of others, his ability to care and to respond."[38] Given these kinds of intense memories—memories with a detail not expected from younger children—it is no surprise that the assassination left a deep emotional scar.

Moreover, the baby boomers could hardly ignore their parents' reactions to the assassination. According to surveys at the time, 90 percent of the public knew about Kennedy's death within two hours of the assassination. The majority of the public said they did not continue business as usual after they heard the news. A majority also said they could not recall any other time in their lives when they had had the same sort of feelings. Surveys showed that most felt what one report from the National Opinion Research Center called an "immense tide of grief, loss, sorrow, shame, and anger." The report showed the intensity of the public feeling: "Nine out of ten Americans felt sympathy for Mrs. Kennedy and the children and deep feelings of sorrow that 'a strong young man had been killed at the height of his powers.' Four out of five 'felt deeply the loss of someone very close and dear.' Five out of six admitted to deep feelings of 'shame that such a thing could happen in our country,' and approximately three out of four 'felt angry that anyone should do such a terrible deed.' "[39]

Those kinds of emotions had to affect children. Indeed, surveys showed that parents did little to explain the assassination to their children, leaving the baby boomers to figure things out on their own. Those parents who did sit down with their children focused most on what one report called the "diseased or wicked character of the assassin."[40] According to psychologist Martha Wolfenstein, "children were exposed to the unaccustomed sight of their parents, teachers, and other adults openly weeping. This emotional breakdown of the grownups was probably quite alarming to the children. At the same time, the grownups, distracted by their own distress, became to some extent withdrawn and less available to the children."[41] Unlike their children, however, the parents would have had some buffers against the grief—perhaps past experience with the death of a parent or relative, perhaps strong religious beliefs—which their children did not yet have.

There is no doubt that the baby boomers felt deeply saddened by Kennedy's death. Three-quarters of Sigel's sample of Detroit-area children said they felt the loss of someone very close and dear, nine in ten felt sympathy for Kennedy's wife and children, eight in ten felt ashamed that such a tragedy could happen in America. Moreover, half of the younger children said they did not feel much like eating over the weekend following the assassination. Another third said they had headaches or an upset stomach; a third said they cried; almost 70 percent said they had trouble getting to sleep.

The deeply felt grief shows in Wolfenstein's sampling of baby-boom memories drawn soon after the weekend:

Boy, twelve: I just couldn't bear the thoughts of having someone take away the life of the heroic John Fitzgerald Kennedy. He was so living at first and then "poof" he's dead. I was grief-stricken when I heard he was shot.

Girl, thirteen: The weekend that followed that tragic Friday was to be the worst one in my life. . . . Things that I usually enjoy doing just weren't fun for me that weekend. . . . The whole world seemed upset and disorganized.

Girl, fourteen: I remember that tears came in my eyes and that I just couldn't control myself. "Oh!" you may say that a fourteen-year-old girl doesn't know too much about things like this. Well, maybe not. I really don't know why I cried. I didn't know President Kennedy very well. President Kennedy wasn't my father. I just can't answer the question, "why?"

Boy, thirteen: While watching his aides and friends file in [to review the casket in the Capitol Rotunda] I first realized that he wouldn't make another speech like he made in West Berlin or wouldn't be back to his family in Ireland every ten years as he promised nor would he address us in a television speech as Dear Fellow Americans.[42]

Beyond these expressions of sadness, the baby boomers seemed to worry more about how the nation would survive the future.

Whereas 40 percent of adults wondered how the United States would carry on after the assassination, 60 percent of the baby boomers in Sigel's sample said they worried about how the United States would get along without its leader. Younger children showed the greatest worry; three-quarters of the fourth graders said they worried about what would happen to the country. At the time, Wolfenstein noted that the feeling of loss seemed to persist long past what should have been a normal period of grieving. Unlike their parents, who had "become more readily reconciled to the loss and able to accept it as *a fait accompli,*" Wolfenstein observed that baby-boom teenagers had difficulty working the assassination through. "The problem of giving up a loved and admired leader coincided with the basic unresolved task of their time in life, that of giving up their childhood attachment to their parents."[43]

It is important to note that the baby boomers did not blame the political system for Kennedy's death. Surveys at the time suggested that the baby boomers were more likely than adults to say that the assassin had acted alone, and twice as likely to say that they did not know why he had shot their president.[44] They were reluctant to say there had been some kind of conspiracy, and appeared more willing to blame Kennedy's death on one man's crazy act.

Thus, what the baby boomers seemed to need most was reassurance that the death of Kennedy did not mean the death of his highly personal leadership. Unfortunately, Kennedy was followed by presidents known more for their aloofness than for their warmth—each considerably older than Kennedy, each eventually leading the nation into a great crisis, each remarkably unpopular, each ultimately forced out of office in defeat and disgrace.

Like a stepfather in a new family, neither Johnson nor Nixon could make contact with the baby boomers. Lyndon Johnson tried to match Kennedy's New Frontier enthusiasm with his own Great Society, even announcing the program in a dramatic speech at the University of Michigan, but was always uncomfortable with television and public displays of affection—the best he could do was to lift his beagle by its ears or show his gall bladder scar. Richard Nixon was hardly warmer, continuing the Vietnam war through secret bombings of Cambodia, and bringing a new vocabulary of deceit into the national dictionary—including a new definition for plumbers. With every move and every lie vivid on television and carefully covered by magazines and newspapers, the baby boomers could not ignore the gap between promise and performance. How could they trust a political system which had replaced their hero and friend with Johnson and Nixon?

Kennedy's death did not cause the baby boom's separation from politics. The baby boomers were confused and saddened by the loss, but not alienated. However, if the baby boomers saw Kennedy's death as the act of a single assassin, they saw the struggle for civil rights, the Vietnam War, and the Watergate scandal as the results of basic flaws in the political system. Thus, when coupled with those issues, Kennedy's death looms as the first in a series of great disillusionments.

The disappointments began in the the summer of 1965. Brookings' scholar James Sundquist argues, "That the national mood did change abruptly can be documented with a wealth of evidence. The Great Society of Lyndon Johnson had been enacted in a wave of popular enthusiasm in 1964 and the spring and summer of 1965, the final measure being the Voting Rights Act signed into law in August. Johnson and the Congress enjoyed extraordinarily high public approval ratings, which continued into the winter of 1965–66. But suddenly the Great Society had run its course. The sensitive ears of congressmen had begun to pick up sounds of discontent in the electorate, and as the sounds grew the reformist urge dissolved."

By the fall of 1966, Johnson's approval rating had fallen 22 points, less than half of the voting age public gave him a passing grade on his handling of the most important national problems, and he lost 47 seats in the House and three in the Senate. As Sundquist concludes, "The war on poverty and civil rights—the noble causes of a year before—had turned sour; they had not led to the racial harmony that had been promised but to riots. And on this, surely, the turning point can be precisely named—Watts."[45]

There had been other riots before—one in Birmingham in 1963, another in Harlem in 1964. But it was not supposed to happen in Los Angeles, not in a city which had been ranked first among 68 cities in the quality of life for blacks, and not so soon after the Great Society had begun. Nevertheless, it happened. During the week of August 11–16, 1965, Watts burned as police and national guardsmen fought snipers and looters. It was the first televised riot in history. As Washington reporter Juan Williams writes, by 1965, the strains of a decade-long struggle were apparent. "Nonviolence was no longer the only tool for change; many blacks had seen too many murders, too many betrayals."[46] When the fires were out, 34 people had died; a thousand more had been arrested. It had taken 14,000 national guardsmen to restore order.

The disappointments continued with Vietnam. Indeed, it is difficult to tell where the impact of civil rights ends and the effect of Vietnam begins. Johnson clearly understood that the war could undermine public trust in his presidency. "I knew from the start that I was bound to be crucified either way I moved," he told his biographer Doris Kearns. "If I left the woman I really loved—the Great Society—in order to get involved with that bitch of a war on the other side of the world, then I would lose everything at home. All my programs. All my hopes to feed the hungry and shelter the homeless. All my dreams to provide education and medical care to the browns and the blacks and the lame and the poor."[47] Nevertheless, within twelve months of his 1964 landslide election, over 200,000 troops were in Vietnam. Within eighteen months, 400,000. Within two years, 500,000. And the casualties mounted.

The baby boomers were clearly aware of the escalation; after all, they were supplying the cannonfodder. According to one study which followed a sample of tenth-grade boys from 1965 through 1970, when first asked "What are some things you're not too happy about these days?" and "Can you tell me some of the problems young men your age worry about most?" only 10 percent said they were personally worried about Vietnam. Four years later, the number had more than tripled. In 1966, only 7 percent of the boys had mentioned Vietnam as one of the problems their age group worried about. By 1970, that number had grown to 75 percent.[48]

Baby boomers did not always agree on why they opposed the war. Baby boomers who went to college were over six times more likely than those who stayed at home to mention moral concerns as the basis for their opposition to the war. Conversely, the high school grads were over three times as likely as their college brethren to mention their concerns about the number of American soldiers being killed or injured as the source of their opposition. Even the baby-boom gender gap shows up in the opposition to the war, with women 15 points more likely than men to mention the danger to American lives as their reason for opposition. Yet, despite these different bases for opposition, the baby boomers were united in their desire to get the United States out of Vietnam.

Even the youngest baby boomers—including those born during the 1964 presidential campaign—may have been affected by the war. According to political scientist Howard Tolley, Jr., "public controversy over the war appears to have accelerated political socialization, leading many young children to question the wisdom of government policy at an earlier age than did their predecessors."[49] Half of these young baby boomers said the United States had made a mistake in Vietnam; almost half said the president did not always tell the truth about the war. And what they did not learn about distrusting government from Vietnam, they were bound to pick up from Watergate.

By the mid-1970s, the baby boomers, young and old alike, had plenty of evidence to support their cynicism toward government. Just fifteen years after Kennedy's inauguration, political scientist Christopher Arterton found that the youngest baby boomers now saw the president as "truly malevolent, undependable, untrustworthy, yet powerful and dangerous." Watergate was the cap-stone.

Comparing 1973 to 1962, Arterton found a number of trou-bling changes. Whereas roughly half of the third, fourth, and fifth graders in 1962 said the president was their favorite or almost their favorite political person, almost two-thirds of the grade schoolers in 1973 said the president was not one of their favorites at all! Whereas most of the children in 1962 saw politicians in general as smarter, more honest, and almost always able to keep their promises, the children in 1973 had turned dramatically. In 1962, a majority of school children said that candidates almost always kept their promises. In 1973, the number was 18 percent. As Ar-terton summarizes the data, "politicians are seen as more selfish, less intelligent, more dishonest, and less likely to keep their pro-mises. . . . the effects of Watergate (and/or the intervening eleven years) have been a diminished respect for the personal characteris-tics of individuals who run for public office."[50]

Ultimately, it may be impossible to untangle the causes of the baby boom's political estrangement. As one pair of researchers have argued, "It is hard to know how much of the disenchantment during the late 1960's can be traced directly to United States involvement in Vietnam. Other events, such as the assassination of three great leaders—John Kennedy, Martin Luther King, and Robert Kennedy—have surely left their mark. These recent ex-periences have been especially traumatic for young people, for they identified closely with the fallen leaders, and youth are the ones who face the prospect of personal involvement in a mean and frustrating war."[51]

Was it memories of the Cuban missile crisis coupled with Watergate? Was it King's assassination coupled with My Lai? Was it a low draft number coupled with the Watts riot? Whatever the answer, the 1960s and early 1970s forged a remarkable genera-tional estrangement. Even if the baby boomers disagreed on the specific events and reasons, even if some said the United States should have been allowed to win in Vietnam while others said the

United States had no reason to be there, the baby boomers agreed on one thing: the system and the leaders failed.

It should not be surprising, therefore, that people born after the 1960s are more trusting of government than those born before. The Harris Poll proves this conclusion. Looking at public trust in 16 institutions in 1985, people under 25 years old showed the greatest confidence in ten, including medicine (60 percent), major education (43 percent), the military (43 percent), the White House (36 percent), and law firms (22 percent). It may be one of the many ironies of the era that President Reagan's strongest supporters are also the most confident in labor unions (20 percent), the executive branch (28 percent), and TV news (27 percent). They may grow more cynical with age, and may find their own lessons about social institutions in the Iran-contra scandal and the stock market crash. For now, it is not clear which leaders of what institutions will fall the farthest.

(It is important to remember, however, that the baby boom is, on average, only about 10 percent less trusting than both younger and older Americans toward their leaders and institutions. Again, everyone was affected by the 1960s and early 1970s. On some questions, the margins are even smaller, reflecting the baby boom's greater education. The baby boomers may be more trusting of some institutions because they know more about how the system works, or because they feel more effective or self-reliant.)

(It is also important to note that the baby boomers show slightly greater trust in the abstract concept of governmental power, perhaps reflecting their once great attachment to Kennedy. They are more trusting regarding governmental intervention in the economy and have somewhat greater faith in the notion of public service. When asked in 1984, for example, how many people in government were crooked, 32 percent of the baby boomers said quite a few, compared to 37 percent of those over 65 years old.)

Moreover, in spite of their distrust of specific institutions and specific leaders, the baby boomers remain unwilling to abandon the American democratic system, perhaps reflecting the lessons learned when they were just children. When asked whether government in a general sense is run for a few big interests, 56 percent of the baby boomers said yes, compared to 63 percent of the elderly. And when asked whether government does right just about always and much of time, 47 percent of the baby boomers said yes, compared to 46 percent of the elderly.[52]

Like their consumer behavior, baby-boom trust in specific institutions and leaders may be linked with performance. While the baby boomers may feel that the government can play a role in society, they may also feel that recent leaders and their institutions have been inadequate. That linkage may explain why trust in government went up during the first years of the Reagan administration. It wasn't called the "Morning in America" for nothing. The Grenada invasion was a success, the United States creamed the world in the 1984 Olympics, and inflation stayed down. The message was that government could act effectively and responsibly.

And, lo and behold, public confidence in government went up.[53] In 1974, for example, just after President Ford's pardon of a disgraced Nixon, 66 percent of the public said government was pretty much run by a few big interests. In 1978, after a year of Carter-style government, the figure was still at 67 percent. By 1984, however, it had fallen back to 55 percent, the lowest level since the mid-1960s. In 1974, for a second example, 50 percent of the public said that public officials did not care much what people like them think. In 1978, the figure was up ever so slightly. By 1984, Democratic campaigns about fairness to the contrary, the figure was down to 42 percent, again the lowest in almost twenty years.[54]

This rebound in public confidence may have been Reagan's greatest irony. After campaigning against Washington, after bashing the federal bureaucracy, he pushed public support for government back to pre-Watergate levels, perhaps paving the way for future administrations, whether Democratic or Republican, to expand government again. Not only has the tax revolt faded, images of waste, fraud, and abuse no longer ring the halls of Congress. "Thus, the ultimate irony of Reagan's presidency," Schneider writes. "He restored people's faith in government, which is certainly not what he set out to do."[55]

Whether that support still remains in the wake of the recent political crises is in some doubt. By the fall of 1985, the Harris Poll had declared "Confidence in Major Institutions Down!" Within another year, the *Washington Post* had found growing worries among the public about national bills coming due. By Thanksgiving 1986, news of an arms-for-hostages deal with secret diversion of the profits to Nicaraguan rebels drove Reagan's popularity down 15 to 20 points overnight. And, by the summer of 1987, a majority of baby boomers told the *New York Times* Poll that they thought the president was lying about what he knew about the Iran-contra connection.

As of now, it is not yet clear whether a different kind of arms deal between the United States and Soviet Union will be able to reverse the reversal of Reagan's renewal of public confidence. For now, the baby boomers remain less trusting than any other Americans toward their political institutions and leaders, maintaining a continuing estrangement from the American system of government.

It may be that the only way the baby boomers can reconcile their low opinion of government with their very real concerns about the future is to place their trust in technology. The baby boomers appear to have great faith in the benefits of technology for solving tomorrow's problems. Not only are the baby boomers more likely than older Americans to be employed in a science- or technology-related job, they expect to reap greater benefits from developments in science and technology over the coming decades.[56]

Some of that trust comes from the baby boom's greater education, some from age, some from experience. The baby boomers will be around longer than older generations to benefit from technology. Having grown up with technology, they may also feel much more confident about the tangible benefits to be derived from it. This may also explain why the baby boomers are so much less likely to be concerned about governmental policy concerning science and technology. Only about 30 percent of the baby boomers say they are very concerned about that policy, compared to 44 percent of the over-65 age group.

That does not mean the baby boomers are unaware of the risks. A 1986 Harris Poll for Congress shows that almost half the baby boomers believe it is either very or somewhat likely that genetically engineered materials will someday represent a serious danger to people and the environment. A significant minority believe that such materials will increase the rate of animal and plant extinction, and a substantial majority say that society has only touched the tip of the iceberg of risk.[57]

Yet the baby boomers are much more concerned about *not* moving ahead with new research than by any risk to health or safety. Asked whether technology ought to be restrained in the interest of society, almost two-thirds said no. There is near-unanimous support for continued research into genetic engineering, robotics, organ transplants, and so forth. Only a fraction believe that federal funding for this research should be cut back.

Part of the support reflects a convenient rationalization—a large number of the baby boomers believe that most of the risks that people worry about with the new technology never really happen. Part centers on the lack of a moral basis for opposing frontier research like genetic engineering. Whether from their greater knowledge or from their weaker ties to religion, younger Americans are less likely to say that humans have no business meddling with nature and that creating such things as hybrid plants and animals through genetic manipulation is just plain wrong. Part of the baby boom's support involves confidence in the potential benefits of new technology, whether in the form of new jobs, better health, or solutions to environmental problems that already exist—acid rain, nuclear waste, pollution, and so on.

Indeed, the baby boomers would never support new technologies if they did not believe the investment carried great social benefits. Large majorities, for example, say that genetic engineering will improve the quality of life for people like themselves. So too, will robots and automation, solar energy, and organ transplants. Most of the baby boomers believe that their lives will be better because of scientific and technological breakthroughs over the next twenty years, and a significant minority—on the order of 40 percent—say that the current rate of investment in new research is too slow.

Thus, asked to weight the benefits against the risks, the baby boomers are the most pragmatic of all age groups, even if many also believe, for example, that there is some likelihood that genetically engineered organisms will someday mutate into a deadly disease or create antibiotic resistant diseases. Among the other new technologies, the baby boomers are more hopeful of some technologies than others, reflecting at least some awareness of the respective risks. Whereas almost all of the baby boomers see personal benefits coming from solar energy and transplants, nearly half express reservations about nuclear energy and robotics.

It is in regulating the risks that the baby boomers also express their strongest support for governmental intervention. Less than 10 percent say society should lessen its control over new technology and scientific research, and a near majority say that control ought to be increased.

The first question is who should do the risk assessments? The baby boom's answer is clear: not the companies who make the new products, nor the trade associations that represent the companies. Asked whom they would be most likely to believe regarding the risks of new technologies, the baby boomers answered that they would believe public health officials first, university scientists second, environmental groups fourth, public-interest groups fifth, local officials sixth, and the companies who made the product dead last just behind the news media. Moreover, even though over half of the baby boomers said they think that the leaders of the environmental movement are "out of touch" with the public, two-thirds would believe an environmental group over a federal agency if there were a disagreement on the nature of a genetic risk.

The second question is, who should do the controlling in the case of an unacceptable risk? Again, the baby boom's answer is emphatic: not the companies involved nor their representatives. The baby boomers prefer either some external scientific body or a governmental agency. It is an important lesson for those who argue for steady deregulation of industry. The baby boomers may see the benefits from new investments and increased research funding for new technologies, but they remain unwilling to let the market economy determine the priorities and the risks. They may be pragmatists, but they are not fools. Even if they do not trust their governmental institutions, they are unwilling to abandon government regulation in favor of unrestrained growth.

This first half of the portrait shows a baby boom separated from traditional social roles and estranged from political and social institutions. Ultimately, the baby boomers remain separated not so much because of old anger but because these institutions and roles may be irrelevant to their lives. The baby boomers still do not believe that participation in politics holds much reward. They are perfectly comfortable remaining on their highly individual course, moving in and out of politics on the basis of their short-term concerns.

6

A Portrait of Separation II

THE BABY BOOMERS came through the 1960s and early 1970s with extremely weak political attachments. They had abandoned their social and political traditions with ease, moving into a state of political limbo which continues to the present. The baby boomers seem quite comfortable with their political *dealignment*, perfectly willing to pick candidates on the basis of fleeting imagery or issues.

The baby boom's volatility may explain the growing popularity of the "perception analyzer" as a campaign tool. The analyzer itself is nothing more than a hand-held dial tied into a computer. In the hands of a group of "subjects" watching a debate or commercial, however, it becomes a remarkably effective device for registering instant, gut-level reactions. The subjects input their positive or negative perceptions whenever they feel the urge and, after the "event" is over, the computer spits out an analysis telling the candidate which gestures, images, and phrases worked best. According to one of the perception analyzer's salesmen, John Fiedler, of Populus Inc., "It enables the speaker, if he's got a healthy ego, to close the loop between himself and the people he's talking to. It's an overall emotional reaction—not terribly cognitive, not terribly rational, to what people are seeing and hearing." Unfortunately, the analyzer cannot tell a candidate much of substance about the public judgment on any issues or their long-term concerns.

In such a short-term, perception-driven system, if a quick summit between the United States and Soviet Union is all it takes to get the baby boom's vote, then perhaps that is all the baby boom will get. Get the candidate to pose with the Soviet premier, and *voilá!* If a promise is all it takes to get votes, why deliver substance? "Democracy is meant to be government by consent of the governed, not government by consent of their guts," Duke political scientist James David Barber argues. The perception analyzer is "a prime illustration of the deterioration of political discourse in this country, the substitution of sentiment for reason."

However, perception analyzers would never sell if the perceptions themselves did not make so much difference in contemporary political campaigns. In the absence of strong party ties, perceptions take over. Such are the consequences of the baby boom's separation—a separation which reflects its detachment from the political parties, its commitment to individualism and self-reliance, and its increasing distance from the very medium which brought it together in the 1960s and early 1970s—television.

Does this mean the baby boom is only interested in political beauty pageants? Has it become a generation of political voyeurs? The answer is not yet. To date, baby boomers appear more likely than older Americans to distinguish between personal issues which affect politics and those which are best left in private. According to a 1987 *Times Mirror* Poll conducted by Gallup, baby boomers and older Americans alike want to know if a candidate has evaded income taxes or exaggerated military service or academic achievements. However, baby boomers were less likely than older Americans to say the press should report if a candidate is having an extramarital affair or is homosexual. Whereas 48 percent of the over-60 age group said the press should almost always report whether a candidate had been arrested for marijuana possession in college, only 32 percent of the baby boomers agreed. Whereas 57 percent of the over-60 age group said the press should also almost always report if a candidate is having an extramarital affair, only 38 percent of the 30 to 39-year-old baby boomers agreed. It seems that older Americans have a somewhat higher level of interest in the private lives of public candidates.

This line between personal/public and personal/private issues showed up in the baby boom's views of a string of campaign scandals in 1987. Seventy percent of the baby boomers said the press went too far in reporting that Republican candidate Pat Robertson's first child was conceived out of wedlock, but only 35 percent said the press went too far in reporting the charges of plagiarism against Joseph Biden. Perhaps most important, almost 70 percent of the baby boomers said the press went too far in reporting charges that Gary Hart was having an affair with Donna Rice, but only 30 percent said that the press went too far in reporting that the Dukakis campaign had "attack" video tapes showing clips of Biden's misstatements.[1]

Why were the baby boomers so forgiving toward Robertson and Hart, but not toward Biden and Dukakis? The answer is not political ideology. Given their views on social issues, one might have expected the baby boomers to be particularly damning toward Robertson's hypocrisy. Yet, they were forgiving. Perhaps the answer is that the baby boomers draw a line between *human* mistakes which should remain private, and *political* mistakes which indicate potential problems in office. Whereas Robertson and Hart made personal errors in judgment, Biden and Dukakis were caught abusing the political process.

Yet, even though the baby boomers draw a public/private line in the campaign dirt, they remain highly dependent on what they read in newspapers and magazines or on what they see on television. If the press only covers the dirt, it is not clear that the baby boomers will have anything else to guide their decisions. Such is the cost of their shallow party identification. If candidates talk about the issues, and the press covers the dialogue, the baby boomers can behave as issue voters. If, however, candidates focus on grand imagery—like the "Morning in America" or "new ideas" —or the press concentrates on mudslinging and personality, the baby boomers are left without the anchor of party identification to make their decisions.

At least for now, however, the baby boomers seem likely to go with the election flow, turning the voting booth into one big perception analyzer. Lacking stable party attachments, they have little choice. There was a time, of course, when political scientists still hoped that the baby boomers would finally decide to support the party system. The Vietnam era was seen by most researchers as a deviant period in history, a disturbance, and the baby boomers were seen as "malsocialized." In that sense, some argued that the baby boomers were just waiting until the dust settled.

The baby boomers were not the only Americans hit by the shock of the 1960s, however. "Hardly any age group escaped the tremendous forces of change," political scientists Helmut Norpoth and Jerrold Rusk note. "Although the young failed to acquire partisan ties to a degree which had been commonplace in the past, voters with acquired ties to a considerable degree abandoned them."[2] The fact that older Americans were jumping ship meant that the baby boomers had fewer role models to follow, inhibiting the natural transfer of party commitments from one generation to the next. The baby boomers must have been puzzled indeed by parents who voted for Lyndon Johnson in a landslide one year only to switch to Richard Nixon or third-party candidate George Wallace four years later.[3]

There is ample evidence, however, that the baby boomers were hit the hardest by the 1960s. As the protest movement gained steam, some scholars even began to wonder whether the political system could survive. There was plenty of talk about the coming of a second American revolution. The Black Panthers were organizing the ghettos; the Youth International Party (yippies), Students for a Democratic Society (SDS), and the Weathermen were working the campuses.

It is critical to remember that the 1960s involved far more than the Woodstock festival and a few peaceful protest marches. It was an exceedingly violent period, with all the warning signs of impending political collapse—conspiracy trials mocked the judicial process, political violence took lives on both the left and the right, "America: Love It or Leave It" became a right-wing rallying cry, and national guardsmen loaded live ammunition to police angry crowds. For every picture of a love-in there were two of protesters moving through a cloud of tear gas toward an inevitable battle. As the riots continued during the summer of 1967 and spread to the campuses, the very survival of constitutional government seemed in doubt. America came precariously close to abandoning its traditional political process altogether.

It is no surprise then, to find that the baby boomers reacted more intensely to these events than did their parents. They were on the frontlines, whether as soldiers of combat in Vietnam or soldiers of protest in the United States. True, only a small percentage actually participated in either conflict. But most were watching and most were at an age when the imagery of conflict had a deep impact. Looking at the overall drop in party identification from 1964 through 1980 in an exhaustive statistical analysis, Norpoth and Rusk offer a simple conclusion about the baby boomers in the 1960s: "Younger voters were more inclined to abandon their partisan ties than were older voters, and the sharpest decline —using the partisanship of previous new voters as a benchmark —occurred among those voters who became eligible to vote in this period of change. Indeed, this group, together with the group of voters who had entered the electorate in the 1950s and early 1960s, contributed nearly 75 percent to the decline in partisanship in the American electorate."

Was this a generational change? Did this mean that the baby boomers were marked for life? As Norpoth and Rusk answer, "if generational is meant to refer to the fact that the young are more prone to change, we would be inclined to agree." Older voters simply had more protection against the impact of the era.[4] They had voted with their party in earlier elections, which got them into the habit of picking candidates on that basis. The baby boomers had no such experience. They were asked to be loyal to their party choices during the worst possible moment. Those who wanted to be loyal Democrats had to vote for Lyndon Johnson; those who wanted to be loyal Republicans had to vote for Richard Nixon. It was a Hobson's choice. Far better not to pick a party at all than to have to violate the commitment in a first or second election.

Political scientist Paul Abramson reports, "Among youths who were Democrats in 1965, only 59 percent were Democrats eight years later, 7 percent were Republicans, and 34 percent were Independents (including Independents who leaned toward a party). Among those who began as Republicans, only 46 percent remained Republican, 15 percent were Democrats, and 39 percent were Independents. But among those who began as Independents, 65 percent remained Independents eight years later, while 18 percent were Democrats and 16 percent were Republicans."[5] That kind of data often led political scientists to a curious, almost nonsensical conclusion: baby-boom independents were more likely to remain "loyal" or "stable" than partisans. Yet, by definition, by saying they were independents, baby boomers were declaring their lack of loyalty and stability.

Perhaps the best way to see the changes over the past twenty-five years is to look at the class of 1965. It is surely the most studied high-school class in political science history. By interviewing the same national sample of baby boomers when they were 18, 26, and 35 years old, researchers at the University of Michigan have been able to compile a remarkable record of early political attachment and subsequent disengagement, a longitudinal diary of continuity and change. Thus, whereas the first survey in 1965 showed a generation about to make lasting party commitments, the second in 1973 found a generation in the midst of political crisis, and the third in 1982 uncovered a generation in a "stable" political dealignment.

However, it is important to note that even in 1965, the study found something amiss with the baby boomers. There was already disturbing evidence that the family socialization process was breaking down. Interviewing the parents as well as the students, M. Kent Jennings and Richard Niemi found one low statistical correlation after another between the two generations within the same families. There were few agreements on religion, drug use, governmental intervention in the economy, and racial equality.

Even in a third of the cases when the parents and students agreed exactly on *both* the party (Democrat, Republican, or Independent) and the level of intensity they felt toward it (strong or weak), there was still evidence of a shallow baby-boom commitment. "On the one hand," Jennings and Niemi explained at the time, "the students simply lack their parents' long experience in the active electorate, and as a consequence have failed as yet to develop a similar depth of feeling about the parties. On the other hand, there are no doubt specific forces pushing students toward Independence."[6] Jennings and Niemi could not have known it at the time, but those forces of independence would never back off.

The results must have surprised those who believed that the family was the primary force in transmitting political values across generations. The most Jennings and Niemi could say about the success of parents in teaching their children was "that there is considerable slack in the value-acquisition process. If the eighteen-year-old is no simple carbon copy of his parents—as the results clearly indicate—then it seems most likely that other socializing agents have ample opportunity to exert their impact."[7] Given that these baby boomers watched television twice as frequently as their parents, perhaps TV could indeed have been seen as the new political parent.

Talking to the same parents and students a second time in 1973, the Michigan team found that even the party agreements were suspect. Looking at the party identification without any measure of intensity, roughly 40 percent of the baby boomers had changed their minds. Adding in intensity—that is, whether the baby boomers still felt they were strong, weak, or leaning partisans —almost 70 percent had changed their minds! Only 24 percent who said they were strong Democrats in 1965 were still strong Democrats in 1973—most had become weak Democrats or independent/Democrats, and four percent had become weak Republicans.[8]

The Republicans were hardly more successful in holding the class of '65 either. Only 32 percent of those who had said they were strong Republicans when they were high school seniors in 1965 were still there when they were 26 years old, eight years later, and five percent had switched completely over to become strong Democrats. What is particularly critical here is to note that the parents mostly stayed put. The baby boomers were shaking free of their party attachments on their own, creating powerful evidence for the those who believe that the Vietnam era produced a unique generational zeitgeist.

The cause of the decline in party loyalty seems clear. In 1973, nearly half of the class of '65 mentioned Vietnam and/or civil rights as being things they were least proud of as Americans. According to a statistical analysis by Gregory Markus, those two issues scarcely affected the baby boom's parents, while exerting an independent and about equal influence on the students.[9] If this is what happened to baby boomers born in 1947, who had spent the better part of their lives in "normal" politics, one can hardly be hopeful about those who came of age immediately in their wake.

By 1983, many of these patterns were hardening. The class of '65, then settling down in their mid-30s, had stabilized at a lower level of party loyalty. Again, it is difficult to use terms like "loyalty" and "stability" in the same breath as "independence." A generation in which the most stable political commitments reflect weak or nonexistent party identification is better characterized as volatile. Barbara Farrah and Helmut Norpoth analyzed baby-boom party commitment, from 1976 to 1986 as, "[first] setting out

on a steady Democratic course, then flirting with the GOP in the
wake of Reagan's victory over Jimmy Carter, only to revert back
to its Democratic origins by late 1983, until being swept into a
virtual tie between the parties in the wake of the 1984 election."[10]
If this isn't volatility, what is? In such a political system, Republican gains under Reagan may have little lasting value. The fact that
the baby boomers moved toward the Republican party in the early
1980s does not mean they will be there in the 1990s.

Indeed, the baby boomers may have changed the very definition of party loyalty. A voter's party identification once meant a
life-long commitment to a choice made in adolescence. For the
baby boomers of today however, it has become little more than a
running tally on issues, a summary of what they did in the most
recent election.[11]

Party identification once also meant making a firm choice
between being something or being nothing; between being a partisan or an independent. Today, even baby boomers who say they
are strong partisans sometimes say they think of themselves as
independents. Part of the reason is simple boredom: asked in 1984
whether there was anything they liked or disliked about either or
both parties, over one-third of the baby boomers could think of
nothing to say. "Increasingly, the image of the parties is just
nothingness," political scientist Martin Wattenberg says.

Party identification once meant a choice between being a
Democrat or a Republican. Those who liked one party generally
disliked the other. Today, political scientists are finding evidence
that voters sometimes think of themselves as Republicans and
Democrats simultaneously. Today, they are also finding that the
number of people who like one party and dislike the other has
fallen dramatically. Among the baby boomers, such feelings are
not because they do not see any differences between the parties,
but rather, they seem to think that the issues they care about most
are not the ones that help separate the parties.[12] Further, even

where the parties are different, the baby boomers can have it all, being Democrats on social issues and Republicans on economic ones. The party that wins is the one that can make an election turn on its particular issue.

Party identification also once confirmed a person's loyalty to other social groups—union members were Democrats, businessmen were Republicans. Today, of course, those connections have much less meaning to the baby boomers. As Joseph Veroff, Elizabeth Douvan, and Richard Kulka argue, the 1970s witnessed "a general loosening of people's social integration, a reduction in the meaning and satisfaction they find in assuming and performing roles in a social organization."[13] Party identification was part of that abandonment.

Party identification once meant a relatively stable outlook on policy issues. Democrats were supposed to support government intervention in the economy, Republicans were guaranteed to be opposed. As such, party identification was a potent source of information on the issues. Today, however, the baby boomers are quite comfortable getting their political insights elsewhere, particularly from television. Political consultant Robert Shrum commented during the 1986 Senate campaign that "a political rally in California consists of three people around a television set." And his colleague Robert Squier complained that "the television set has become the political party of the future."

Moreover, the baby boomers may even be willing to make political choices on the basis of no information at all. They watch fewer television programs about politics than older Americans, read fewer newspaper and magazine articles and, at least in 1984, watched less of the debates between Reagan and Mondale. So how does a baby boomer, who doesn't have any party commitment and doesn't know much about politics, make a reasoned choice in an election? At least for some, the answer has to be on the basis of fleeting campaign imagery.

Finally, party identification once meant an almost automatic choice in the voting booth. A voter connected the candidate to the party label and pulled the lever, repeating the decision down the ticket. People made their decisions early. They had no need to wait for the campaign. Today, the baby boomers seem more willing to make their decisions on other bases. They are much more willing to wait until the last moment to decide. In 1984, for example, only 26 percent of the baby-boom voters said they knew how they were going to vote all along, compared to 40 percent of the over-65 age group. Moreover, 55 percent of the baby-boom voters split their state and local votes between the parties, compared to 43 percent of the over-65 group.[14] (It is the combination of such split-ticket voting and the declining voter turnout that led MIT political scientist Walter Dean Burnham to conclude that the party-organized political system "has ceased to exist in our time.")

There should be little doubt that party identification has less meaning for Americans today. First, as Harvard scholar Morris Fiorina concludes, "identification with the parties has declined in importance as a variable that influences—indeed, that at one time *structured*—the voting decision. . . . The ties that bound in the past seem to bind less tightly today." Party identification is simply not the great predictor of elections it once was. "A second facet of party decomposition is the decline in the importance of parties as organizations. Ignoring such older 'reforms' as civil service, consider that the spread of direct primaries and open caucuses has stripped the parties of much of their power over nominations. Public financing and political action committees, or PACs, have lessened the financial importance of the parties. Active political participation by a large, leisured middle class dwarfs the manpower resources of the parties. Television provides cheap information. Increasingly, the parties grow irrelevant to the conduct of political campaigns."[15]

The expert opinion is nearly uniform on one point: the days of strong parties are gone forever. "We will never return to a time when people identify themselves as strong partisans and vote straight tickets," Republican pollster Robert Teeter says. Lee Atwater agrees "there will not be a permanent majority party again in American politics anytime soon."

The result is a much more unstable electorate, led by the most unstable voters of all, the baby boomers. As Seymour Martin Lipset puts it: "the American electorate has become more volatile . . . a large part of it can be easily moved from one party to another." Brookings' scholar James Sundquist says that the "electoral swings are more abrupt now, more massive." William Schneider argues that "results, not ideology, are what count for Americans voters." Public opinion expert Everett Carll Ladd even talks about a new kind of American political soap opera: "As the Realignment Turns." *Washington Post* columnist David Broder may have put it best over a decade ago with his book entitled *The Party's Over.*[16]

And what of the future? Are the parties dead or merely irrelevant? There is a curious debate within political science over the answer. One side believes that the parties are the victims of the baby boom's overall cynicism toward political institutions, its *negativity,* as one scholar put it. The other side believes that the parties are their own worst enemies, victims of the baby boom's *neutrality,* as another scholar put it.

In fact, both approaches may be right, but for different periods in time—the baby boomers abandoned their early party ties because of their cynicism, but likely continued their distance because of the unmistakable lack of social value in calling themselves Democrats or Republicans. As such, their lack of commitment reflects an estrangement rather than an irrevocable divorce.[17]

If this assumption is accurate, the parties would have to do much more than just wait for the baby boom to get over their old disappointments. They would have to make themselves relevant over the long term. Martin Wattenberg makes the case: "In order to reinvigorate political partisanship in the future, then, the public must be convinced that political parties perform a useful function in the American political process. The challenge that the parties face is not merely to espouse programs with popular appeal, but also to demonstrate that they play a crucial political role—from the recruitment of leaders to the implementation of policies."[18]

This theory of performance-based politics has great merit for understanding the baby boom's political future. As political scientist Samuel Popkin and his colleagues suggest, scholars who assumed that voters kept their party loyalties in spite of poor party performance were just plain wrong. "They were wrong when they assumed that voters took their cues from party and candidate lines and ignored cues from their daily lives and self-interest. The events of the 1960s proved them wrong: the changes of party, the growth of black participation, the success of issue-based protest movements in toppling at least one president [Johnson] from within his own party, and certainly the rise of George Wallace— perhaps even the rise of George McGovern."[19]

In this view of voting, people are more concerned with what a candidate can deliver if elected, and therefore look for signs of competence. In 1984, for example, even if the public had agreed with Mondale's policy positions, they had little confidence he could deliver once in office. Mondale's leadership "negatives" were a source of constant frustration, forcing him to prove his strength by promising tough choices, including a tax increase. It made him look stronger, but hardly helped his popularity.

Mondale was not the first presidential candidate to suffer from leadership negatives. In 1972, for example, McGovern's vacillation over the fate of his running mate, Sen. Thomas Eagleton (D-MO), sapped confidence even among his natural supporters. When Eagleton first revealed he had once received electroshock therapy, McGovern said he was behind his vice presidential nominee 1,000 percent. Within days, however, Eagleton was gone, replaced by Sargeant Shriver. As Popkin and his coauthors argue, using McGovern's own polls, "McGovern was deserted by large numbers of his own issue publics. They left him because of the widespread perception of his incompetence, a perception fostered largely by the Eagleton affair in July and August, problems of general campaign style, and the constant campaign crisis of July and August, 1972."

Among McGovern's natural supporters—the 25 percent of the registered voters who said Vietnam was the most important problem facing the nation, and who also said they favored a guaranteed national income—65 percent favored him in June, but only 52 percent by September. Moreover, among first-time voters, mostly younger baby boomers, 56 percent favored McGovern in June, but only 37 percent by September.[20] Even though these voters may have opposed Nixon's proposed timetable for peace in Vietnam, at least they felt he would deliver. What good was McGovern's promise if he was incompetent?

Instead of blaming the baby boomers for abandoning the parties, perhaps the parties are to blame for assuming that the baby boom would remain loyal to them in spite of poor performance. Unlike older Americans, who often rely on their party identification in deciding where they stand on issues, baby boomers rely on their issue beliefs to determine where they stand on the parties. It may be the most important difference between the two generations.

Thus, looking at changes over the 1960–1980 period, for example, political scientists Charles Franklin and John Jackson argue that party loyalties are best seen as a reflection of policy preferences, not vice versa. "They are a person's accumulated evaluations from previous elections and are dependent upon the events and actions of political leaders during these elections and during subsequent terms in office. In this way, each campaign leaves its imprint, or residue, on individual identifications."[21] This "endogeneity" of party identification, as Franklin and Jackson call it, puts the burden squarely on the parties and candidates to be relevant to the individual. Gone are the days when the parties could count on stability among their followers in the absence of performance.

The key to a performance-based view of party identification is the explicit link between what parties and candidates say in campaigns and what they produce in office. More important, even if the baby boomers choose a party, their support is never going to be permanent. If the party does not deliver, the baby boomers are perfectly willing to switch. "If citizens are responsive to the positions of the parties and the preferences they hold on issues," Franklin concludes elsewhere, "then we have the basis for models which place the burden of maintaining support, or gaining it, on party leaders."[22] It is exactly what one might expect from a more educated generation.

And why not? Why shouldn't the parties be held accountable? Just as the American automobile industry found it could not compete with the Japanese just on the basis of old brand loyalties, that quality and reliability were the keys to the baby-boom dollar, perhaps parties should concentrate on recruiting candidates who can deliver on their promises, possibly through stronger ties between presidents and members of Congress before the election. If there is one phrase to describe the difference between party loyalty of the 1950s and the loyalty of tomorrow, it is "performance matters."

This political and party estrangement does not mean that baby boomers somehow feel powerless to shape their futures. This is a generation that places a premium on individual achievement and self-reliance, a generation that believes it can do fine on its own.

Nor does their abandonment of party politics mean that the baby boomers believe they are helpless to influence government either. Quite the opposite. They have confidence in their ability to both influence government and understand the issues of the day. They are about 10 percent less likely than people over age 65 to say people shouldn't vote if they don't care about how an election comes out, and almost 20 percent less likely to say that public officials don't care much about what people like them think. They are about 10 percent less likely to say that politics and government sometimes seem so complicated that people like them can't really understand what's going on, and almost 20 percent less likely to say that people like them don't have any say about what the government does.

The figures reflect the baby boom's high levels of education—it is much easier to feel confident about knowledge and ability with a high-school diploma or a year of college in hand. Indeed, the numbers might have been higher if not for Vietnam, as Patrick Caddell notes. "Their expectations of a massive social consciousness movement were not fulfilled. By the time they were in their early twenties, they did not seem to have accomplished what they thought could have been accomplished. You had all these political assassinations and the war. The war finally ended, but it went on for 10 years and seemed unstoppable." There was a sense that no amount of protest mattered to Washington. The lesson seemed clear to some: the baby boomers could shape their own individual lifestyles, but not national policy.

Nor are baby boomers frightened by governmental power. When asked in 1984 whether government had grown too powerful, less than half of the baby boomers said yes, compared to roughly 70 percent of both those over 65 years old and those under 25. It is a clear generational marker, distinguishing the baby boomers from older and younger Americans alike. "Much has been made lately in the mass media about a potential generational polarization," political scientists Linda Bennett and Stephen Bennett suggest in writing about the economic issues that affect both older and younger generations. "How ironic, then, to discover in the '80s the elderly are more likely than the young to opine that the federal government has become too strong."[23] Though the elderly clearly benefit from programs like Social Security and Medicare, and though baby-boom taxes have been going up steadily to cover those costs, it is the elderly who think government has grown too big, and the baby boomers who feel comfortable with the exercise of strong government power.

Clearly, the baby boomers feel government has some business meddling in people's lives. They believe that society should ensure an equal chance for everyone. Nor do they believe that the country has gone too far on equal rights or that Americans should worry less about equality for women and minorities. In fact, the baby boomers are almost 20 percent less likely than older Americans to say that it is no big deal if some people have more of a chance in life than others. Only 30 percent of the baby boomers agreed with that notion, compared to over 55 percent of the over-65 age group.[24]

Most Americans, baby boomers or not, feel there is a time and a place for government intervention. Everyone believes in self-reliance, according to political scientists Paul Sniderman and Richard Brody, unless their problems are beyond their control. "By far the overwhelming majority of those facing a personal life problem feel they should cope with it on their own: over 80 percent of those who feel their most important problem is the quality of their personal lives feel it is entirely up to themselves to deal with the problem." So, too, for the baby boomers. They have been perfectly willing, for example, to work out their marital problems on their own, and clearly believe government has no business regulating their private lives.

In the case of a national economic crisis, however, Americans believe government should become involved. If people are fired from their jobs because they are lazy or incompetent, that is their fault. But if people are fired because of unfair trading practices in Japan or a deep recession, government should step in. As Sniderman and Brody conclude, "Less than 5 percent believe the responsibility for coping with such problems is theirs alone. By far the largest number who regard societal economic problems as their prime concern—indeed nearly 80 percent—feel government ought to help."[25]

Americans of all age groups feel there are some problems that should be handled by the individual (personal and family), some that should be addressed with the help of government or private charities (health and personal economic distress), and still others that should be the responsibility of government alone as national priorities (social issues like drugs and crime, economic crisis, and public health and safety). Again, this too applies to the baby boomers; they may want government out of their own bedrooms, but not off the backs of polluters and corporate tax cheats.

Self-reliance is clearly a broad social value held by all Americans, traceable to the earliest days of the nation. As authors Robert Bellah and his colleagues write in *Habits of the Heart*, "Self-reliance is a nineteenth-century term, popularized by Ralph Waldo Emerson's famous essay of that title, but it still comes easily to the tongues of many of those to whom we talked. . . . What, if not self-reliant, were the Puritans, many of whom, like John Winthrop, left wealth and comfort to set out in small ships on a dangerous 'errand into the wilderness'? They felt called by God, but they had to rely on themselves."[26] However, the baby boomers appear to be more willing than any other age group to stand alone. Three reasons merit explanation.

First, at least for now, the baby boomers are more willing than any other age group to blame failure on the individual, not society. They can be particularly unforgiving in this regard. If people fail in life, the baby boomers are more likely than older generations to say it is their own fault. Not society's. Not bad luck. Not a poor education. As such, they may see their current poor economic performance as an individual-level problem unworthy of government intervention. To the extent that Democrats can persuade them that it is instead a system-wide problem, they may then decide to ask for help.

The baby boomers have clearly taken self-development seriously. "Brought up in an environment of change," Michael Maccoby writes of a new generation of workers, "they have learned to adapt to new people and situations, and to trust their own abilities rather than parents or institutions. They value independence, and they accept responsibility for themselves. They try to stay in competitive condition, physically as well as mentally, to grasp opportunities, and enjoy life to the fullest. Their weakness is the reverse of their strength: detachment, reluctance to commit themselves and to take parental-type leadership roles."[27]

When asked in 1984, for example, whether most people who do not get ahead in life work as hard as people who do, 48 percent of the baby boomers said no, compared to 33 percent of the over-65 age group. More important, when asked whether they agreed that even if people try hard they often cannot reach their goals, three-quarters of the baby boomers said yes, a very high figure to be sure, but still 10 percent less than the elderly.[28] The pressure is on the individual first. Daniel Yankelovich summarizes the baby boom's consumer style as, "You have to think a little harder, shop a little smarter, know when to hold back a little; you have to figure out how the system works in order to win." By implication, when you lose, you have no one to blame but yourself. You must not have been thinking or trying hard enough.

Second, the baby boomers are hardly ready to say they are failing as individuals or that their poor economic performance is yet deserving of government intervention. In 1986, for example, almost 60 percent of the under-30 age group said they were better off financially than they had been the year before, and three-quarters said they expected to be better off in the next year.[29] To date, the baby boomers have worked their way through poor economic times with credit cards and optimism, keeping up with the cost of living mostly by borrowing money or by not saving.

Moreover, whatever their feelings about the state of the economy, baby boomers feel in control of their own financial lives. Nine out of ten say they are either very well or fairly well informed about financial matters and, as one study concludes, "Virtually all members of this generation believe they are capable of handling their own financial affairs, with the majority considering themselves *very* capable in this area."[30] Perhaps the baby boomers see their poor economic performance as something they can take care of themselves.

But, that does not mean the baby boomers have been doing well in an objective sense. In 1984, 34 percent of the baby boomers borrowed money to supplement their incomes, 30 percent put off medical care because of the economy, and almost half looked for a new job or part-time work to make ends meet.[31] Nevertheless, in a relative sense, they felt they were doing better. As one housing expert says, "It's a strange situation where interest rates on 30-year mortgages are barely creeping under 10 percent and everyone thinks the millennium has come, but recent thinking has so colored our experiences that we think this is good."

Indeed, as Veroff, Douvan, and Kulka argue, while the basis of personal happiness may not have changed from the 1950s to the 1970s, "saying that one is 'not too happy' does not seem to be as demoralized a response as it was a generation ago." More "unhappy" people in 1976 were optimistic about the future; more were confident about their ability to work out the tasks they had set for themselves.[32]

Despite this short-term optimism, the baby boomers remain worried about the distant future. Social Security is a prime example. In a fiftieth anniversary report card on Social Security, pollsters Yankelovich, Skelly, and White found that most of the baby boomers felt the program should be continued. Most also understood that Social Security is essential for many elderly Americans, and only a small number said the program had outlived its usefulness. Yet, 35 percent of the baby boomers also said the country could no longer afford the system, and an astounding 70 percent had little confidence that they would ever see any benefits. More troubling for the future perhaps, three-quarters of the baby boomers also said it was either very or somewhat likely that Social Security would no longer even exist when they retired in the next century.[33]

This blend of short-term optimism and long-term worry is made particularly evident in the book *The Inner-American*. Younger Americans were much more concerned about their future in 1976 than their peers had been in 1957, leading Veroff and his colleagues to conclude: "The young are both worried (especially in 1976) and optimistic. This contradiction may arise from their recognizing both the potential and the limitations of their futures."[34] The worries about the future clearly increased between the 1950s and 1970s, perhaps reflecting the nuclear era and the social crowding of the baby boom. In 1957, for example, 32 percent of the under-30 age group said they worried a lot or always. By 1976, the number was up to 51 percent.

As such, worry is not exactly the opposite of optimism. It contains a considerable amount of uncertainty and doubt. It is more a sense or a feeling that something out there is not going to work out. While the baby boomers are pretty sure next year is going to be okay, they aren't at all sure about the distant future. And what they do know about programs like Social Security is not promising.

The question is whether a candidate or party can build a winning coalition based on this worry. For now, the answer appears to be no. The worry does not appear strong enough to attract the baby boom to a specific party or candidate. Mondale certainly hoped to be the first. As his pollster, Peter Hart, said after the 1984 defeat, "It was clear to me that if the election were a referendum of the present versus the past, the Democrats were going to lose. The only possibility we had was to stress the future. When we talked to the voters, our figures showed they were very satisfied with the present. But when we asked them about the future they were uncertain. That was the open ground."

Nevertheless, a campaign based on gloom-and-doom about the future runs directly counter to the baby boom's optimism about the short term. And given their lack of trust in government, perhaps that is all that matters. What is the point of voting on the basis of long-term promises if leaders and institutions cannot deliver even today?

Third, and perhaps most important for explaining their overall societal separation, the baby boomers are more likely than past generations to see their strength as coming from within. They are also more likely than previous generations to say they are unique from other people. This is a generation which derives greater strength from intimacy than from participation in traditional social or political connections. This introspection may be a natural reaction to the baby boom's social crowding. Having been labelled and numbered from the very beginning, perhaps the baby boomers are simply looking for a little individual distinction.

This is a generation which focuses on the self as the key social unit, not the family, peer group, church, or community. When baby boomers are asked to describe themselves, they focus on individual characteristics. According to Veroff, Douvan, and Kulka, young Americans were more willing in 1976 than in 1957 to focus on personality in describing how they differed from others. "They seem to be actively working out identity issues, to be intensely aware of their unique qualities, shortcomings, and strengths. . . . Young people—both men and women—more often than older people, wish they had more friends. Yet, in listing sources of strength, young people also more often allude to their social skills. Thus, they are not reflecting a deep sense of social insecurity in their wish to be liked more and have more friends. Rather, they are in the process of building social networks and are striving to enlarge their circles."[35]

This introspection may explain why, for example, the baby boomers rely less on prayer in times of trouble than their parents do. When they get into trouble, the baby boomers seek highly personal solutions—for example, individual therapy rather than the comfort of a community. "The shift from prayer to more intimate help-seeking," Veroff and his colleagues suggest, "is a clear example of the shift away from more organized formal institutionalized forms of integrating to the social world to a much more personal form through intimate interpersonal relationships."[36]

The closest many baby boomers come to belonging to a community are their highly personal networks of friends. As *The Inner-American* concludes, "One of the most dramatic findings in our study is the degree to which people in 1976 now talk to friends and other people in their support system about their worries and periods of unhappiness. Not only do they report such help-seeking much more often than they did in 1957, but when they do seek out help of this sort, they are more likely to select a *variety* of such people."[37]

Their introspection may also explain why baby boomers have been shifting from things public to things private, toward a privatization of experience and involvement, a kind of social and political survivalism. As they abandon the commons—the town square —in pursuit of private solutions, national policy becomes fragmented into a thousand state and local issues. The question is not, for example, how to solve the hazardous waste problem, but who can yell "Not in my back yard" the loudest. Thus, historian Paul Starr argues that the shift "is not from open sociability to personal intimacy, but from civic virtue and political participation to the pursuit of self-interest. . . . It is striking, although perhaps coincidental that the United States in recent years has seen a public-to-private transition in both individual involvements and the aims of public policy."[38]

Their introspection may also explain the baby boomers' drift away from the national community. "The nation-state is remote," Yankelovich explains, "the person you are living with is not. Your community is not. You can develop bonds in your community, with ethnic groups, and others." Indeed, when asked in 1987 which people in government they trusted most, 37 percent of the 25- to 34-year-old baby boomers said local people, 27 percent said state, and only 19 percent said federal. Though the baby boomers were not particularly trusting about any level of government, they were clearly willing to give local leaders the edge if they had to deal with any officials at all.

Finally, the introspection may even explain why the baby boomers still want a high degree of personal service in the marketplace. In life insurance and banking, for example, the baby boomers still want to be served one-on-one by live agents, even if it might be easier to get the information they need elsewhere. Unlike grumpies—grim, ruthless, upwardly mobile professionals who demand efficiency at any cost in human contact—most baby boomers resist mechanizing even routine transactions. Three-quarters of the baby boomers still want to deal with a person, even if it raises the cost of those services.[39]

Some of this introspection may erode with age. The baby boomers may eventually decide they know enough about their selves. "Older people have probably resolved many of their doubts about their own selves," Veroff and his coauthors suggest. "In some ways, raising questions and criticisms about the self in old age is a meaningless activity. The same kind of interpretation can be offered for the fact that older people do not often wish for greater social acceptance or want more friends. They have already negotiated social adaptations and are not about to question them now."[40]

Moreover, the baby boomers may soon tire of being out there on their own. As Albert O. Hirschman argues, investments in things public and things private are both acts of consumption, and are both subject to disappointments. "Acts of consumption, as well as acts of participation in public affairs, which are undertaken because they are expected to yield satisfaction, also yield disappointment and dissatisfaction. They do so for different reasons, in different ways, and to different degrees, but to the extent that the disappointment is not wholly eliminated by an instantaneous downward adjustment of expectations, any pattern of consumption or of time use carries within itself, to use the hallowed metaphor, 'the seeds of its own destruction.' "[41]

Just as wars don't end quickly and Great Societies sometimes fail, the baby boom may eventually find the private networks wanting too, prompting a swing back toward the commons. In this cycle of public-to-private and back again, Hirschman argues that "public action is undertaken by the individual as an alternative to the disappointments, the narrowness, and selfishness of the quest for purely private happiness."[42]

Indeed, Yankelovich's tracking polls seem to be picking up at least the initial elements of a renewed commitment to things public. Perhaps the baby boomers have grown tired of the endless search for perfection. "There are signs that Americans are taking a more reasoned approach to the self and its potential and growing more self-accepting. There is more willingness to say, 'This is who I am.' There is more interest in gradual self-improvement toward specific, realistic ends, and correspondingly less belief in the prospect of radical or instant self-transformation." Perhaps the baby boomers are learning firsthand that no matter how hard they try, sometimes people simply cannot reach their goals.

Finally, the baby boomers may yet discover that they cannot solve their problems by building higher fences and creating a greater isolation. Try as the baby boomers might to defend their own backyards, national problems have a way of intruding upon individualism. Hazardous wastes have a tendency to migrate, threatening the ground water of everyone. Acid rain can affect even the most pristine New England ponds. Nuclear waste has to be buried somewhere. The corrosion of urban infrastructures in New York or Chicago eventually affects economies in California and New Mexico.

Nevertheless, for the immediate future, the focus on introspection and privatization of experience will continue. Indeed, even as the baby boomers form their own social networks, they are building without the traditional social foundations. It is a much more intimate process, working one friend at a time. Whereas members of previous generations found it easier to join a church or social club, and in doing so make a hundred friends at a time, the baby boomers appear to be working at a much more personal level.

The baby boom's introspective nature has profound implications for the political process. It makes the generation more difficult to reach, and more difficult to hold. Already, the "inner-directed" or "self-developed" baby boomers have reshaped the consumer marketplace, forging an entirely new industry designed to find out just who and what the introspective baby boomers want. Part demographics, part psychology, advertisers are increasingly dependent on *psychographics* to sell the baby boom. Politics is not far behind.

Psychographics are designed to reduce hundreds of values and demographics into a small number of typical lifestyles. "In our research we have looked at well over 800 facets of people and find that different lifestyle groups have unique patterns in almost every area," one of the discipline's founders, Arnold Mitchell writes. "We now have powerful evidence that the classification of an individual on the basis of a few dozen attitudes and demographics tells us a good deal about what to expect of that person in hundreds of other domains."[43]

The result of Mitchell's work is the Values and Lifestyle Survey, or VALS for short. Using one form or another of a statistical technique called multidimensional analysis, VALS takes hundreds of questions and reduces them into nine neat categories, or what Mitchell calls "The nine American lifestyles." Like any trade secret, no one really knows what specific questions go into the nine lifestyles. And, like any trade secret, no one knows what the statistical equation says about "goodness of fit"—that is, how well the nine lifestyles really match the data.

However, everything else about VALS is available for a price. The orientation alone costs $7,500, and a two-year subscription to what VALS calls "leading-edge" research on how the lifestyles are changing costs $26,000. Psychographics are big business mainly because advertisers are terrified of not knowing where the baby boomers are headed. Surely, it is not that VALS and the other psychographic programs tell advertisers a great deal more than they already know. "One of the most frustrating aftermaths of any research is a result that is so obvious everyone is thinking 'So what's new?' " Campbell Soup's Tony Adams says. Take an elderly woman living in a retirement hotel: "Do we need a battery of lifestyle questions to label this consumer as a light user of Gucci shoes, Jordache jeans, Chivas Regal, and Godiva chocolates?"[44]

Nevertheless, psychographics are the hottest thing to hit Madison Avenue since the creative revolution of the 1960s. The question psychographics answers is how to market to a generation which believes so strongly in individualism and self-reliance. For

VALS at least, this answer is to break the baby boom into a hierarchy composed of three huge segments, and to design distinctive advertising for the top two. People who care about self-development (the Inner-Directed) are not likely to identify with a Merrill Lynch "Run with the Herd" campaign. People who care about what others think (the Outer-Directed) are not likely to respond to a Clairol "Inner Beauty" campaign. People who are struggling just to get through the day (the Need-Driven) are not likely to respond to any campaign at all—they do not have the economic resources. There are smaller segments within each of these three categories—the Inner-Directed, for example, are defined by the I-Am-Me's, the Experiential, and the Societally Conscious—but the general themes are the same.

The Need-Driven, according to VALS's own advertisements, "are people so limited in resources (especially financial resources) that their lives are driven more by need than by choice. Values of the Need-Driven center around survival, safety, and security. Such people tend to be distrustful, dependent, unplanning." There are no examples of ads for this group. Most advertisers concentrate on the Inner- or Outer-Directeds. Moreover, at least with the baby boom, only 10 percent or so fall into this group and most are blacks and/or women.

In contrast, the Outer-Directeds clearly have enough income to care what other people think of them. As VALS puts it, "The Outer-Directeds conduct their lives in response to signals—real or fancied—from others. Consumption, activities, attitudes—all are guided by what the outer-directed individual thinks others will think. Psychologically, outer-direction is a major step forward from being Need-Driven. Life has broadened to include other people and a host of institutions." Dr. Pepper's "Be a Pepper" campaign is a classic example of an Outer-Directed approach: "You may feel lonely at first drinking a Dr. Pepper, but you're really part of a very hip crowd." In 1982, over half of the baby boomers fell into the Outer-Directed categories. However, as other psychographic programs have discovered, the Outer-Directed baby boomers are increasingly expressing themselves in the language and style of the Inner-Directed.

Indeed, the Inner-Directeds almost invariably come from an Outer-Directed background, either rebelling in childhood and adolescence or switching over in response to an increasingly introspective culture. They contrast with the Outer-Directed "in that they conduct their lives primarily in accord with inner values—the needs and desires private to the individual—rather than in accord with values oriented to externals. Concern with inner growth thus is a cardinal characteristic."

Foremost within the Inner-Directed lifestyle, according to VALS, are the Societally Conscious. "A profound sense of societal responsibility leads these people to support such causes as conservation, environmentalism, and consumerism. They tend to be activistic, impassioned, and knowledgeable about the world around them. Many are attracted to simple living and the natural; some have taken up lives of voluntary simplicity."

In 1982, exactly one-third of the baby boomers fell into the Inner-Directed category. As a spokesperson for Dr. Pepper says, "We currently see 30 percent of the young population as being Inner-Directed; it's the most rapidly growing segment. Our projections indicate Inner-Directeds will make up 60 percent of the population by 1990." That is one reason why Dr. Pepper switched its ad campaign to "Hold Out for the Out of the Ordinary." At least within the consumer marketplace, there is a "realignment" underway from the Outer-Directed to the Inner-Directed, with the baby boomers and their younger siblings at the front.

Ultimately, of course, VALS would be of little interest if the baby boomers, whether inner- or outer-directed, adhered to traditional buying cues. "Sure it may oversimplify," one advertising executive says of VALS. "No matter what classification system you use, you're distorting everybody's individuality. But the alternative is to tailor advertising to 80 million individual households."

The rise of the Inner-Directeds led Merrill Lynch to its "Lone Bull" campaign, with its stark imagery of a bull wandering down

Wall Street. For corporations that cannot afford two separate ad campaigns, the challenge is to find a theme which calls to the Inner- and Outer-Directeds at the same time. That is precisely what Clairol did in its Nice'n Easy hair color campaign which could run in *Reader's Digest* and *Cosmopolitan* simultaneously. According to consumer reporter James Atlas, the ad "had the challenging tone that Inner-Directeds like and the endorsement that Outer-Directeds like. 'Color and Condition that should have been yours can be,' declares the new creative. 'Make it happen. Sells the most. Conditions the most.' Outer-Directeds are reassured that Nice'n Easy is popular, and Inner-Directeds feel in charge of their own lives."[45]

Psychographics has even affected state lottery ads. Even though lotteries might appeal mostly to the Need-Drivens who hope to break out of their economic struggle, former VALS vice president Stephen Crocker says that the Inner-Directeds can be hooked by a good cause. In Colorado, lottery revenues are set aside for parks and recreation. "We found that the inner-directed groups participated much more in Colorado because they felt that by buying a ticket, they were making a meaningful contribution. One Colorado man we interviewed said, 'When I buy a lottery ticket, I feel like I win either way.'" In Maryland, lottery ads depict a couple searching for a missing child, while viewers are told that lottery revenues are paying for the police helicopter that eventually saves the day.

Psychographics are about to penetrate politics, too. After years of trying to make baby boomers fit traditional demographic and political categories, strategists are beginning to use *poligraphics* to define distinctive electoral styles.

Poligraphics are certainly the basis for determining what political pollster Stanley Greenberg calls the new middle-class voter: "a growing pool of independent voters, the defectors who left the Democratic party in 1984 and the now-dominant generation of baby boomers." According to Greenberg, there are four characteristics that define this new middle-class profile: (1) a strong populist orientation, (2) a sense of life being played out just above the economic margin, (3) a reconstructed image of the Kennedy era which suggests a government of limits and self-reliance, not idealism and public commitment, and (4) a view of government, as Greenberg puts it, "as a perverse irony—a necessary and positive entity, but one that now belongs to others, that has come to embody special interests, big things, support for the undeserving, and disregard for the middle class."[46] These new middle-class voters are clearly different from traditional Democrats in their sense of separation from politics.

Poligraphics are also the underpinning for what the *Times Mirror* Poll calls a new typology of politics—one based on values, not demographics. Using data collected by Gallup in 1987, along with a statistical technique called factor analysis, *Times Mirror* found eleven distinctive poligraphic types, including Enterprise Republicans, Moral Republicans, Disaffecteds, Seculars, and the Passive Poor. A generational view of politics is implicit in the *Times Mirror* approach. The eleven types are defined in part by the era in which a voter's first political contacts occurred, and by a voter's political heroes.

In looking for such potential generational differences, roughly half of the baby boomers are captured by four categories:

• Twelve percent of the baby boomers are Enterprise Republicans—pro-business and anti-government, but still tolerant on social issues—compared to 10 percent of the total adult population. Their heroes are Lee Iacocca and Ronald Reagan. Key events were Vietnam and the Reagan presidency.

• Eleven percent of the baby boomers are Seculars—highly educated, moderate on social issues, committed to personal freedom, expressing religious beliefs—compared to eight percent of the population. Their heroes are Martin Luther King, Jr., John F. Kennedy, and Franklin D. Roosevelt. Key events were Vietnam and Watergate.

• Ten percent of the baby boom boomers are Partisan Poor—low income, concerned about social justice, and solidly Democratic—compared to nine percent of the population. Their heroes are John Kennedy, Martin Luther King, Jr., Franklin D. Roosevelt, and Edward Kennedy. Key events were the Kennedy presidency, the assassinations, and the civil rights movement.

• Fourteen percent of the baby boomers are Sixties Democrats —upper-middle class, identified with the peace and civil rights movements of the 1960s, highly tolerant—compared to eight percent of the population. Their heroes are Martin Luther King, Jr., and John Kennedy. Key events were Vietnam, civil rights, and the assassinations.

The baby boomers are underrepresented in four other *Times Mirror* categories, suggesting the decline of certain kinds of political thinking as one generation passes out of the electorate and another takes over:

• Ten percent of the baby boomers are Bystanders—poorly educated, uninterested in current affairs, non-participants in American politics—compared to 11 percent of the total adult population. Their only hero is John Kennedy. Key events were Vietnam and the Reagan presidency.

• Eight percent of the baby boomers are Moral Republicans— very conservative, very religious, anti-abortion, anti-big government, anti-communist—compared to 11 percent of the population. Their heroes are Billy Graham and Ronald Reagan. Key events were Vietnam and the Reagan presidency.

• Six percent of the baby boomers are New Deal Democrats —blue collar, union members, in favor of government intervention in the economy, in favor of a strong national defense, against aid to minorities—compared to 11 percent of the population. Their heroes are Franklin D. Roosevelt and John Kennedy. Key events were the Great Depression and the New Deal.

• Five percent of the baby boomers are Passive Poor—older, committed to social justice, favor all forms of increased social spending—compared to seven percent of the population. Their heroes are the Kennedys, Franklin D. Roosevelt, and Martin Luther King, Jr. Key events were Vietnam, the assassinations, and the Great Depression.[47]

This poligraphic portrait confirms the importance of the baby boom's tolerance and social liberalism for future politics, and also shows the generation's somewhat higher willingness to participate in politics when compared to older generations. Looking at past voting histories across the groups, and not calculating who is more or less likely to turn out in a given election, roughly 73 percent of the baby boomers fit into Democratic categories, and only 27 percent fall into Republican territory. The secret to a Democratic success, of course, is to get the vote out, and that involves breaking the baby boom's introspection. For, while Enterprise Republicans are aggressive at the polls, the very definition of a sixties Democrat involves a separation from political tradition.

Yet, poligraphic research may reinforce that separation even further. By targeting highly selective baby-boom groups, it may provoke the kinds of polarization that may divide the generation against itself. And by leaving out groups like the Bystanders, it may also reinforce the potential conflict between the haves and have-nots. Poligraphic research is based in large part on the proposition that the baby boomers should be addressed in separate social enclaves. However, the growing agenda of baby-boom problems can only be solved by a broad generational commitment to stewardship and patience, values which are currently in short supply and which rarely show up in poligraphic profiles.

However they approach the baby-boom voters, parties and candidates may have to develop new channels of communication. The baby boomers are becoming increasingly estranged from time-honored advertising conduits, especially TV, making them much more difficult to contact. Network viewership is down, cable and alternative programming is up.

Much of the separation reflects the growing clutter of television. For one thing, there are more commercials per minute today than ever before. In the early days of television, for example, most commercials were sixty seconds long. By the late 1960s, however, advertisers had figured out they could make more money if they broke "sixties" in half, creating the thirty-second ad. And in 1985, they broke "thirties" in half again. There is even talk now of 7.5-second ads.

For another thing, television executives found more time for commercials at the top and bottom of the half hour, and cut programs accordingly. Not only were there more commercials per minute, there were more minutes of advertising in each hour of prime time. Between 1967 and 1981, according to the Newspaper Research Bureau, the number of network commercials jumped from 1,856 per week to 4,079, an increase of 119 percent. At the same time, the number of local commercials also rose 119 percent, from 2,413 to 5,300 a week.[48] Moreover, the number of promotional advertisements, public service announcements, and ten-second breaks also rose. Even within a single commercial, the number of cuts of information increased as advertisers sought to put more information and imagery into a smaller time frame.

Take a look at old reruns of "I Love Lucy" or "Andy Griffith" on local TV as simple proof of the changing world of television. The programs simply will not fit into contemporary time frames, and are cut to ribbons to accommodate the new commercial regimen. Twenty-eight minutes of old programming will not fit into twenty-two minutes of modern television time.

For a third thing, the 1970s brought new competition to the television industry. As television expert Kenneth Hey argues, "technological gadgets expanded viewer choices and destroyed the concept of a concentrated audience. Superstations, cable stations, cable networks, pay-per-view outlets, and every possible specialty station from sports to religion now compete for people's attention. Viewers eagerly bought into these new options. Between 1980 and 1984, for example, the revenues of cable and pay-TV companies grew by 278 percent." As a result of the increasing options, the number of American households tuned in during prime time to ABC, NBC, or CBS fell from 50 percent in 1980 to 44 percent in 1986. As Hey concludes, "Viewers, who were once thought of as docile 'couch potatoes,' had become adept manipulators of their media environments."[49] And the baby boomers led the way.

Does the clutter make any difference? The answer is yes. Clutter clearly reduces what viewers remember. Even before the 30-second era, viewers were having trouble with recall. Back in 1965, for example, one study showed that a scant 18 percent of viewers could remember the specific name of the product they had just seen advertised. By 1974, even after easing the test, just 12 percent could remember the specific name of *any* product they had just seen advertised in a *cluster* of commercials. By 1981, only seven percent could pass that simple test.

Indeed, by the early 1980s, recall tests showed that viewers could hardly remember a product long enough to make a quick trip to the refrigerator. In one study, viewers were asked only four minutes after viewing a commercial if they could remember the product they had just seen. Only 12 percent could pass the test. After eight minutes, none could identify any product correctly from any of a cluster of commercials. Now was it Comet or Ajax, Coors or Bud, Coke or Pepsi, Chevrolet or Ford? Viewers simply couldn't answer right.[50]

Will the clutter continue into the future? Again, the answer is yes. After interviewing a group of 250 advertising executives in 1985, Leo Bogart reports that most "expect the total number of advertising messages disseminated annually to double again by the year 1997. Similarly, they expect that a typical individual will be within sight or hearing of twice as many advertising messages each day as at present. Most of those who expect this to happen are disturbed by the prospect of what this means for advertising effectiveness . . . since there is no way that the public's time and attention can keep pace with advertisers' capacity to produce ads."[51] The ad executives also predict that network viewership will continue to drop, down from its high of 95 percent in the 1960s to 78 percent in 1985 to perhaps 40 percent in 1998.

Has the clutter affected baby-boom viewing habits? Again, the answer is yes. The clutter has increasingly relegated television to background noise. Almost 30 percent of the baby boomers say they use TV as a background for other things, compared to just 11 percent of those over 65. Further, the baby boomers have a tendency to spin the dial at random—almost half say they tune into programs by accident, compared to just 30 percent of those over 65. And cable is cutting deeply into network viewership.

More important, the baby boomers are increasingly using their VCRs to combat commercial advertising. The baby boomers are becoming experts at "zapping" ads. They pre-record their favorite programs and then speed past the ads with the fast-forward button. All a zapper needs is a VCR and a blank tape. And the baby boomers have plenty of both. In fact, half of all American households now have VCRs, and well over 250 million blank tapes were sold in 1987 alone.

The rise of zapping has created a fair degree of panic among television advertisers. As marketing professors Carrie Heeter and Bradley Greenberg show, zappers are clearly separated from the traditional model of a careful television viewer. "In every study we have done, zappers are less likely to know what shows they are going to watch before they sit down to watch. . . . They check more channels when deciding what to watch. They are more likely to check them in numerical order, 2,3,4,5,6, . . . 36. They are more likely to stop at the first show that looks good to them. Zappers then are channel-checkers when they turn the set on. . . . Zappers are less likely to watch a show from start to finish. They are more likely to change channels between shows, during shows, and at commercials."[52] And just who are the zappers? Heeter and Greenberg pinpoint the average age at 30, right in the middle of the baby boom.

Political advertising may be the most vulnerable to zapping.

Most commercials are "talking heads," with little creative imagery. Though Mondale and Reagan both produced several highly creative ads in 1984, the very limited viewership data suggest that the baby boomers and their younger peers either spun the channel or hit the fast-forward at the first sign of a political commercial. Moreover, with a TV tuner in hand, 130 channels for the picking, the baby boomers can end-run even the most sophisticated commercials. Indeed, the latest addition to the baby boom's defense against advertising is a VCR attachment which actually senses commercials and zaps them automatically.

Parties and candidates appear to have two options in responding to the baby boom's separation from television advertising. One is to continue the ads anyway, dropping from 30-second spots to 15 seconds and 7.5 seconds, in spite of growing evidence that fewer and fewer people are watching, and in spite of the loss to the democratic process. As Sen. Bob Graham (D-FL) said during his 1986 campaign, "We may have reached the point where instead of staying on your front porch like candidates once did, you spend all your time in a television studio. It's a very frustrating commentary. I'd like to see Alexander Hamilton and Thomas Jefferson debate the French Revolution in 30-second spots."

The other option is to get out of the studios and back to the grassroots, building political loyalty the old-fashioned way, by earning it through performance. Unfortunately, many candidates define performance as a "a public presentation or exhibition," as in style and imagery, not as "the fulfillment of a claim, promise, or request," as in action on a baby-boom agenda.

That may explain why so many contemporary candidates are drifting toward video politics. For them, the medium is the message. Not only is it a good way to be in a hundred places at the same time, it is supposed to be the next best thing to a personal visit. As the creator of Gary Hart's campaign videos remarked in 1984, "People aren't going to spend a lot of time reading in-depth stories anymore, because we're all tube oriented. How many housewives in Oshkosh really have the time to sit down and read

A New Democracy? But they do have the time to plug in a videocas-
sette that very graphically shows them: 'Here's a smokestack, and
here's Silicon Valley—no smoke. We'll rebuild this.' It's in a
format that's more enjoyable to 'read.' "

Yet, whether they use cassettes or 30-second spots, parties and
candidates have a choice between exploiting short-term imagery
or promoting long-term brand loyalty. Given the cost of continued baby-boom volatility, perhaps parties and candidates would
be wise to concentrate more on the long-term commitment.

That is certainly what the churches are doing. After two
decades of declining membership, churches are finally turning to
advertising in an effort to rebuild their congregations. Ads from
the Episcopal Church show a picture of the ten commandments
under the heading "For fast, fast, fast relief, take two tablets." The
Catholic Archdiocese of New York calls out "Come home all ye
faithful—Find what you're missing." The Sacred Heart Seminary
says "We want to collar a few good men." The Religion in American Life Campaign says "Over 1 million kids run away from home
each year . . . Give them something to Believe In. Bring Your
Family to church or synagogue this week." Advertisers do not
know whether the ads are working, but their clients believe it is
an investment worth making.

That is also what car manufacturers are doing. Chrysler
switched to a brand-loyalty pitch in 1985: "We have one and only
one ambition. To be the best. What else is there?" Only five years
earlier, Chrysler was still in what its marketing vice president
called survival marketing. "We faced an industry that was dying,
an economy that was in bad shape, interest rates that ran past 20
percent, consumer confidence at an all-time low, and the inability
of the American economy to support its major industries. So we
couldn't sell product values. We were too busy saying 'get a car,
get a check.' "[53] Back from the edge of bankruptcy, Chrysler
changed its focus to quality, backed by a five-year, 50,000-mile
warranty.

For the national parties, the answer is not drafting Chrysler chairman Lee Iacocca to be a presidential nominee, but in stealing some of his industry's hard-learned wisdom. As Chrysler knows, a long-term warranty is only a selling point if owners do not use it. If all Chrysler provides is repeated trips to the service department, no slogan will rebuild the brand loyalty. They know how Honda penetrated the United States market in the first place— with its straightforward slogan "Honda, We Make It Simple," and the quality to make it stick.

This portrait of separation creates a new reality in American politics. "We have gone from a ward and precinct structure, where there is a real bond, to a situation where the tie is a lot less strong," pollster Peter Hart says. "Party ID continues to be the single best predictor of what an individual will do, but to look only at how people identify themselves and expect that that will not change is a false god to worship." Why would politics be any different from marriage, parenthood, or jobs? Why would the baby boomers stick with one party or one candidate over time when they do not stay with one spouse, one career, or even one town?

Beside the split-ticket voting and the short-term thinking, the question is whether the continued baby-boom separation really matters. Who should care? The first answer is that the baby boomers themselves should care. Like it or not, somebody will have to make the crucial choices about the baby-boom future. Public policies basic to their quality of life do not spring full blown from thin air. By separating from the political system the baby boomers allow these choices to be made by unaccountable representatives. Do they want all the decisions to be made without their input?

The second answer is that the candidates and parties should care. Presidential candidates who take advantage of the baby boom's volatility eventually foster a system in which they cannot move without fear of short-term retribution. By exploiting short-term thinking in elections, they sow the seeds of their own failure. What goes around comes around in politics, too. Moreover, volatility based on random imagery is hardly the kind of demo-cratic goal American politicians can court with pride.

Yet, what have the parties and candidates done in their search for baby-boom votes? They have created giant campaign ma-chines, incapable of one-on-one contact, spending more time in the television studio than at the grassroots. No wonder the baby boomers are not connected to politics on any permanent level. Ultimately, candidates and parties must decide what kind of politi-cal marketplace they wish to establish for baby-boom political consumers: one that emphasizes voter volatility and party-brand disloyalty or one that emphasizes candidate and party perform-ance on a long-term agenda. For now at least, the parties are still struggling with the short-term pressures of winning the next elec-tion.

Republicans, for example, seem content to savor the recent victories, even as their leading candidates court the right wing with an agenda that is antithetic to that of the baby boomers. The party's top strategists have become specialists in the new media campaigns, unwilling to acknowledge the potential impact of short-term politics on the baby boom's political separation.

Consider the comments of Charles Black, one of the hottest young Republican consultants, as an example: "There is sort of a conventional wisdom that you can overexpose your candidate in ads, and people will get tired of hearing about the campaign. I've never seen any data that showed that to be true. If you think about it, government and politics are a whole lot more important to people than which hamburger stand they eat at. Yet, McDonald's advertises 365 days a year, far heavier than any political campaign, and it doesn't get them overexposed. People still go to the counter and buy hamburgers."

Democrats, in contrast, are desperately trying to find their soul, struggling to create an agenda which might appeal to baby-boom voters. In dealing with what Caddell calls their "death wish" to drive the baby boomers away, Democrats seem content to parrot Republicans on economic issues—what Walter Dean Burn-

ham calls "yuppification" of the party—and to court the disaf-
fected with an ambiguous agenda of new ideas.

Consider the Democratic Policy Commission's 1986 report,
New Choices in a Changing America, as an example. Drafted to
show the party's intellectual vitality, the report first tells its readers
that "individuals must be responsible for their own lives" and that
"basic moral values are the bedrock of individual responsibility,"
then moves on to the notion that "opportunity is the key to a free
society" and that "a growing economy is the foundation of a
society." All true no doubt, but all in some conflict with each
other.

The baby boomers may strain to find a coherent agenda within
the report. In one chapter titled "Investing in People," the Democratic Commission promises national training accounts to help
displaced workers, but muddles about on just where the money
would come from—perhaps higher payroll taxes on the baby
boomers? In another chapter titled "Making It Work," the commission reaffirms the value of mutually assured destruction as the
basis for nuclear policy, waffling on the strategic defense initiative,
while supporting the Stealth bomber, the Midgetman nuclear missile, and the Trident submarine as "second-strike" weapons capable of surviving a Soviet attack. It is not a comforting picture. All
weapons and no solutions. Even if the strategic defense initiative
does not work, at least the Republicans offer some hope to worried
voters.

Both parties might be more successful in courting the baby
boomers by offering fewer promises and more performance. To
the extent the parties sell themselves like hamburgers, they ensure
that the baby boomers will continue to treat politics as a fast-food.
To the extent they talk about politics at a higher level of sophisti-
cation, they may guide the baby boomers toward a more reasoned
decision. It may seem uncomfortable at first—after all, the parties
are used to volatility. However, it may provide the kind of political
cushion parties ultimately need to govern. By getting the baby
boom to invest in politics on the basis of long-term performance,

presidents and members of Congress alike may find that they finally have the breathing space to make choices about the nation's future.

That does not mean that the parties cannot learn from Madison Avenue. What it all boils down to is a quality product. Media and slogans do not appear to matter even a fraction as much as a good idea. Chrysler can talk all it wants about being the best, but until it can produce a car or truck that runs as well as a Nissan or Toyota, the baby boomers won't believe it. Let the parties offer their products on the basis of a good performance, and the baby boomers may begin to reconnect, elevating their choice of a president to the importance it deserves.

7

The Baby-Boom Agenda

Baby boomers are already in the habit of holding some of their
politicians accountable for performance. Carter's performance, or lack thereof, on inflation and foreign policy clearly mattered to the baby boomers in 1980. Reagan's performance on the
same issues clearly mattered to the baby boomers four years later.

At least for now, however, the baby boomers only seem capable of retrospective voting. Instead of looking forward to what a
candidate might do in the future, they look back to what the
incumbent has done in the past. That is one reason for the baby
boom's electoral volatility. If every election is a referendum on the
last six months, why should a president care about either the
immediate or distant future? It may be troubling to think that the
United States boycott of the Moscow Olympics was one reason
Carter did so poorly among baby boomers in 1980, while the
Soviet boycott of the Los Angeles games was one reason Reagan
did so well four years later.

It is not that retrospective voting is always bad. In the worst
of times, it may be perfectly reasonable to "throw the bums out."
Nor is it that short-term politics doesn't get politicians elected.
Nor is it even that political scientists don't like it. Some say it's

not perfect issue voting, but it's close enough. Rather, it is that the kind of short-term thinking that feeds a retrospective system creates a political process in which the winners often feel like losers, living in constant fear of public retribution, rendered unable to maneuver in the straightjackets they tailored, incapable of satiating the special interest appetites they created. More important, in the better and best of times, short-term voting could reward the very policies which may bring the worst of times back.

The question is whether the baby boomers are ready for prospective voting. Can they commit to a long-term agenda, and give a party or candidate the time needed to make that agenda succeed? The answer depends in large part on the leadership—that is, what the parties and candidates offer. Do they want a system based on short-term support, where voters abandon parties and candidates at the slightest notice, or one based on a long-term commitment? Do they want a system which caters to instant gratification, in which the public gives a winner but a moment to succeed, or one based on patience? The answers may all boil down to a choice between volatility and stability, between instant gratification and commitment.

Politicians, particularly presidents, have always been torn between long-term visions and short-term rewards, between images of the future and the reality of the present. They are pols and prophets at the same time. Unfortunately, after two decades of "what-have-you-done-for-me-lately" politics, they may have forgotten how to develop a long-term agenda. They may have become so focused on political survival that they no longer remember how to create a vision of the future; so dependent on the cluttered world of television that they can no longer imagine beyond a 30-second time frame.

Nevertheless, a long-term agenda is exactly what the baby boomers need. Their future is cluttered with problems that cannot be solved overnight. If the parties and candidates opt for stability, they will have to gamble that the baby boomers are smart enough to accept a long-term agenda designed to address those concerns. It is certainly worth a try. After two decades of short-term politics, the baby boomers remain adrift, unwilling to commit to the future, absorbed in their private interests, while their problems continue to grow. Their own backyards and enclave communities may seem well protected, but hazardous waste is still piling up at the hiden dumps, the nation's infrastructure is still decaying at an alarming rate, poverty among children is still growing, and interest on the national debt is still spiralling upward.

People may have turned their backs on government, as *Washington Post* pollster Barry Sussman says, but the government's role in solving a growing list of national problems exists nonetheless. Baby-boom trust in government may be down, but demands for action can only go up in the coming years.

Prospective voting on a long-term agenda would certainly alter the way elections are contested. The parties and candidates would have to address the question, performance on what? And the baby boomers would have to be more willing to wait for results. They would have to lengthen their political time horizon, thereby cutting the pressure on instant gratification.

Ultimately, prospective voting would involve a truce between parties, candidates, and the baby boomers. The parties would have to develop a long-term agenda, and hold their candidates to it. The candidates would have to make steady progress forward even if it means that they will not be around when success is achieved. And the baby boomers would have to give their permission for a more reasonable pace in addressing their growing policy problems.

Before developing a political agenda for the baby-boom future, however, the parties and candidates would have to know more about where the baby boomers stand on the issues and how the issues fit together. Once the parties and candidates recognize that the baby-boom agenda is based on a constellation of issues that no longer fit the traditional liberal/conservative rhetoric, the question becomes whether the current political system has the capacity for change.

Back in the early 1970s, there was no question about what the baby boom wanted, at least not for social historians like Charles Reich, who hailed the rise of a society based on new introspective values. In place of the agrarian values of the 1800s and the organizational values of the 1950s, the values Reich envisioned in his *Greening of America* were to spring from the very essence of the baby-boom experience. "In place of the world seen as a jungle, with every man for himself (Consciousness I) or the world seen as a meritocracy (Consciousness II), the world is a community. People all belong to the same family, whether they have met each other or not. It is as simple as that. There are no 'tough guys' among the youth of Consciousness III."[1]

There may have been no "compassionate guys" in Consciousness III either. As the counterculture faded over the 1970s, Consciousness III collapsed into what historian Christopher Lasch identified as the "culture of narcissism" and what others called more familiarly the Me Decade. The baby boomers seemed more committed to self than to community. By 1980, according to Washington's Cato Institute, a self-described, baby-boom think tank, there were four distinct baby-boom ideologies, not one consciousness:

• Liberals who support government economic intervention and expansion of personal freedoms, an approach generally supported by younger Democrats, and held by roughly a third of the baby boomers.

• Conservatives who oppose both intervention and expanded freedoms, a set of attitudes more typical among older Republicans, but still held by roughly one in seven baby boomers.

• Populists who oppose expansion of individual freedoms but support government economic intervention, a view typically held by New Deal Democrats, but supported nonetheless by a quarter of the baby boomers.

- Libertarians who oppose economic intervention but support expansion of personal freedoms, a kind of every person for him or herself approach, usually held by young Republicans, and supported by roughly one in five baby boomers.

What happened to Consciousness III? Apparently, it was eclipsed by the new economic realities of oil embargoes and double-digit inflation, and fresh memories of the American humiliation in Iran. As one 28-year-old college graduate told the *New York Times* in 1985, "My generation is only aware of Republican presidents—we were very young when Kennedy was assassinated and we only vaguely remember LBJ. Nixon may have been a crook, but we didn't have runaway inflation. Carter's presidency was a disaster. Reagan is doing well, so our history tells us that the Republican party is the one that keeps the economy moving and keeps prices under control. I have nothing against the Democrats, I just think the Republicans are looking out for people like me— they are good to young people."

According to Cato researchers William Maddox and Stuart Lilie, the baby boom and libertarianism may soon by synonymous. "As populism has declined as a reflection of the decaying nature of its support in various social groups, so has libertarianism prospered. The near doubling of support [from 12 to 22 percent] evident for the libertarian view in eight years (1972–80) can in large part be traced to the increasing proportion of the electorate that is from the newer political generations, is earning more income, and has high levels of education."[2] Some of these new libertarians may have even started out the 1970s in the vanguard of Reich's Consciousness III, only to later drop the notion of a world community, while becoming ever more committed to taking care of number one, and number one alone.

Such a shift away from Consciousness III and toward libertarianism would have significant implications for politics. According to Cato vice president David Boaz, the challenge of the 1990s is how to attract the "baby-boom or libertarian vote." He uses the terms interchangeably.[3] Politicians of both parties should stop talking about the world and the common good, he says, and start talking about opportunity and tolerance. "The GOP needs to combine its fiscally conservative constitutency with the baby boomers instead of the social reactionaries, creating a forward-looking rather than a backward-looking coalition. Clever Democrats would challenge this approach by moving toward an opportunity-oriented economic policy, thus trying to add the baby boomers to their traditional peace and civil liberties constituencies." The ideal candidate would combine the free-market economy of a Rep. Jack Kemp (R-NY) with the social liberalism of a Sen. Paul Simon (D-IL).

How could the baby boomers have changed so quickly? How could they switch from the vision of community and interdependence of Consciousness III to the emphasis on freedom and individualism of libertarianism in only eight years? One answer is that Consciousness III always carried the seeds of self-absorption. But for the economic collapse of the late 1970s, Consciousness III might have flourished. Another answer is that Consciousness III may still be alive and well within the baby boom, albeit channeled through the New Age movement and EST. Still another answer is that the baby boom is large enough to accommodate proponents of both Consciousness III and libertarianism.

Will the real baby boomers please stand up? Before the parties and candidates can speak to a long-term baby boom agenda, they are going have to know where the generation is today. And that may be a very difficult task indeed.

It is not that Reich and Cato are both completely wrong. In fact, Cato has good evidence on the rise of the baby boom libertarians, even though the numbers are still too small to draw grand conclusions. It is just that both views of the baby boomers are so limited. Cato's analysis does not leave room for baby-boom libertarians who just happen to believe in a little bit of government regulation, whether of pollsters or biotechnology. And Consciousness III does not accept baby-boom liberals who just happen to be struggling to pay their bills.

There has been a lot of talk lately about the baby boom's role in the Reagan revolution. After voting for a right-wing conservative twice, some commentators naturally concluded that the baby boomers had become staunch conservatives. Yet, in survey after survey, the baby boomers show their liberalism, refusing to budge on Reagan's social agenda, aid to minorities, abortion, or defense spending.

There is no doubt that some of the old liberalism is gone, mugged by the reality of the life cycle and new issues; no doubt that Vietnam is fading ever deeper into baby-boom memories. After looking at a host of data on Vietnam protestors in the class of 1965, M. Kent Jennings concludes that "these baby boomers did become more conservative in a number of politically relevant ways over time. The more ideologically extreme segments, the protestors, underwent more movement than the less extreme ones. . . . Given the highly politicized nature of the protestors, there is little reason to think that these shifts are simply an expression of 'what's in the air,' all the more so because they could render reasonably articulate reasons for having become more conservative. Popular impressions had a basis in reality, though exaggerations abound."[4]

That does not mean the protestors have become right-wing Republicans. Indeed, they retain many of their liberal positions. Rather, as Jennings concludes, it is hard to stay different from the rest of the generation for so long. "Bearers of the generational ethos are vulnerable to the same general societal drifts and major events as are other segments of the population. They are also susceptible to life-stage demands that can undermine that ethos. As has been observed in a number of contexts, time often has a way of smoothing out certain prior differences within a population, including those of a generational sort."[5]

Moreover, this has been a highly volatile period in American politics. There is no such thing as a pure liberal or conservative position, and the underlying structure of public opinion remains in flux. Which direction should the parties and candidates take?

The libertarian path or the liberal? Populism or enterprise Republicanism? "These apparent contradictions in polls have been giving opinion analysts fits in recent years," Barry Sussman wrote in 1985. "It is hard to explain how people can dislike Reagan's policies and distrust what he says, yet give him high ratings. It is equally baffling when majorities take the most pessimistic view of public affairs, yet say that things are going in the right direction."[6]

Consider the following opinion riddles offered by James Sundquist as examples.

• People want less government, but also say government should guarantee a job to everyone who wants to work.

• People say government should do more for the poor, but not for people on welfare.

• They say they favor lower taxes, but support a balanced budget.

• They say they want the United States to stand up to the Russians, but also say the two nations should cooperate more.

• They want to protect the environment, but not if it costs jobs—conversely, they want new jobs, but not if it hurts the environment.

• They want the courts to be tough on criminals, but want to protect the innocent.

No wonder the parties and candidates are confused. The public wants it all—great taste *and* less filling. The question is how did American public opinion get this way?

A first answer is that the *parties and candidates did it.* In one election after another, they never said no. Everything was possible —welfare reform, tax reform, and hospital cost containment all in one easy package; a balanced budget, tax cuts, and a defense buildup all in four short years; a "get-tough" foreign policy and no combat. In fact, the current structure of opinion tends to favor politicians who work both sides of the issues. As Sundquist argues, "The fact that people want it both ways on most issues gives an advantage to the political candidate who is willing and able to promise it both ways, while the one who feels bound to choose—like Walter Mondale with his promise of a tax increase—gets clobbered."[7]

A second answer is that *strategic political consumers did it*. After three recessions, two Iran crises, two Social Security rescues, two oil embargoes, one $150 billion budget and trade deficit after another, they were bound to take stock, engaging in a kind of decade-long political "self-audit" trying to figure out which issues to keep and which to jettison.

A third answer is that the *programs did it*. The Great Society just did not work as well as planned. As one president after another announced the latest reforms, the public just might have gotten an idea that things were not working particularly well. Between 1970 and 1985, for example, there were four grand announcements of welfare reform (Nixon's Family Assistance Program, Carter's Program for Better Jobs and Income, Reagan's Workfare, and Sen. Daniel Moynihan's JOBS package), two Social Security reforms (one based on the recommendations of a National Commission on Social Security Reform), at least three major and a half-dozen minor tax reforms (culminating in the celebrated rise and fall of the new W-4 form in 1987), two budget process reforms (one creating an entirely new process and fiscal year in 1974, and the Gramm-Rudman-Hollings package in 1985), countless procurement reforms (one based on the recommendations of a Blue Ribbon Commission on Procurement Reform), one civil service reform, a new education department, a war on energy, as well as trucking, banking, airline, and consumer deregulation, all sold to the public under the label of reform. Reform seemed to be the most popular political term in Washington, often packaged as a set of new ideas—as in new military reform, new welfare reform, and new budget reform.

Whatever the reason, American public opinion is in flux. For parties and candidates who hope to lead the nation in the coming decades it is a disquieting time. Sociologist James Davis called it conservative weather in a liberal climate. Looking at National Opinion Research Center data from the 1972–78 period, Davis detected "a slow, long-term trend toward liberalism in the opinion climate, plus a sharp, short-term shift toward conservatism in the opinion weather."

The conservative shift seemed clear across a number of fronts —from support for the death penalty to anti-communism, from greater respect for authority to concerns about pornography. As Davis concluded, "increased backing for Arms and Space, decreased priorities for Health, Blacks, Drugs, Environment, and Cities, and a stalemate on Abortion are not likely to generate much applause from the left—new, old, or middle-aged."[8] According to Davis, that sharp change in temperature hit all generations "at exactly the same time and with exactly the same strength."

On some issues, Americans did become more conservative. They began to worry more about inflation and government spending. They began to wonder more about government aid for minorities and became more supportive of defense spending. At the same time on other issues, however, Americans actually became more tolerant, perhaps reflecting the baby boom's social influence. They were increasingly willing to say that premarital sexual relations were not always wrong, that they would vote for a woman presidential candidate, and that birth-control information should be made available to teenagers.[9]

And where are the baby boomers? It is critical to remember that the baby boomers began the era in a much more liberal position than older generations. Therefore, if the conservative cold wave hit everyone at the *same time* and with the *same strength*, it stands to reason that the baby boomers would end up still more liberal than older generations. That is exactly what happened.

On issues of social tolerance, there is no doubt that the baby boomers are the liberal anchor of American political opinion, becoming ever more tolerant over time. On questions of political tolerance, they also mark the liberal epicenter, though they clearly became more conservative on the economy and crime during the 1970s and early 1980s. Nevertheless, in 1984, 11 percent of the baby boomers still identified themselves as strongly liberal, compared to just six percent of those over 65. The differences show up at the other end of the liberal/conservative continuum, too, where 14 percent of the baby boomers said they were strongly conservative, compared to 19 percent of those over 65.

That does not mean the baby boomers did not change. They were hit by the conservative cold wave, too. Only 41 percent were still liberals of one degree or another in 1984, compared to two-thirds in the early 1970s. As Davis added up the gains and losses in 1980, "the long-term liberal (warming?) trend in attitudes and opinions continued through the early 1970s, but politicians and practical opinion analysts were wise to wear policy overcoats and mittens since the attitude and opinion weather was dominated by a large-scale conservative cold front."[10]

There is a tendency to overdraw the baby boom's conservatism, perhaps because scholars need to find a reason for the generation's support for Reagan. There is no question that the baby boomers became more conservative between 1975 and 1985. The trend is clear on a wide range of issues, including capital punishment, the courts, gun control, pornography, and federal spending for blacks and the cities. Indeed, looking at a list of 14 different policy issues, the baby boomers became more conservative on eight, stayed the same on four, and grew more liberal on two.[11]

Yet, it is one thing to find a trend, quite another to draw a sweeping conclusion that the baby boomers are the leading edge in the age of conservatism. At least for the baby boomers, it is hardly the beginning of an ice age. Consider the following examples drawn from Thomas Exter and Frederick Barber's article, "The Age of Conservatism:"

Trend: The baby boomers became more conservative on gun control.

Facts: In 1975, 20 percent said gun-control legislation was unnecessary; by 1985, the figure was up five percent.
Conclusion: A trend of sorts, but hardly an age of conservatism.

Trend: The baby boomers became more conservative on spending for blacks.
Facts: In 1975, 10 percent said spending on blacks was excessive; in 1985, the figure was 23 percent.
Conclusion: Another trend, but hardly evidence of racism.

Trend: The baby boomers became less tolerant of pornography.
Facts: In 1975, 21 percent said pornography should be illegal in all cases; in 1985, the figure was 30 percent.
Conclusion: Some evidence of change, but still very little support for this kind of censorship.

Trend: The baby boomers stayed steady on defense spending.
Facts: In 1975, 13 percent said defense spending was inadequate; in 1985, the figure was unchanged.
Conclusion: Hardly evidence of support for the Reagan defense build-up.

Moreover, on attitudes toward spending for the environment, education, and space, the baby boomers remained firmly liberal. After five years of the Reagan revolution, less than 10 percent of the baby boom said spending on education and the environment was excessive, perhaps in part because of Reagan's own record with the Environmental Protection Agency, and his highly visible problems with Ann Gorsuch-Burford and Interior Secretary James Watt. Moreover, they became somewhat less conservative toward spending for foreign aid, perhaps because such programs were cut down in the early years of the administration.

There are two possible conclusions in the data: either the underlying baby-boom liberalism remains solid, albeit tempered by age and experience, or the underlying conservatism remains intact, albeit softened by the Reagan revolution. Obviously, the facts fit the first conclusion. Reagan was hardly a champion of liberalism. Much as he tried to shake the baby boom's liberalism on issues like Social Security and the environment, the generation remained strong in its support.

Further, the fact of the matter is that Americans did not cash in their social consciences in the 1980s. "Their sympathy toward the poor still runs deep," James Sundquist writes. "Despite their disillusionment about governmental programs, they still believe that government should be doing more for the poor, not less, and are even willing to pay higher taxes for the purpose."[12] They may not think government is the most efficient way to lift people out of poverty, but they want it done nonetheless.

These patterns of social liberalism hold among the baby boomers. Even after giving Reagan huge majorities in 1980 and 1984, they were still unwilling to abandon their social concerns. However, they were not overwhelmed with confidence about government's effectiveness in addressing poverty either.

For example, when asked in 1984 whether government should see to it that every person has a good job and a good standard of living or just let each person get ahead on his or her own, the baby boomers were the most likely of all age groups to take the middle position, neither saying government should intervene, nor that it was every person for him or herself. When asked whether government should make every effort to improve the social and economic position of women, the baby boomers were again the most likely to take the middle ground, neither overwhelmingly supportive of government involvement nor willing to say that women should take care of themselves. Finally, even on the issue of United States involvement in Central America, where one might expect the generation to be most worried about a new Vietnam, the baby boomers appeared to be the least ideological of the age groups, neither the most concerned about getting out nor the most enthusiastic about getting in.[13]

These views may reflect a lack of confidence in government's ability to solve national problems. Indeed, the baby boomers appear to be more selective about when and where government should get involved. On the one hand, when asked in 1984 whether the country would be better off if people just stopped worrying so much about how equal people are, 48 percent of the baby boomers said yes, compared to 67 percent of those over 65. Yet, when asked whether it was not really that big a problem if some people have more of a chance in life than others, only 30 percent said yes, compared to 56 percent of those over 65. Perhaps there is a role for government in making sure everyone gets a fair start. Once the race is on, however, the baby boomers seem to believe government should stay out of the way.[14]

Even on those issues where the baby boomers have taken a more conservative position—crime, the economy, welfare spending—according to Peter Kim, "It's a new kind of conservatism. It's more a resurgence of individualism, being pragmatic and solution oriented, and a reluctance to accept cliché liberalism of the 1960s. It would be a mistake to say these groups were returning to strict, traditional values as earlier defined by the Republican vs. the Democratic parties." As Lee Atwater says, "They do understand the concept of family, and the family's very important to them, but they understand the very structure of the family unit has changed. The concept of hard work is still intact, but it's not hard work for the sake of money or for materialism; it's hard work with a notion of success in mind, instead of just money. On the other hand, on issues such as sexual mores, smoking marijuana maybe, cohabitation, and so on, you find them liberal or open minded."

The contradictions are apparent in the 1980 and 1984 elections. The baby boomers may have voted for Reagan, but they clearly disagreed with his policies. Thomas Ferguson and Joel Rogers, in an article entitled "The Myth of America's Turn to the Right," argue that for Americans of all ages, "there is little direct evidence that mass public sentiment has turned against the domestic programs of the New Deal, or even the most important components of the Great Society, and little evidence of a stable shift to the right in public attitudes on military and foreign policy. On the contrary, poll after poll demonstrates that the basic structure of public opinion in the United States has remained relatively stable in recent years. To the extent that there have been changes in public opinion on particular issues, most have tended to run *against* the direction of public policy."[15] Such is the problem of interpreting elections based on image or volatile short-term issues. Democrats and Republicans alike can create mandates on votes which reflect little more than fleeting perceptions.

Nevertheless, liberals dare not write off the baby boom's conservatism as some temporary fluke. The class of 1965, for example, clearly became more conservative between 1973 and 1982. Among the Vietnam protestors, the number who considered themselves liberals dropped from 83 percent to 63 percent, the number who said marijuana should be legalized fell from 83 percent to 61 percent, and the number who said government should do the utmost to protect the rights of the accused fell 35 points, from 81 percent to 46 percent. Among the non-protestors, the drops were less dramatic, mainly because they started from somewhat more conservative positions in the early 1970s. The number who said they were liberals, for instance, fell from 45 percent to 28 percent, while the number who supported the legalization of marijuana declined 21 percent, from 55 to 34 percent.[16]

These patterns show up in Exter and Barber's survey data, too.

Trend: The baby boomers took a hard line on crime.

Facts: In 1975, 57 percent said capital punishment was a necessary weapon in the war on crime; by 1985, the figure was up 25 points to 82 percent. In 1975, 66 percent said the government was not spending enough on crime and that spending was inadequate; in 1985, the number was 67 percent.

Conclusion: The baby boomers have clearly become much tougher toward criminals.

Trend: The baby boomers became more conservative regarding the rights of the accused.

Facts: In 1975, 78 percent said the courts were too lenient; by 1985, the number was up by eight percent.

Conclusion: The baby boomers have always been conservative on this issue.

Trend: The baby boomers became more conservative regarding welfare spending.

Facts: In 1975, 41 percent said welfare spending was excessive; by 1985, the figure was up by seven percent.

Conclusion: A substantial number of baby boomers were skeptical about welfare spending in both periods.

Trend: The baby boomers became more liberal on foreign aid spending.

Facts: In 1975, 74 percent said government was spending too much on foreign aid; by 1985, the number was down to 66 percent.

Conclusion: Hardly much evidence here of a shift back to liberalism, even if the trend is in the right direction.

Again, the baby boomers carried trace elements of the 1960s. The class of '65, for example, became more, not less supportive of equality for women. However, if the Reagan era was not exactly the culmination of the age of conservatism, it was hardly a temporary detour either. Americans may not have completed a full right turn, but they are on somewhat of a curve. The question is whether the Democrats will figure out that the era of straight-and-narrow liberalism is over. One 26-year-old blue-collar worker told the *New York Times* Poll, "It's not what the Republicans are doing for me, it's what the Democrats aren't doing. They have no organization, the party is in shambles, they're holding on to 20-year-old programs. I think more and more people my age feel this way —the day of the liberal Democrat is gone . . . and good riddance to it." William Schneider warns his Democratic colleagues that they are only deceiving themselves when they take "consolation from polls indicating that Reagan's appeal is wholly personal, that people feel better about government, or that the welfare state is alive and well. The message seems to be, none of this is really happening, and if we just wait a couple of years, it will all blow over."[17]

What do these patterns mean for the baby boom's political future? The answer is that it may be time for a sorting through of the issues. The challenge is figuring out which issues are important, and which are merely public-opinion chaff. Sussman likens contemporary public opinion to a porcupine: "The porcupine is not very aggressive. It extends its spines when aroused or attacked. The rest of the time the spines just lie there, and the porcupine lets the world go by." The challenge lies in finding out just which issues raise the generation's spines.

Given the baby boom's separation from traditional politics, perhaps the first step is to ask whether parties and candidates can still use the liberal and conservative labels. Perhaps the terms have lost their meaning over the past fifteen years. Just as the baby boomers no longer call themselves Democrats or Republicans, perhaps they abandoned the old-time ideological labels, too. In fact, one of the reasons the baby boomers have been so hard to understand—and the political future so hard to predict—is that they view issues in a very different way than previous generations.

Instead of thinking in one liberal/conservative dimension, the baby boomers appear to think in multiple dimensions. The Cato Institute, for example, believes that the baby boomers think in two dimensions—government economic intervention and personal freedom. However, even a two-dimensional approach may be too limiting. After all, the baby boomers are interested in more than just economics and personal freedoms. They are worried by foreign affairs and environment, the social safety net and child care. Thus, at the very minimum, it appears reasonable to suggest that the baby boomers think in at least three political dimensions—opportunity, safety, and meaning.

The baby boomers are clearly capable of thinking in more than one political dimension. For one thing, they are more educated than other generations, giving them a better grasp of how issues may or may not fit together. For another, they grew up with the clutter of television, teaching them how to keep track of multiple cuts of information at the same time. For still another, from 1968 on, candidates of one party or another have been encouraging the baby boomers to abandon single-dimension politics. Wallace, McGovern, Carter, John Anderson, Hart, and Reagan all worked to get the baby boomers to think beyond traditional categories.

The first dimension of the baby-boom agenda involves a search for opportunity—personal and economic. The search reflects what Daniel Yankelovich sees as a baby-boom anthem: " 'I want to live my life according to my own lifestyle. Other people ought to be able to live theirs according to their own lifestyle.' " According to Yankelovich, this search for space is not quite conservative, not quite liberal. Rather, "it is the legitimization of free choice. They would say 'Why should people be deprived of a choice simply because it is traditional?' " As the data clearly suggests, the baby boomers are far more likely than previous generations to express their demand for personal space. From gender roles to marriage, from sexual mores to parenthood, the baby boomers believe government has no business meddling in their private lives.

In the search for personal opportunity, the baby boom's concern for individual freedom and privacy reconciles what seem to have been a number of contradictory baby-boom political positions in 1984:

Abortion: 43 percent of the baby boomers said that women should always be able to obtain an abortion as a matter of personal choice.

Busing: 84 percent of the baby boomers said that letting children go to their neighborhood schools is more important than achieving racial integration through busing.

School Prayer: 59 percent said that it is all right for schools to start each day with a prayer.

National Health Insurance: 43 percent said medical expenses should be paid by individuals or private insurance plans, rather than a government insurance for everyone.[18]

In each case, the baby boomers erred on the side of individual choice, even if it costs them more for health care or limits racial integration. What may be truly remarkable is the baby boomer support for school prayer. Though they are less supportive than older Americans, they may still believe that an individual school child should have the freedom to pray in school if they so desire. That does not mean they support a national religion. As long as the prayer issue is discussed as an individual right rather than a national requirement, the baby-boom tolerance may hold fast.

Of these issues of individual freedom, none is more important to the baby boomers than abortion. As Patrick Caddell warns the Republicans, "The social issues will really come to the fore politically for the Democrats when the Supreme Court begins to move on social issues. If you start tampering with the *Roe v. Wade* abortion decision, you threaten an entire generation of women who believe that abortion is their right. If you want to see political activism, you will see it then."

This baby-boom concern about individual space also includes privacy. According to Yankelovich's data, the baby boomers are more likely than any other age group to believe that the right to privacy is threatened by big business and big government. They tend to see a laziness in Washington toward corporate invasions of privacy, whether in the rising use of polygraphs to test employee honesty or drug screening. Indeed, as noted earlier, the baby boomers are the least supportive toward the use of drug tests, and the most likely to say they would quit a job if they were asked to take one. Even though the Republicans have been able to avoid these issues in the past, Caddell warns that "Sooner or later, the conservatives are going to demand that their loyalty and support be rewarded in terms of public policy. And when that moment comes, that's when you'll start striking political sparks because when you threaten people, they begin to react politically."

The economic side of the search for opportunity clearly favors the Republicans. To date, Republicans have been very successful indeed with the concept of an "opportunity society." According to Atwater, "As long as inflation rates are down, interest rates— a big, big deal to baby boomers—are down, the Democrats are going to be sucking wind with the baby boomers."

Despite significant economic divisions between baby-boom men and women, and blacks and whites, Atwater is on target. Whether because of their general optimism or real economic gains, the baby boomers felt they were benefiting from Reaganomics. In 1984, for example, the baby boomers were 10–15 percent more likely than older Americans to say the economy had gotten better over the year leading up to the election. They were also 10–20 points less likely to say that it had gotten harder to find work. They were almost half as likely to say that the costs of things had gone up a lot over the previous year. Finally, they seemed more willing to give Reagan the credit: 43 percent said that the government's economic policies had made the nation's economy better, compared to 28 percent of those over 55 years of age.[19]

The baby boomers also seem to agree with the Republican view of trade. They are less likely than older Americans to say that competition from foreign countries has hurt the economy in their communities. Quite the opposite. Over half of the baby boomers say such competition has had no impact, compared to just a third of those over 65 years old.[20] Whether they would be willing to pay higher prices for imports to protect the rust-belt industries is in doubt. "First of all," says Caddell, "they have a much greater world view. They're not as interested in protectionism to preserve dying industries that won't help themselves."

If the issue is framed as one of limiting the right to the quality products they want, the baby boomers will remain opposed. They don't care where the car comes from as long as it works. Indeed, protectionism hardly makes sense to a generation of which 72 percent believe future economic growth will come from computers and high technology, 11 percent from revitalization of old industries, and only 15 percent from import restrictions.[21]

If, however, the trade issue is framed as one of unfair trade practices and the lack of a level international playing field, the baby boom's search for individual opportunity may come into play. "These people have a notion about excellence and being number one, and competing" Caddell concludes. "If they believe that the United States is being treated unfairly, they're going to be like other Americans: they're going to respond to it."

Reagan's success in courting the baby boom does not mean the Republicans have a permanent lock on the economic opportunity dimension. The baby boomers remain strongly committed to a level playing field, reflected in their support for equal opportunity and a fair start for all Americans. Over 80 percent of the baby boomers still support the Equal Rights Amendment.[22] Indeed, this concern for economic opportunity may even involve a role for government in ensuring that corporations treat baby-boom employees fairly. "When we talk about the need for child care, the need for pregnancy leave, these are not only feminist issues," Rep. Barbara Boxer (D-CA) says. "These are human rights and family issues."

Because dual-earner couples will eventually represent two out of three baby-boom households, the demand for flexible work schedules, pregnancy leave and sabbaticals, job sharing, and company-sponsored day care is likely to grow. "By the mid-1990s," one business group predicts, "many more business leaders will not only be members of working-couple or single-parent households, they may even be second-generation products of them. This coming generation of employers is likely to be far more sensitive to the complexities of balancing work and family responsibilities—and to believe that their business interests are well served when company policies are responsible to the personal and family needs of employees."[23] Government may still need to get involved, both to spur those corporations that do not join the movement, and to make sure new employment policies are fair. Moreover, because dual-earner couples by definition include women, there may even be a role for government in ensuring pay equity—that is, equal pay for work of equal or comparable value.

The second dimension of the baby-boom agenda involves the concern for personal safety, which appears to be linked to the fears of crime highlighted earlier, as well as concerns about public health and fears of war.

The baby boom's support for environmental protection is a prime example of this concern for safety. The baby boomers are consistently more willing than older Americans to say that protecting the environment is so important that requirements and standards cannot be set too high, that environmental improvements must be made regardless of cost.[24] They are less likely than other generations to support a relaxation of pollution controls to help weak industries, and more likely to say that environmental protection laws have not gone far enough. The baby boomers are also more concerned about the risks of nuclear power, and the problems of disposing of radioactive waste. On virtually every environmental and safety issue, baby boomers show high levels of personal concern. And there can be no doubt that these issues will remain hot into the future. Already, almost half of all Americans live in counties that contain at least one of the 500 or so toxic waste sites on the Environmental Protection Agency's priority clean-up list. And given the current snail's pace of clean-ups, those sites may well exist long into the baby boom's future.

The baby boom's concern about safety also reflects the fear of nuclear war. In 1984, two-thirds of the baby boomers said they were worried about the United States getting into a nuclear war, and just over half were worried about a conventional conflict. "Baby boomers do understand that there's a threat out there," Atwater says. "They are conservative, but they want a more efficient defense."

Perhaps so, but the baby boomers are much less confident that the Reagan build-up is the answer to international tension. Even if they understand that there is a threat out there, they also see the dangers of United States nuclear policy. The baby boomers were almost 20 percent more likely than older Americans to say Reagan was not doing as much as possible to limit the build-up of nuclear weapons. And though they were congratulatory regarding the 1987 United States-Soviet intermediate arms agreement, they were still among the strongest supporters of a freeze on all nuclear weapons. Moreover, the baby boomers were skeptical about the exercise of United States conventional power in places like Nicaragua and the Middle East. Following the 1986 bombing of Libya, for example, the baby boomers were more likely than other Americans to say that Reagan's action would make it more difficult to bring about peace in the Middle East.[25]

Ironically for Democrats, who have long supported the nuclear freeze and arms reduction, the baby boom's fear of nuclear war also translates into support for Reagan's multi-billion dollar strategic defense initiative, "Star Wars." In a detailed 1985 *Los Angeles Times* Poll, the baby boomers were more likely than other age groups to know that the United States had started research on a defensive system to protect the nation against attack by intercontinental ballistic missiles. However, asked whether Star Wars would be leakproof or merely a way to reduce the number of missiles that might get through to their targets, only 10 percent of the baby boomers thought the system would work perfectly. Further, the baby boomers were somewhat more likely than older Americans to see Star Wars as a threat to international peace, while two-thirds said it would cost too much, and 60 percent said it would alter the concept of mutually assured destruction.

Obviously, the baby boomers knew enough about Star Wars to have an opinion about it. Despite their reservations, when asked at the end of the survey to take all things into consideration, 62 percent of the baby boomers said the United States should move ahead, compared to 54 percent of the over-40 age group.[26] That baby-boom support has been confirmed in other polls, too. According to a 1985 Gallup Poll, despite fears that Star Wars would decrease the likelihood of reaching an arms agreement with the Soviet Union, 60 percent of the baby boomers still said go ahead.

Although baby boomers might agree with Democrats who say Star Wars won't work, their concern for safety overrides their natural skepticism. On the one hand, the baby boomers support the nuclear freeze and virtually any suggestion for cutting strategic weapons. On the other hand, the baby boomers are not fools. They know that nuclear weapons will be part of the international reality for some time to come, and therefore support any effort to provide some kind of defense. Also remember that baby boomers have more confidence than older Americans in the potential benefits of technology.

The baby boom's concern for safety also converts into basic support for Social Security and Medicare, the two cornerstones of government help for the elderly. Despite their own doubts about the future of the program, the baby boomers do not want to see the current generation of retirees hurt. According to a 1985 Yankelovich, Skelly, and White survey, 98 percent of the baby boomers recognized the importance of Social Security as an essential source of income for the elderly, and just 16 percent said Social Security had outlived its usefulness. More important, nearly all of the baby boomers acknowledged that some elderly would be forced to go on welfare or to rely on their children if Social Security were no longer to exist. And when asked whether current Social Security benefits were adequate, 43 percent of the baby boomers said no. In fact, the baby boomers were more likely than the elderly to say that Social Security should provide an adequate standard of living, rather than just a minimum standard.[27]

Moreover, there is little evidence that the baby boomers view Social Security as an obstacle to their own economic opportunity. They know that the program is not a grand savings account, that their taxes go directly into benefits for the current group of retirees. They also know more than older Americans about the payroll tax that finances the program—they know it is high, and that it takes a greater bite of their earnings each year. Yet, most believe the tax is fair, that it "buys" a quality program.

Given a choice of staying with or leaving the Social Security system, three-quarters of the baby boomers would stay. The reason seems to be that the baby boomers recognize their responsibilities to the current generation of retirees. It is not that they see the program as a great long-term investment for their own retirements in the next century—indeed, 75 percent say it is either very or somewhat likely that Social Security payments will not be available when they retire. Rather, they clearly understand the program's importance to keeping their parents and other elderly safe. As the Yankelovich survey concludes, "widespread support derives from beliefs that the demise of Social Security would lead to undesirable consequences, including dependence of some elderly on welfare."

In addition, focus-group discussions held as part of the survey revealed that, for the most part, neither children nor parents wish to live in the same household. As the participants themselves put it: "Older people need their space and we need ours." "The thought of my mother-in-law living with me sends pure fear through me."[28]

This demand for government help to the aged is not likely to abate any time soon. Even now, according to gerontologist Robert Binstock, "Many adult children—aged in their 40s, 50s, and 60s —are confronting intractable dilemmas. Faced with the choices of expending (currently) $25,000 a year for high-quality institutional care, or institutionalizing a parent in a Medicaid warehouse—the 'space age' version of the British Elizabethan poorhouse—or absorbing the economic, psychological, social, and other costs of maintaining a chronically ill person in their own home (perhaps while raising children or sending them to college), they may push strongly for new alternatives."[29]

The final link in the baby-boom agenda is a growing search for individual meaning. "There is a hunger for another kind of experience," Florence Skelly says of the baby boom. "People like to cry a little here and there—to feel things. This group is not impervious to that—but they want it now. They want a big experience, like the 1960s, again."

In their personal lives, the baby boomers seem to want a return to what Yankelovich data characterize as "good old-fashioned romance and happy endings." Indeed, a 1985 Yankelovich survey found that the baby boomers were far ahead of other generations in their feeling that modern life tends to be more routine and dull than life in earlier times, and that life needs more "sparkle and excitement."[30] Their continuing search for meaning may also explain other polls that have found that an overwhelming majority of baby boomers wanted more emphasis on traditional family ties, as well as more respect for authority.[31]

In their political lives, the baby boomers may link the search for meaning to social and economic justice. One example is their concern over South Africa. "The social consciousness that developed in this group in the 1960s has stayed intact," Atwater concludes. "That's why you see issues like South Africa emerging now, as well as the hunger issue and others. This keen social consciousness is unique to this group." Not only are the baby boomers increasingly aware of what apartheid means, they are the most likely to be sympathetic toward the black population in South Africa. They are more likely than older Americans to say the United States should put more pressure on the South African government to end the policy of racial separatism; they are the least approving of Reagan's handling of the issue.[32]

This support for social and economic justice can also be seen at home in baby boom support for the remnants of the Great Society, concern for those in poverty, and support for spending on the cities. Given such concerns, a move toward the right on economic issues may be the worst move the Democrats could make. First, such a move would cut against the concern for fairness among even the successful baby boomers, all of whom responded strongly to the party's 1982 slogan "It's not fair, it's

Republican." Second, a rightward turn on economics would work against the search for economic opportunity among the baby-boom have-nots. At least in 1984, as Ferguson and Rogers argue, "the mistake the Democrats made . . . was not their alleged 'reaching down'—that is, their efforts to expand the electorate through voter-registration drives—but the fact that they did not reach down nearly enough. On economic issues the Democrats offered voters almost nothing in 1984. . . . There is no particular mystery as to why voters, faced with a choice between someone who promised them little besides a rise in taxes and a candidate who at least verbally championed economic growth and lower taxes, deserted Mondale for Reagan or declined to vote at all."[33] As such, economic justice remains a powerful component of the baby-boom agenda.

As for the future, the baby boom's search for meaning might be best tapped by a reemphasis on civilian, not military space policy. Before the shuttle *Challenger* disaster, the baby boomers were among the most supportive of the National Aeronautics and Space Administration (NASA), the most excited by the American presence in space. Even after the accident, and the subsequent revelations about administrative bungling with the NASA bureaucracy, however, almost 90 percent of the baby boomers said that the shuttle program should continue, compared to 71 percent of those over age 50. The limited surveys on space policy suggest that the baby boomers are still captivated by the scientific nature of the NASA program—the space telescope, with its ability to see to the edge of the universe, the missions to Jupiter and beyond, with their brilliant pictures of distant planets, and the possibilities that research in space might hold the answers to problems on earth.

There is also some evidence that the baby boomers are concerned about the militarization of space, as well as the growing use of the shuttle for secret missions. Nevertheless, that seems to be precisely where space policy is headed. As space expert Erasmus

Kloman writes, "Although the 1958 Space Act stressed the civilian nature of the US space programme, the military space budget has grown to over twice the size of NASA's. Military influence on US space policy has grown accordingly."[34] Indeed, looking at current and projected budget figures, the military side of space will be three times as large as the civilian side by 1992. Continued development of Star Wars and anti-satellite weapons assure that the civilian side will be dwarfed.

However, money is not the only problem in civilian space policy. There is a clear lack of leadership for a reinvigorated civilian program. Politicians seem frightened of the price tags, while NASA itself seems torn between programs like the space telescope and a joint American-Soviet mission to Mars—both of which emphasize the peaceful uses of space—and programs like Star Wars and the space station—one of which uses the shuttle as a kind of delivery truck, and the other which envisions a giant industrial park in space.

To the extent that space policy is guided by the search for new knowledge or adventure, it will receive strong baby-boom support. To the extent that it is used to find opportunities for cooperation between the two superpowers, it may generate renewed baby-boom enthusiasm. However, to the extent space emerges as a new superpower battleground, the baby boom's fear of war and lingering distrust of the military will come into play, and support for NASA and the civilian program will continue to wither.

The preceding agenda, with its emphasis on opportunity, safety, and meaning, holds at least some hope for engaging the baby boomers in their political future. However, the issues the agenda includes are not new issues for American politics. Indeed, many are old staples (e.g., trade, Social Security, and space). But, what makes this agenda different is that it frames those issues in baby-boom values. While baby boomers don't have a unique hold on the search for opportunity, safety, or meaning, given their political separation, they may be more comfortable putting seemingly contradictory issues together—like support for both abortion and a return to respect for authority.

The question is whether the parties or candidates are willing or able to use this baby-boom agenda. The parties, for example, could go in one of two ways: they could either ignore the baby-boom agenda completely, continuing to play short-term politics, or they could drop significant parts of their current platforms in the effort to reconcile the New Deal or Reagan revolution with the baby-boom agenda. On the one hand, the Democrats would have to strengthen their economic opportunity agenda, and answer the Star Wars issue. On the other hand, the Republicans would have to abandon their social agenda, and address the public health and safety plank.

In the short term at least, the two parties may find it easier to stay put—Republicans hoping for elections based on economic opportunity issues; Democrats wishing for campaigns centered on threats to personal freedoms perhaps. The baby-boom agenda just does not carry the kind of controversy that realigns parties. For example, James Sundquist argues that a realignment of the parties based on the conservative social agenda is unlikely. "Separately, no one of the crosscutting issues is sufficient. . . . Together, they do not cluster well. Initially, they divide into two distinct issues complexes—social and moral questions, and military and foreign policy questions—that cut across the electorate in different directions. And each of these is diffuse, made up of somewhat separable, discrete issues that engage different individuals and groups with varying degrees of intensity. Collectively, they may at times be powerful enough to dominate political debate—one of the necessary qualities of a realigning issue—but not with the simplicity and clarity necessary to polarize the community, which is another of the required attributes."[35]

Indeed, the baby boomers have not felt much passion toward any issue lately, let alone the kind of intensity that forces a party realignment. Thus does their political separation work against their long-term interests. Unlike the Great Depression realignment of the 1930s, or the pre–Civil War realignment of the 1850s, the issues on the baby-boom agenda have yet to provoke a great outcry from the public, young or old alike.

Moreover, in times of poor economic performance, social issues fade in importance. "For most people, moral causes are something to indulge in when times are prosperous and inflation is held within the bounds of tolerance," Sundquist concludes. "But when the economy is sick, those issues must be put aside. For the jobless and the anxious and those whose incomes have not kept pace with the cost of living, a political party that concentrates its energies on moral questions is a useless instrument; morals then are something for the churches to worry about, while restoring economic prosperity and stability become perforce the overriding responsibility of government."[36]

If the parties are unlikely to adopt the baby-boom agenda, perhaps one or more candidates will. As Peter Hart predicts, the nation is about to jump a generation in political leaders: "If you look at the people who have governed this country for the last quarter century—all come from the same era, and the seminal event in their lifetime was the Depression." As an older generation of leaders retires from service, they will be replaced by a younger corps who know nothing of the Depression, whose major life experiences came in the post-war period.

Yet, these candidates will have to be more than just young to claim baby-boom support. In 1984, as pollster Hart remembers, "We asked voters how much a candidate who 'is a younger person who stresses that it is time for a new generation of leadership and who is known for seeking fresh solutions to America's problem' appealed to them. This description of Gary Hart in July of 1983 showed us that he was potentially a strong candidate and underlined the potentiality of the 'future' dynamic. As the campaign developed, Walter Mondale became the candidate of the present and Gary Hart the candidate of the future."

Youth alone was not enough, however. Otherwise, Mondale, not Reagan, would have received the lion's share of the baby boom's votes in the fall. Rather, the secret was in becoming the candidate of the future. Hart was seen as bringing a fresh perspective to the policy debate, willing to try out nontraditional solutions to the nation's problems. Though Mondale was able to shake that image to a certain extent with his "Where's the Beef?" ads, Hart attracted the baby boomers precisely because he fit their nontraditional approach to politics. Unfortunately for Hart, the more the baby boomers probed his new ideas, the less they found. He was unable to deliver the substance to fit the style.

Thus, the way to engage the baby boomers is not just to be young nor just to have a good slogan. It involves leadership and communication. It involves both what the baby boomers want and what they need. As political scientist V.O. Key wrote, "The voice of the people is but an echo. The output of an echo chamber bears an inevitable and invariable relation to the input."[37] If the parties and candidates make promises they cannot keep, the baby boomers will remain very much a short-term electorate, demanding immediate rewards for their votes.

Ultimately, the baby-boom agenda presented above deals with the problems of today. The baby-boom agenda presented in the next chapter deals with the problems of tomorrow. The question is simple: will the baby boom be remembered as a generation of self-absorption and instant gratification or a generation of stewardship and commitment to the future? If the baby boomers are to take their place as the stewards of the future, they are going to have learn to be patient, and in a hurry.

8

The Golden Days

ALL GENERATIONS have their golden days. For the baby boom's grandparents, the golden days came in the 1920s; for the baby boom's parents, the 1950s and early 1960s; and for the baby boom itself, they will come in the 1990s. Most baby boomers will be working, many will finally own their own homes, and many will have children. Those who want an intergenerational accounting between young and old should wait until the 2000s. The baby boom's best decade is supposed to be just around the corner. Already, the Social Security system is showing the surpluses that the baby boom's full employment can bring to government coffers.

All generations also have their days of crisis. For the baby boom's grandparents, those days came with the Great Depression of the 1930s and World War II; for the baby boom's parents, it occurred in the late 1960s and early 1970s. Unfortunately, for the baby boomers, their golden days and the days of crisis appear to be coming at the same time. The 1990s threaten to bring a health-care crisis for the baby boom's parents and, therefore, for their children. Continued crowding in the labor force threatens to bring a slowdown in promotions for the baby boom itself, forcing a reevaluation of what it means to have a successful career. And the

continued deterioration of the nation's infrastructure and environment threatens to bring a crisis for the baby boom's own offspring,
which may someday raise the question of how well the baby boom
performed as a steward, or protector, of the nation's resources.

Luckily, these are all solvable crises. The question is not whether the nation can provide affordable health care for the elderly,
new job opportunities for baby boomers in mid-career, or the
renewal of rusting infrastructure and overcrowded national parks,
as well as answers to the hazardous waste problem.

Rather, the question is whether the baby boomers have the
patience to tackle these problems with the kind of energy and
commitment that is necessary. These are not the kinds of problems
that can be fixed overnight. If the baby boomers expect quick
results, they will be disappointed. Patience, diligence, commitment, self-sacrifice, endurance, and forbearance are the values that
the baby boomers must bring to the 1990s to ensure that those
years become the golden days the generation deserves. If they
press for instant returns, they will emerge from this century having wasted their potential to make their homes, communities, and
nation better places to live.

The answer depends in part on whether the baby boomers are
willing to settle for something less than self-perfection, and
whether they can find personal redemption in contributing to
community. Are the baby boomers ready to let go of the Me
Decade?

Philosopher Peter Marin was the first one to caricature the
baby boom's introspection as the "new narcissism." "A broad
retrenchment is going on," he wrote in 1975, "a pervasive and
perhaps unconscious shift in values—not only on a national level
but in the moral definitions and judgments we make as individuals."[1]

Marin was particularly critical of the human potential movement and its new psychological therapies that he said "provide
their adherents with a way to avoid the demands of the world, to
smother the tug of conscience. They allow them to remain who

and what they are, to accept the structure of the world as it is—but with a new sense of justice and justification, with the assurance that it all accords with the cosmic law." In describing Werner Erhard and EST, Marin created the dominant caricature of the 1970s—the solitary baby boomer in search of a new psyche, willing to pay $250 to be stuffed into a room full of hundreds of other sweating, crying, yelling, regressing, and rebirthing solitary baby boomers, willing to be jammed into a weekend-long encounter session, and forced to endure full-day psychological batterings without even a break to go the bathroom.

The rise of charismatic leaders like Erhard, L. Ron Hubbard, and Sun Myung Moon, reflected what Marin called "the growing solipsism and desperation of a beleaguered class, the world view emerging among us centered solely on the self and with individual survival as its sole good. . . . a retreat from the worlds of morality and history, an unembarrassed denial of human reciprocity and community . . . the desire to defend ourselves against the demands of conscience and the world through an ethic designed to defuse them both. . . . What disappears in this view of things is the ground of community, the felt sense of collective responsibility for the fate of each separate other. What takes its place is a moral vacuum in which others are trapped forever in a 'private' destiny, doomed to whatever befalls them. In that void the traditional measures of justice or good vanish completely. The self replaces community, relation, neighbor, chance, or God. Looming larger every moment, it obliterates everything around it that might have offered it a way out of its pain." It was Tom Wolfe who captured this narcissism as the Me Decade.[2]

Yet, it is important to remember that the Me Decade began in the aftermath of Vietnam and with the rejection of traditional social and political labels. People became more aware of individual differences, more tolerant of others, more likely to seek help when they got into trouble. The Me Decade was not all negative. As Joseph Veroff, Elizabeth Douvan, and Richard Kulka wrote in

1980, it is one thing to note the increasing social fragmentation and introspection, quite another to generalize from the tiny numbers in EST to an entire generation. "Facts are observed correctly. The divorce rate has increased; women have left families in order to realize their individual talents or needs; the best-seller lists are dominated by books on self-improvement, personal growth, narcissistic preoccupation. But the facts are then interpreted too broadly, accorded a centrality and power in the broad population which they may in fact hold only for a part, for a highly articulate, 'leading,' powerful subgroup—but a subgroup all the same."[3]

While there were baby boomers who were absorbed in self-indulgence and perfection, there were so many more who were merely seeking to break free of the old traditions. Some of the search for self-knowledge was and is destructive. Yet, some was healthy. Witness the baby boom's rejection of race and creed as a basis for judging an individual's value; witness its tolerance for those who do not fit traditional stereotypes. Surely no one wants to return to the social straightjackets of the 1950s?

It is also important to remember that the Me Decade was in part the result of the baby boom's search for meaning. The fact that the search was perverted in some cases does not mean it was always negative or that it cannot be redirected even now toward a new political and social community. What the narcissist critiques ignored, as psychologist Paul Wachtel wrote in 1981, "is that these movements did begin with a moral impulse, however much they may have subsequently strayed. In the 1960s, concern with self-awareness and personal growth reflected a rejection of the materialism that was seen as the basis for a social system that oppressed its minorities and wrought havoc around the globe. Today, this psychological and therapeutic emphasis continues to represent (at least potentially) an alternative to dominant values that point toward productivity instead of experience; that tell us that we can't 'afford' social programs though we somehow still can afford new cars, gadgets and weapons; and that painfully push us to scrape raw our body politic against the rough edges of limited energy, toxic pollution and misordered priorities which require us to make things we don't need in order to provide jobs."[4]

There is no question that the baby boomers once felt a duty to get in touch with themselves, as Florence Skelly says, "Now that is unique. Instead of looking outside for cues, they looked inside. In fact, if you didn't know if you were happy every moment, and didn't ask yourself every day, you weren't fulfilling your responsibility as a human being." However, as people grow older, they have less energy to look inside. They become more comfortable with who and what they are. As the baby boomers move into the middle range of the life cycle, they may be more willing to look outward for meaning, if not to the traditions of the 1950s and early 1960s then perhaps to expanding networks of peers and friends, and possibly a sense of national community.

There is no doubt that the introspective style puts tremendous pressure on individuals to define and redefine themselves. As the authors of *Habits of the Heart* suggest, "if selves are defined by their preferences, but those preferences are arbitrary, then each self constitutes its own moral universe, and there is finally no way to reconcile conflicting claims about what is good in itself. All we can do is refer to chains of consequences and ask if actions prove useful or consistent in light of our own 'value-systems.'"[5] The constant demand for self-audit, as Yankelovich calls it, is exhausting, and may eventually force individuals to streamline their decisions, separating those demanding personal attention from those better made in the context of a family, community, or nation.

Ultimately, no one, no matter how self-confident and well-educated, can handle the pressure to make every decision on the basis of inner-knowledge. Indeed, there is increasing evidence that the baby boomers are growing weary. "There's something frightening about all this strategic thinking," Skelly says of the baby boomers, "because there's no commitment to what's right, only to what works—and I think if you look back in history, there's a lot of evidence that, while America may not always do the right things, Americans are very concerned about being moral. There's something like an *American character* and it's just as powerful in this group."

Finally, if ever a generation needed patience and a commitment to the long-term and community, it is the baby boom. The baby boomers face problems that are neither easily nor quickly fixed. Without a willingness to defer instant returns, the baby boomers are likely to be very frustrated in the coming three decades and beyond.

In the near term, the baby boomers face a series of problems which demand forbearance. Consider job plateaus, infrastructure renewal, and care-giving to the elderly as three examples.

The baby boomers will certainly need patience to handle their emerging problem with job plateaus. Because of their sheer numbers, there is less room at the top, indeed in the middle. More and more baby boomers will be trapped in dead-end jobs, or waiting ever longer for promotions. They will spend more time on each plateau up the promotion climb. They will need to redefine what it means to be successful, be more willing to wait in line for upward movement, and learn to deal with the frustrations of being left behind. It is the most serious personnel issue facing United States business in the 1980s and 1990s, according to Arch Patton, a former McKinsey and Company management consultant. Baby boomers face "the virtual certainty that the promotion rate will fall dramatically. Executives are likely to stay on the job longer, because they cannot afford to retire; at the same time, the number of candidates for their jobs will expand at the highest rate ever."[6]

The facts seem clear. During the past decade, according to the Bureau of Labor Statistics, the number of people aged 35 to 44 has increased roughly twice as fast as available management jobs. According to Anthony Carnevale, chief economist of the American Society for Training and Development, the "leading edge of the baby boom has just turned 40 and won't be retiring for another 30 years. Over that period of time, employers will face a curious demographic twist in their internal labor markets."[7]

On the one hand, there will be fewer younger workers to fill the entry-level jobs. The baby bust which is following the baby boom, will be able to demand a higher wage for the jobs they take, and many jobs will go wanting. On the other hand, there will be fewer mid-level jobs to accommodate the advancing baby boomers. As a result, there will be tremendous internal pressure for older workers to move out of the way. Putting the two trends together, the baby boomers will clearly be spending more time in the same jobs before advancing while facing competition at their heels from the baby busters.

Expectations may have to change within the baby boom. Given their higher levels of education, the baby boomers are more likely than other generations to demand self-development in their jobs. And that means new challenges and opportunities, not just money. For a generation accustomed to moving quickly, the plateaus will be difficult indeed. For those who thought their years in college would pay off with rapid upward mobility, this new employment reality will be a profound disappointment. "Unfortunately, the baby-boom group enjoyed unusually rapid promotion rates during the 1970s and therefore entered this decade with very high expectations," Patton says. "Cooling the expectation level will require time and innovative modes by top management."

Unfortunately, the plateaus exist as far as the eye can see. There are only so many top jobs in America, and many will be occupied by those born just before the baby boom or those at the very front end of the generation itself. The baby boomers are going to have to redefine their timetables for success. "In America, the notion of success is heavily oriented toward a linear career path," says business professor Kenneth Brousseau. "The common belief is that the only good move is a move upward. If you stay where you are or if, God help you, you take a position at a lower level, you are quickly seen as a failure."

How will the baby boomers react to the plateaus? Brousseau warns of more stress, more burnout, more psychological withdrawal. One recent study suggests that plateaued workers tend to either withdraw from their jobs entirely or spend more time thinking about home or leisure.[8] The resulting "on-the-job-retirement" is hardly the answer to the United States competitiveness problem.

The plateaus are already creating a new language among personnel experts. They talk about downward mobility and ways of easing the pain of demotions. Indeed, according to organizational psychologists Douglas Hall and Lynn Isabella, there are at least seven ways a baby boomer can tell whether he or she is on the way down:

1) The downward promotion
2) The lateral demotion with a salary cut
3) The lateral demotion without a salary cut
4) The temporary step-down
5) The later-career move away from the front lines
6) The demotion as an alternative to being fired
7) The demotion for plain old incompetence[9]

No matter how a corporation says it, a demotion is not a promotion. Nor is a termination. No matter how many ways a corporation does it, hundreds of thousands of baby boomers are going to be told they are washed up in coming years.

Already the plateaus and downward mobility are evident. Just before Christmas, 1986, AT&T fired 25,000 mid-level managers, most of them baby boomers. Ford Motor Company hopes to cut 9,000 mid-level workers over the coming five years. Eastman Kodak has a hiring freeze on at its mid-level ranks. "There is a good deal of cost and overhead in the middle-management, and it's being squeezed from two directions," says D. Quinn Mills, a Harvard Business School professor. "The first is the competition both domestically and internationally—companies simply can't afford to carry people who don't directly contribute to the bottom line. The second is that it's become increasingly clear that, if they reorganize, they can push middle-management functions lower down into the work force and save a good deal of money. I think companies are going to continue to seek to reduce the number of employees they have. . . ."

Moreover, the baby boom's bad economic luck seems to be continuing in a new bottom-line management philosophy. Says Edward Mazze, dean of the Temple University School of Business Administration, "although economic conditions have improved, American business in general is staying lean and mean. Two or three managers are being asked to do jobs that took at least five in the past. Foreign competition and the fast-changing economic climate have kept corporations from 'staffing up.' " And just which age band of workers is most likely to suffer in such a climate? Why the baby boomers of course.

The plateauing problem is most severe in no-growth industries. Public-sector employment is a prime example. After growing from seven million in 1955 to a peak of almost 17 million in 1980, federal, state, and local employment had fallen back to 15 million by the mid 1980s. As public management expert James Wolf writes, "it is impossible to avoid the conclusion that baby-boom demographics and the public employment bust will severely constrict career opportunities in the public sector. The obvious, and perhaps most damaging, consequence will be the number of plateaued public employees whose potential for movement into positions in the organizational hierarchy will be severely limited. Opportunities for career success, as currently defined by title, status, and bigger paycheck will diminish."[10] Again, even though baby boomers are less likely to care about title and status, they do care about the opportunity to grow. And those opportunities are clearly constrained by job plateaus and downward mobility.

The plateauing is growing in the private sector, too. Growth in the computer industry is flat, academia is tenured-up, the automobile industry is looking for cuts, the health-care industry is consolidating. In an era of mega-mergers, corporations are staying lean, both as a way to free capital for takeover defenses and as a signal to stockholders that management means business. Profit margins are tight, and middle-management ranks are an attractive target for quick cost savings. Peter Van Hull, an automobile industry expert predicts that overall employment will fall five percent a year through 1990, and most of the cuts will be at the mid-level or in clerical staffs. "There is a view that middle-management and clerical groups are involved in work that doesn't add value to the product. They tend to become self-perpetuating bureaucracies. In international competition, jobs that don't add value to the product are not needed."

The baby boomers will also have to deal with America's rapidly deteriorating public infrastructure—the roads, bridges, rails, dams, underground storage tanks, sewers, water treatment plants, and pipes that are the hidden underpinning of America's economy. Indeed, the decaying infrastructure may be the single greatest threat to the baby boom's economic future. Having neglected the repairs in a two-decade binge of short-term cost savings—if the infrastructure ain't yet broke, why maintain it?—the bills are now coming due.

Infrastructure may be the dullest topic on the national agenda, but it is important nonetheless. The baby boomers may not yet understand the term, but they will be spending plenty of time waiting for repairs in the coming years. And they already hit the potholes every day. Given the state of the nation's roads and highways, one thing is absolutely clear: the baby boomers will be wasting away their days in future traffic jams. "Rebuilding the nation's public infrastructure," says economist Pat Choate, "promises to be the single most expensive government challenge of the 1980s and 1990s."

The 42,500-mile interstate highway system, for example, stands as a remarkable public achievement, a testament to the optimism of the 1950s and early 1960s. By the early 1980s, according to Pat Choate and Susan Walter, the highways were deteriorating at a rate of 2,000 miles per year. "Because adequate funding for rehabilitation and reconstruction was not forthcoming in the late 1970s, over 8,000 miles of this system and 13 percent of its bridges are now beyond their designed service life and must be rebuilt."[11]

Yet, maintenance is easier said than funded. It is the easiest thing to cut in times of tight budgets. Just delay it another year —or at least until a chunk of bridge falls in Connecticut. The title of Choate and Walter's book may say it all: *America in Ruins*. By the early 1980s, as many as a third of the nation's 1.5 million underground storage tanks were leaking gasoline or chemicals, threatening many community wells and aquifers.

By any calculation, the infrastructure problem is huge and growing. It cannot be solved on an ad hoc basis. According to a 1984 report for the Joint Economic Committee of Congress, it will take over one trillion dollars to just maintain and rebuild the national infrastructure between now and the year 2000, to say nothing of the cost of new development. As the report concludes, "the immediate and projected infrastructure needs are considerable, and the gap between capital expenditures and capital needs is growing." Under current estimates, the government will fall roughly $400 billion short.[12] Unless the baby boomers are willing to tolerate closed bridges, detours, rough highways, and unreliable water supplies, the infrastructure repairs must be made. It may not be as exciting as a mission to Mars perhaps, but it is part of the responsibility of their stewardship.

The infrastructure problem is analogous to a host of other environmental challenges. The national parks are in disrepair, new hazardous waste sites are leaking faster than the old sites can be cleaned up, and nuclear waste continues to pile up waiting designation of a national storage facility. None of these are one-time problems either. Once the parks are restored, they will need care—the baby boomers are visiting in record numbers. Once the hazardous waste is contained it must be monitored. Once the nuclear waste is stored it will stay hot for generations.

The baby boomers will have to be careful. Very careful. Take nuclear waste as an example. According to investigative reporters

Donald Bartlett and James Steele, "Nuclear waste will be stored for up to a century—if not forever—in some two hundred cities and towns throughout the country. Chunks of real estate will be rendered permanently uninhabitable in some states and placed off limits for much of the twenty-first century in others. Tens of billions of dollars will be spent to correct mistakes of the past and present, a massive financial burden that future generations will have to bear."[13] Not only will the baby boomers be responsible for stewardship of the nation's infrastructure, they will be responsible for its waste.

The baby boomers may have no other choice but to accept the responsibility for these future problems. How this single genera- tion manages its economic and social progress over the next dec- ade will determine whether future generations inherit a land of spent resources or a renewed economic infrastructure. Whether in cleaning up the nation's waste dumps or protecting America's reservoir of natural resources, the baby boomers face a choice: either continue their search for short-term gratification or make a long-term commitment to preserving something for future gener- ations.

The baby boomers will also need patience to cope with their care-giving responsibilities to the nation's dependent elderly. The good news is that America's elderly are more independent than ever, living longer, staying healthy for a larger proportion of their lives. With Social Security available as a source of income and Medicare as a bulwark against illness, poverty has fallen dramati- cally among those over 65. And so has mortality. Indeed, geron- tologists now talk of several different groups among the aged—the young-old, generally from 65 to 75 years old, who are vital and active, and the old-old, generally over 75 years old, who are more likely to be disabled and in need of intense care.

The bad news is that the elderly still become disabled, with all that means for the decline in their quality of life. "People are undoubtably living more healthy years," says Jacob Brody, of the National Institute of Aging, "but the problem is they are living more unhealthy ones, too." And most of the care given during those unhealthy years comes from American families, not nursing homes or hospitals.

The baby boomers have not yet faced much of a care-giving burden for their parents and grandparents. Because their parents were so young when the baby boomers were born, many of them are just now entering retirement. Moreover, most projections suggest that they will stay healthy and energetic through their first 15 to 20 years of retirement, entering a time of increasing illness and vulnerability only toward the end of the second decade. By 85 years of age or so the elderly reach "a kind of turnaround point," says policy analyst Elizabeth Kutza. "After that, the problems come faster: How healthy will I be? Who is going to be around to take care of me? How do I keep the income stream going?"

The facts on the increasing number of elderly dependents are clear. In 1900, one in twenty-five Americans was over age 65. By 1950, one in twelve. By 1985, one in nine. It is no secret why the increase has occurred. As *Wall Street Journal* reporter Alan Otten writes, "the current surge in the ranks of the oldest old stems primarily from the increased numbers of children born and surviving in the late nineteenth and early twentieth centuries, and secondarily from declining deaths from epidemics, heart attacks, strokes, and other diseases that used to kill people in youth or middle age."[14] Whereas there were 12 million elderly in 1950, there are now 28 million. People now survive the heart attacks, accidents, strokes, and cancers that once would have killed them.

These new survival rates have a number of obvious impacts. First, children can expect their parents and grandparents to live longer. According to a population model developed by demographer Jane Menken, the number of women who could expect to reach age 50 with their mothers still alive jumped from 37 percent in 1940 to 65 percent in 1980. As Menken writes, "It is indeed new to human experience that a large majority of fifty-year-olds would still have living mothers. . . . we can expect that a lot of them would still have mothers-in-law as well—or, given divorce rates, ex-mothers-in-law." The number of years a child could expect to spend with at least one parent over age 65 increased from thirteen years in 1940 to nineteen years in 1980.[15]

Second, the survival rates also imply a changing menu of illness from acute disease to chronic infirmity, from life-threatening crisis to long-term impairment. As more elderly survive to their eighties, more will require care. As Elaine Brody of the Philadelphia Geriatric Center says, it is in this population of the old-old that one finds "most of the million and more who are so disabled that they require round-the-clock care in nursing homes, the two million who are equally disabled but who are not in institutions, and many of the six million more who require less intensive services."

Much of the care that will be given to the oldest-old in the next century will come from baby boomers. And it is likely to be hard work. Consider the current care-giving network as one scenario of just what the baby boomers will be asked to do in coming years. According to authors of the most comprehensive study to date, most of the nation's care-givers are female, with adult daughters providing almost one-third of the long-term care. "Three-quarters of the care-givers live with the care recipient and the majority provide assistance seven days a week. They spend an average of four extra hours per day on caregiving activities."[16] It is no small task.

For the daughters now providing care for elderly parents, one-quarter have competing family obligations. Although less than 10 percent have quit their jobs to provide these levels of care, the study concludes that "a sizable proportion of female and male caregivers have had to rearrange their schedules, reduce their work hours and/or take time off without pay to fulfill caregiver obligations." Further, a third of all care provided today is given by people already over age 65 themselves, whether the "young-old" caring for an older spouse or parent, or the old-old caring for a husband or wife. Sooner or later, that burden will pass on to the baby boomers.

Because such care is almost entirely voluntary, it requires great compassion and commitment. Because it is so often given to those who are frustrated with their own incapacity, it requires great patience. Because it is so intensive, it creates great stress. According to gerontologist Pamela Doty, this stress may be particularly acute for adult children who are called upon to care for an aging parent. Compared to elderly spouses who are called upon to care for a disabled husband or wife care-givers who "show a strong tendency to maintain care-giving whatever the social/emotional costs and stop only when deterioration in their own health physically prevents them from providing the services," adult children "appear to have a lower tolerance for stress, especially continued high stress over time."[17]

Part of the lower tolerance for stress may reflect the fact that sons and daughters often have competing responsibilities both at home and at work. They are more likely to have children and spouses of their own to care for, and are more likely to be employed in either full- or part-time work. Finding an extra four hours a day is simply more difficult.

Part may also come from the rising baby-boom divorce rates. As Peter Morrison suggests, divorce creates ambiguity about who is responsible for whom. "To what extent is a father responsible for both his natural children and his stepchildren? What if the stepfather of his natural children is far more prosperous? Should a stepdaughter be held responsible for the support of a needy stepmother? To cite a familiar example, laws requiring the children of Medicaid recipients to help pay for their parents' nursing home care have touched off intense debate over such 'family responsibility' laws: Which parents? What children? To what extent? And why?"

Finally, part of the lower tolerance for the stress of care-giving may come from the baby boom's short-term focus. Having been able to easily separate from traditional roles in the past, some baby boomers may find it hard to commit to the kind of intense care-giving that their parents may someday need. Nevertheless, stressful or not, America relies on the family to provide long-term care for the elderly. The nursing care beds simply do not exist. Moreover, as the baby boomers themselves reach retirement, they will find that their care-giving responsibilities to husbands and wives, perhaps past and future, will also increase. With current longevity projections, it is entirely possible that the baby boomers will reach retirement with care-giving responsibilities to aging parents and to aging spouses.

Perhaps some of the fortitude and patience baby boomers will need can come from a commitment to their children. By making a commitment to future generations, the baby boomers may be able to find the will and endurance to deal with their own problems.

There is little doubt that America's children could use the baby boom's help. There is no doubt that baby-boom divorce rates have made childhood a very uncertain experience. Whereas only 19 percent of the baby boomers born in 1950–54 saw their parents split up, as many as two-thirds of the children born in 1980–84 will see their parents divorce. "With more children being born to unmarried couples and to couples whose marriages subsequently dissolve," Morrison says. "Children increasingly live with only one parent (typically the mother). . . . Nontraditional (single-parent) families are becoming more common, and traditional families are not enduring as long as they once did. Proportionally more children than before will be spending some part of their childhood in a single-parent or blended family." That does not mean these children will be somehow maladjusted or unhappy. But it does suggest that they may be more in need of financial and emotional support.

In addition, whatever their needs for support, children have been on the budget chopping block for almost a decade. Writing

in 1986, social policy experts Harold Richman and Matthew Stagner report: "The percentage of children in poverty today is one-
and-a-half times the percentage of all people in poverty. Our
unemployment rate for youths ages sixteen to nineteen is nearly
three times greater than the unemployment rate for adults over age
twenty. And while the adult suicide rate has declined, the suicide
rate for children has risen dramatically over the last twenty-five
years."[18]

One reason children are so easy to ignore in the policy-making
process is that they have no one to lobby on their behalf in Washington. Unfortunately, as politicians search for ways to trim budgets, children's programs are easy targets. According to Madeleine
Kimmich, of the Urban Institute, recent cutbacks in children's
programs have slashed both the quantity and quality of services.
"Where do we go from here? Which promises to our children will
we keep? The problems of income, education, employment, and
family functioning cannot be adequately handled piecemeal and
through crisis intervention; many believe that there must be a
national mandate, a service agenda to enlist the aid of both the
public and the private sectors." Perhaps the baby boomers can take
the lead, not only as parents of young children themselves, but as
stewards of the future.

The answer is not to be found in artificial trade-offs between
programs for the young versus those for the aged. Children need
not benefit only at the expense of the elderly. As Alan Pifer notes,
"Such a tradeoff is hardly necessary, since the few billions needed
to broaden the support of children could, if the will were there,
certainly be found in a wealthy nation such as ours, without
seriously penalizing the elderly."[19] Moreover, the notion that children can only rise if the elderly fall ignores the potential for cuts
elsewhere, including the defense budget. "Add it all up on the
domestic side and make sure we get our share," groups like Americans for Generational Equity (AGE) seem to say in defining
intergenerational equity in the narrowest terms possible. In fact,
the intergenerational equity argument may be the ultimate in

short-term politics. Instead of asking how the nation can help the young and old alike, AGE seeks an immediate accounting and restructuring, no matter how costly in the long run.

Ultimately, the baby boomers have ample cause to care about the all the nation's young. If not out of love and compassion for their own children, perhaps out of long-term self-interest. According to Pifer, the most powerful case for investing in children "is that the nation will be enormously dependent on them as prime-aged workers when the baby-boom generation begins leaving the work force two or three decades from now. Because of the demographic twist of a period of exceptionally high fertility being followed by a sustained period of low fertility, today's and tomorrow's children promise to be the most heavily burdened generation in the nation's history. On their small numbers will depend the vitality of the economy, the defense of the nation, and the support of the elderly and children of that time."[20]

Ironically, the baby-boom divorce rates may someday haunt the generation. "The majority of today's young children will, at some stage of their youth, become distanced from the economic support and care of one of their natural parents," says Morrison, thereby eroding the kinds of family connections Americans have long relied upon for care-giving. "Filial, parental, and grandparental responsibilities will become more complex and open to legal dispute as reconstituted families (containing stepchildren, half-siblings, and stepparents) become more prevalent."

At the very least, however, perhaps the baby boomers can be interested in making the kinds of public investments today that will provide the wherewithal for future generations to help the baby boomers tomorrow. If the baby boomers cannot earn their children's compassion, perhaps they can earn their respect. Without their children's help, the baby boomers face a very rough retirement indeed.

9

2016

MOST BABY BOOMERS could not care less about the year 2016. It is just a year in the distant future. Yet, two things make the year very significant. It is the year the baby boom will turn 70 years old, marking the beginning of a huge retirement wave. Assuming current fertility rates hold, by the year 2030 one out of every fifth American will be over age 65.

It is also the year the baby boomers will celebrate a half century of political participation. It will be their thirteenth presidential election. By 2016, the baby boomers will have cast on the order of 700 million votes.

For now, 2016 is not very important to the baby boomers. They are still in their first jobs, their first marriages, and changing the diapers on their first children. Nevertheless, unless the baby boomers start paying at least some attention to the future, 2016 may herald the beginning of a 20-year social and economic crisis. Unfortunately, by allowing politicians to exploit their short-term focus, baby boomers are making key choices today that may make their retirements difficult at best tomorrow. The average baby boomer may not be thinking much about the future, but it is coming nonetheless. If the baby boomers continue on their present course, the 2016 election may bring the intergenerational conflict many worry about in the present—not between the baby boomers and their parents, but between the baby boomers and their own children.

If current projections hold true, the baby boomers will be asking a lot from their kids. Today, there are roughly twenty people over age 65 for every 100 adults under 65. By 2030, the ratio of old to young will nearly double—to forty people over age 65 for every 100 adults under. In cold economic terms, there are roughly five workers to cover every Social Security beneficiary today, but there will be only 2.5 when the baby boomers are fully retired in the year 2030. The baby boomers may discover that they need more than self-development to survive. Born in an era of unlimited opportunity, they may find themselves isolated and alone.

The question, as Ebeneezer Scrooge once put it, is whether this is the future that will be or just one of several futures that may be. The answer depends entirely on what the baby boomers do in the decades leading up to 2016. Will they wake up in time?

If they stay on their present path, the baby boomers may finally be held accountable for their lack of stewardship. If they remain disengaged from the political process, voting only on the basis of "what-have-you-done-for-me-lately" promises, the baby boomers will drift toward retirement with little to show for their once great potential but a social and economic crisis. Having gone it alone throughout their working lives, they will go it alone in old age, spending their last years jammed into crowded retirement homes and hospitals, looking for one-on-one comfort that may never come.

For now, this is just one future that might be. There is still time for the baby boomers to create a different outcome. Lost in the baby-boom caricatures is a portrait of the generation's great potential for public good. Lost in the search for individual achievement is a tolerance and commitment to social justice. Lost in the focus on instant gratification is a possible commitment to stewardship.

The baby boomers still have great possibilities, not as some great political monolith, but as a collection of individuals, each willing to give at least something to the future. If these baby boomers accept their role as stewards of the future, if they begin to invest as much attention in selecting their presidents as they invest in buying their cars, if they start voting on the basis of "what-will-you-do-for-the-nation-tomorrow" promises, their children and grandchildren should be more than willing to shoulder the burden for the baby boom's retirement.

Obviously, no one can be sure what will happen over the next fifty years. Indeed, as Thomas Espenshade says of demographic forecasting, "most economists project a quarter or two ahead, or maybe a couple of years. That's a piece of cake for demographers. Our problem is we're trying to project to 2020."

Nevertheless, the baby boomers appear to face two very different futures. One is rosy, dominated by economic growth and intergenerational compassion. The other is dark, plagued by economic stagnation and the erosion of family care-giving networks.

The two futures contain very different images of the 2016 election. One sees more than enough children to support the baby boomers in retirement, more than enough economic growth to provide investment income and adequate pensions. Social Security looks fine far into the next century, and the Medicare program maintains its health. The 2016 election is not much different from any other presidential election. The second scenario shows too few children being born and too little economic growth to keep pensions even with inflation. Medicare collapses in the late 1990s, with Social Security gone around 2020. The 2016 election becomes a referendum on Social Security tax increases with the aging baby boomers aligned against their children, and with the have-nots within the baby boom fighting against the haves.

One might expect the Democrats to be the most pessimistic about the baby boom's future. After all, they have been gloomy for almost a decade. Wasn't it Mondale who promised the tax increase? Aren't the Democrats the party of sacrifice?

One might also expect the Republicans to be the most optimistic about the baby boom's future. After all, they have been celebrating the Morning in America for almost eight years now. Wasn't it Reagan who promised the balanced budget by 1984? Aren't the Republicans the party of economic growth?

In fact, the parties are exactly the opposite of where one would expect them to be. Democrats are the party of long-term optimism, predicting more than enough fertility and economic growth to cover the baby boom's retirement, while Republicans are the party of long-term pessimism, predicting gloom-and-doom for the future. The reason has less to do with good long-term forecasting than with short-term politics. Republicans have been looking for ways to cut Social Security for years, using pessimistic long-term projections to sell benefit cuts to the public, all the while undermining baby-boom confidence in the program's future. In defending against those proposals, Democrats have been using optimistic long-term forecasts to calm the panic, even if they ignore problems which might be better addressed now rather than later.

Because forecasting the future involves both political and technical judgments, and because it is so difficult to predict what kind of society will exist fifty years from now, it is hard to know just which future is most likely. That is one reason why Social Security forecasters do not assign probabilities to their estimates. At best, they can only create scenarios of the future, of what tomorrow might bring. Then it is up to policy makers to decide just how much they care about preventing one scenario or encouraging another. As such, all futures are possible, if only because, as Eric Kingson, Barbara Hirshorn, and John Cornman write, policy makers have the tools to shape the future.

Monetary and fiscal decisions can significantly affect the economy of the future. Workers can be encouraged or discouraged to stay in the labor force past what are today the early and normal retirement ages. Changes are already scheduled in Social Security—including liberalizations of the delayed retirement credit and the earnings test, and the gradual increase in the eligibility age for full retirement benefits—that will encourage increased work effort among the elderly. Tax policies that encourage firms to offer early and very early retirement options in their private pension plans could also be changed, and several incentives could be developed to encourage private employers to offer part-time employment opportunities to elderly workers. Moreover, encouraging research for prevention and treatment of chronic conditions such as Alzheimer's disease, other dementing illnesses, osteoporosis, osteoarthritis, and urinary incontinence is likely to both reduce the anticipated rate of increase in future public and private expenditures needed to treat these debilitating conditions and to improve the quality of life for the children, young, and middle-aged workers of today who will be tomorrow's elderly.[1]

At least for now, one thing is absolutely certain about the future: the baby boomers will get older. And that means that they will someday cross the age threshold for Social Security. Despite the baby boom's lack of confidence in Social Security's future, the program will still exist in 2016, short of some massive social or economic catastrophe on the order of nuclear war. The more relevant question is whether the baby boomers will get much in the way of benefits. Just how much will American society be able to afford?

The answer depends on two key demographic variables: the baby boom's own fertility and its longevity. The fertility rate says a great deal about how many workers will be around to pay the baby boom's benefits, while longevity says everything about how long the baby boomers be will around to draw the checks.

Consider the impact of fertility first. If fertility remains at its current level of 1.8 or so births per woman—or roughly 0.3 births *below* zero population growth—Social Security taxes will have to rise. If children are never born, they never grow up. If they never grow up, they never go to work. If they never go to work, they never pay Social Security taxes. Moreover, if they are never born, they will never have kids of their own, who also never grow up and pay taxes. Harvard University economist David Bloom estimates that as many as 20 percent of the younger baby boomers will remain childless, compared to under 10 percent in previous generations. Among women corporate managers, the number who remain childless may hit 30 percent. "In the past," Bloom says, "career women thought of themselves as mothers who had careers. Now they think of themselves as career women who happen to have children."

These fertility rates "should scare the hell" out of the baby boom, according to American Enterprise Institute researchers Ben Wattenberg and Karl Zinsmeister. Not only do larger populations produce larger economies, they produce a better national defense, providing a larger base of people, industry, infrastructure, and taxes to pay the bills.[2] The growing fear that the United States is being both de-populated by itself and out-populated by the Third World has even led to a new lobbying group called the Committee on Population and Economy to unite Americans who believe in the "injunction to be fruitful and multiply."[3]

However, there is virtually no way to force women to have babies if they don't want to. "The fertility will remain very, very low indefinitely," predicts demographer Charles Westoff. "I don't see any of the forces that operated historically to keep fertility high turning around. I don't see women giving up jobs and going back to the kitchen or nursery. I don't see any great return to religion and tradition. I don't see any reduction in the availability of contraception. I don't see any particularly available cheap housing." Whether the United States will decline to the 1.3 birth rate of West Germany is still not clear. But it is not likely to surge back toward the 3.7 birth rate of the baby boom either.

Yet, by itself, low fertility is not enough to destroy Social Security. Even at the current 1.8 birth rate there may be enough taxpayers to cover the baby boom's benefits. It will all depend on the total number and the mix of dependents. It is important to remember that the elderly are not America's only dependents. Children are dependents, too. As the fertility rate falls, so does the number of dependent children. Indeed, the number of dependent children per 100 adults has already fallen from 77 in 1965 to 51 today, and will continue to fall to 44 by 2030. That means there will be fewer maternity wards, fewer teachers, and fewer schools in the future, perhaps allowing a redistribution of resources to the retiring baby boom. Another way to note the change is to add the two dependency ratios together. Even with the baby boomers fully retired in 2030, America will still be far below the 1965 post-war high of 95 dependents per 100 adults. At its peak in 2030, the total dependency rate will only be 83 per 100.[4]

It is also important to remember that taking care of some dependents costs more in federal dollars than taking care of others. It may be that the elderly and children cost exactly the same amount, but the money comes from very different pockets. Whereas parents cover the costs of raising their children mostly from personal earnings, American society covers the cost of support for the aging mostly through payroll and income taxes—plus some payments by the elderly themselves. Thus, as the proportion of elderly rises as part of the overall dependency ratio—moving from 17 per 100 adults in 1965 to 40 in 2030—government expenditures may have to rise or benefits will have to fall.

Unfortunately for the baby boomers, to get from one pocket to the other, Congress will likely have to use tax increases as the redistributive instrument. The degree to which future workers will tolerate higher Social Security payroll taxes depends in large part upon their commitment to what Alan Pifer calls the "traditional unwritten compact under which each generation supports the one above it in exchange for support in its old age by the generation below it."[5]

Consider the impact of increasing longevity—what some demographers prefer to call declining mortality—on the baby boom's retirement as the second factor in how much American society will be able to afford to support the baby boom's retirement. If current experience is any guide, the baby boomers can expect to live at least two full decades past their retirement. According to Pifer, "the startling increases in longevity that we have experienced in recent decades have forced us to develop wholly new perspectives on the human life span. A person at the age of fifty, instead of being close to the end of life, may have nearly half his life still to live, and can look forward to the likelihood of at least a quarter of a century more of vigor and good health. In many cases, a newly retired worker can anticipate half as many years again in retirement as he spent in employment."[6]

Under current Census Bureau estimates, baby boomers who make it to retirement will have another 17 to 22 years of life left. That is an increase of almost six years since 1900. More important, more baby boomers will make it to retirement in the first place, in large part because they survived their very first year of life.

The results of this longevity are two-fold. First, as Peter Morrison argues, population aging will "concentrate older persons at the more extreme elderly ages, where chronic health conditions become more prevalent and activity limitations increase the need for long-term care. People over age 85 now make up only nine percent of all the elderly, but their numbers will grow to 13 percent by 2015 and peak at 24 percent by 2050. This increase in the extreme elderly population means that older persons will be more likely themselves to have a surviving parent; four- and five-generation families will become more common."

Second, not only will the baby boomers need Social Security and care longer, but they will have plenty of time on their hands. The question is what they will do with it. The potentials are enormous. The baby boomers may find the final quarter of life the most rewarding for, according to gerontologists Matilda White Riley and John Riley, Jr., longevity 1) prolongs the opportunity for accumulating social, psychological, and biological experiences; 2) maximizes a person's opportunities to complete or to change the role assignments of early and middle life—for example, to change jobs, marriage partners, or educational plans, and to take on new roles in the later years; 3) prolongs a person's relationships to others—to spouse, parents, offsprings, friends—whose lives are also extended; and 4) increases the potential structural complexity of a person's social networks—for example, of kinship, friendship, community—as all members survive longer.[7]

This longevity is a great gift. The baby boomers will have plenty of time to think back over their lives, to take stock of what they did or did not accomplish, to undo past mistakes, and to build completely new care-giving networks. But they will need support. The added years will hardly be rewarding if they are spent in poverty.

Moreover, the increasing longevity does not necessarily mean the baby boomers will be in good health through the end of life. Though Riley and Riley argue that "medicine is improving its command over the timing of death, enabling dying persons and their caretakers to contemplate the event, and to prepare for it," medicine has not yet solved the causes of disability.[8] As more and more people survive past 80, more and more will need care.

Ideally, people would be healthy to the end of their lives— "physically, emotionally, and intellectually vigorous," as medical researcher James Fries writes, "until shortly before its close, when, like the marvelous one-hoss-shay, everything comes apart at once and repair is impossible." According to Fries, medicine may be on its way to such a rectangular survival curve in which all babies survive past infancy, all teens make it to 20, and the elderly are healthy and lucid to the very end.[9]

For now and into the foreseeable future, however, most researchers believe that average health expectancy will remain fixed, that the added years of retirement do not equal added years of vigor or freedom from disability. One can hope that the baby boomers will be different, that their obsession with physical fitness will pay off, that their exposure to countless toxic chemicals will not hurt them. However, it is a safe bet that the baby boomers will need their children and grandchildren for more than Social Security taxes. They will probably also need them to care.

The question of how much America can afford for the baby boom's retirement also involves a number of economic variables. How much inflation will there be over the next thirty years? The answer affects the size of benefits. How much will wages grow?

The answer shapes the amount of revenue collected by taxes. How high will interest rates go? The answer says something about how much the Social Security Trust Fund will earn before the baby boomers start to retire. How much immigration will be permitted? The answer affects the number of potential taxpayers.

Because the future is mostly uncertain, it is best to think in terms of different possible futures, rather than any precise prediction. For example, Social Security actuaries use four different scenarios to portray the future: one impossibly optimistic, one optimistically possible, one right in the middle, and one highly pessimistic.[10] Lest that seem too much, population experts Jacob Siegel and Cynthia Taeuber use five: from an optimistic outlook featuring high fertility/high mortality/high immigration to a pessimistic model using low fertility/low mortality/low immigration, with a low-middle fertility/extremely low mortality/middle immigration in between. It may seem curious that increases in longevity are seen as pessimistic. That is the way of the Social Security world—anything that keeps people alive longer means they get benefits longer, and therefore falls into the pessimistic scenario.

These various scenarios suggest two basic questions for the baby boomers: which one is more likely? and, what kind of world would the baby boomers face if the worst case came true? It is always possible, for instance, that the most optimistic scenario will actually occur. If so, perhaps the baby boomers need not worry about what their children will think.

Unfortunately, the pessimistic scenario is more likely to occur than the optimistic. The baby boom's fertility is low, mortality is falling, and immigration is restricted. After examining the 1986 Social Security estimates, Morrison concluded as follows:

The so-called "pessimistic" demographic assumptions strike me as more than remotely possible. The total fertility rate has hovered around 1.8 since 1975. Perhaps it will rise to 2.0 [as the mid-range Social Security estimate projects]. Perhaps it will sink to 1.6 or below and stay there, as has already occurred in a number of Western European nations (Switzerland, the Netherlands, West Germany, and others). . . . As for future life expectancy, a number of recent studies raise disturbing doubts in my mind about the assumed future levels. They may understate future life expectancy in old age, lengthening considerably the period over which retirees would be eligible to receive Social Security benefits. Misjudging this possibility could prove to be an extremely expensive error.[11]

Moreover, even under the mid-range forecast—the optimistically[11] possible scenario—the Medicare program will enter a funding crisis in the late 1990s or early 2000s as medical costs continue climbing, and Social Security starts a downward turn in the mid 2020s as more and more baby boomers retire. The good news is that Social Security will accumulate a huge surplus in the next thirty years as the baby boomers pay far more in taxes than the current generation of retirees take out in benefits. The bad news is that the surplus will be exhausted long before the baby boomers pass on. And that assumes that Congress will allow the surpluses to even accumulate. There is a growing debate over whether Social Security should be allowed to build the surpluses, a debate in which the baby boomers are not involved. If Congress decides to cut Social Security taxes back to a more modest level, the baby boomers will be even more dependent than before on their children and grandchildren's willingness to pay.

What would the baby boom's retirement look like if the really bad scenarios came to pass? Not good at all. Under Siegel and Taeuber's two more pessimistic scenarios—low-middle fertility/ extremely low mortality/middle immigration, and low fertility/ extremely low morality/low immigration—"the nature of American society in 2050 would differ vastly from the way it is today. Very high proportions of elderly persons and very high dependency ratios, accompanying continuing low fertility and very low mortality, could have profound social and economic consequences."

Consider their list of possible impacts. "There could be serious dislocations in the economy as it tries to adjust to changing needs for jobs, goods, and services. Societal aging calls for increasingly larger financial contributions to the federal treasury by workers on behalf of older non-workers. Tax rates could become oppressively high and serve as a disincentive to work. The productive capacity of the economy could be diminished as the proportion of persons of working age shrinks and vast expenditures have to be made for the 'maintenance' of the burgeoning number of elderly persons."[12]

Should the baby boomers plan for the worst case? Probably not. The kind of society envisioned by highly pessimistic projections won't have much room for Social Security anyway. It would be a very different world. Furthermore, the kinds of draconian measures that would have to be taken now to anticipate such dislocations might actually make the pessimistic scenario come true.

Should the baby boomers plan for the optimistic case? Absolutely not. There is no evidence at all to support the rosy scenarios presented above. Fertility is low and looks likely to stay there. Mortality may not yet be extremely low, but it is still falling. Should the baby boomers plan for something in the middle? Again, probably not. Under the current Social Security middle scenario, fertility is still too high. The difference between a fertility rate of 2.0 and 1.8 births per woman may seem trivial, but it actually translates into several million children who will never be born.

Ultimately, the baby boomers should plan for a future somewhere between the worst-case and the mid-range—a future in which Social Security benefits are highly dependent on the willingness of the baby boomers' own children to shoulder the burden, but in which there is enough economic growth and past investment to make the burden bearable.

What matters most in such a scenario, of course, is their children's willingness to pay the bills. Social Security is a social insurance program and relies on the government's power to tax. Unlike a private pension, it does not need all the money on hand at one time. It is a "pay-as-you-go" program—one generation pays, another gets the benefits. Given the facts presented above, there is little doubt that the future will hold a sizable federal tax increase of one kind or another. According to John Palmer and Stephanie Gould, "In order to pay for everything that current policy entails (aside from any effort at reducing the existing federal budget deficit), federal tax revenues would have to rise by as much as 5 percent of GNP [Gross National Product]. . . . Roughly speaking, it would mean that the purchasing power of the average taxpayer's after-tax income would rise by 135 percent, rather than by 150 percent over the next fifty years."[13]

The willingness to be taxed depends on more than just the amount of taxes to be paid, of course. The public currently supports the Social Security tax because they see it as fairer than other federal taxes, and as a source of important support for the elderly as well as part of a social contract. Will the baby boomers have done anything to create a willingness to pay among future taxpayers? The answer is still unclear.

It is not that the baby boomers cannot win a fight over Social Security in 2016 if they have to. Not if 60 percent of the likely voters happen to be either in retirement or very close to it. But at what cost? Enforcing a steep Social Security tax increase is hardly the way to earn the compassion the baby boomers will need in 2030 or 2040. The baby boomers might be able to win the short-term battle, but not the long-term retirement war. The way to make sure the social compact remains intact for the future is to first honor the social compact between generations that exists today and to make sure the next three decades boast a record of stewardship and social investment that will make future generations thankful.

Ultimately, the 2016 election, indeed all of the elections in the early to mid-2000s, will be about the baby boom's leadership in the coming decades. As the baby boomers enter their final decades, they will confront a series of questions about their own contributions to society. Did they ever make a commitment to their own children? Did they give the kind of care they will expect to receive? Did they measure their leaders against performance on a stewardship agenda or on the basis of their short-term gratification? Did they create a world in which their children and grandchildren can flourish?

Thus, the baby boom's future involves a subtle social contract. Just as the baby boom's parents made a decision in the 1940s and 1950s to invest in their children—saving for their children's college, supporting federal aid to education, building the interstate highway system, etc.—the baby boomers must decide whether to invest in their children's future. If they maintain their current focus on themselves, it is not clear whether anyone will care much how they do in retirement. If they don't care much for others during their working lives, why should the baby boomers expect anything different from their children?

Notes

1. The Real Baby Boomers

1. Quoted in *U.S. News and World Report*, September 16, 1985, p. 60.
2. Population Reference Bureau, *America's Baby Boom Generation: The Fateful Bulge* (Washington, D.C.: Population Reference Bureau, April 1980), p. 4.
3. Louise Russell, *The Baby Boom Generation and the Economy* (Washington, D.C.: The Brookings Institution, 1982). p. 11.
4. See in particular Frank Bean, "The Baby Boom and Its Explanations," *The Sociological Quarterly* 24, no. 3 (Summer 1983), pp. 353–65.
5. Charles Westoff, "Some Speculations on the Future of Marriage and Fertility," *Family Planning Perspectives* 10, no. 2 (March/April 1978), p. 80.
6. Bean, "The Baby Boom and Its Explanations," p. 464.
7. See Richard Easterlin, *Birth and Fortune: The Impact of Numbers on Personal Welfare* (New York: Basic Books, 1980); for a shorter paper outlining Easterlin's theory, see Easterlin's "What Will 1984 Be Like? Socioeconomic Implications of Recent Twists in Age Structure," *Demography* 15, no. 4 (November, 1978), pp. 397–432.
8. Landon Jones, *Great Expectations: America & the Baby Boom Generation* (New York: Coward, McCann & Geoghean, 1980), p. 90.
9. Vern L. Bengston and Joseph A. Kuypers, "Generational Difference and the Developmental Stake," *Aging and Human Development* 2, no. 1 (Winter 1971), p. 253.
10. Poll reported in the *New York Times*, September 2, 1986.
11. Poll reported in the *Washington Post*, May 27, 1986.
12. American Council of Life Insurance, *The Baby Boom Generation* (Washington, D.C.: American Council of Life Insurance, 1983), p. 30; thanks to Jack

Katosh, former research director at ACLI for his assistance in explaining the methodology of the survey.

13. See Teresa Carson, "Fast Track Kids," *Business Week,* November 10, 1986, pp. 90–92, for the complete list.

14. Elaine M. Brody, Pauline T. Johnson, Marck C. Fulcomer, and Abigail M. Lang, "Women's Changing Roles and Help to Elderly Parents: Attitudes of Three Generations of Women," *Journal of Gerontology* 38, no. 5 (September 1983), pp. 597–607.

15. Lillian Troll and Vern Bengston, with the assistance of Dianne McFarland, "Generations in the Family," in W. Burr, R. Hill, Ivan Nye, and I. Reiss, eds., *Contemporary Theories about the Family* (New York: Free Press, 1979), p. 129.

16. Barry M. Staw, William W. Notz, and Thomas D. Cook, "Vulnerability to Draft and Attitudes Toward Troop Withdrawal from Indochina: Replication and Refinement," *Psychological Reports* 34, no. 2 (April 1974), pp. 407–17.

17. Karl Mannheim, "The Problem of Generations," in K. Mannheim, *Essays on the Sociology of Knowledge* (London: Routledge and Keagan, originally published in 1923, new edition in 1952).

18. M. Kent Jennings, "Residues of a Movement: The Aging of the American Protest Generation," *American Political Science Review* 81, no. 2 (June 1987), pp. 367–82.

19. Phillip Converse, *The Dynamics of Party Support* (Beverly Hills: Sage, 1976), p. 110.

20. Myra MacPherson, *Long Time Passing: Vietnam and the Haunted Generation* (New York: Doubleday and Company, Signet Edition, 1985), p. 35, 33.

21. Kingsley Davis, "Wives and Work: The Sex Role Revolution and Its Consequences," *Population and Development Review* 10, no. 3 (September 1984), p. 405.

22. Theodore Caplow and Howard Bahr, Bruce Chadwick, Reuben Hill, and Margaret Holmes Williamson, *Middletown Families: Fifty Years of Change and Continuity* (Minneapolis: University of Minnesota Press, 1982), p. 329.

23. Ibid., p. 288.

24. Davis, "Wives and Work," p. 406.

25. Ibid., p. 411.

26. Kingsley Davis and Pietronella van den Oever, "Demographic Foundations of New Sex Roles," *Population and Development Review* 8, no. 3 (September 1982), pp. 507–8.

2. Intergenerational War or Peace?

1. Frank Levy and Richard Michel, "The Economic Future of the Baby Boom," Report to the Joint Economic Committee of the U.S. Congress, December 5, 1985.

2. Finis Welch, "Effects of Cohort Size on Earnings: The Baby Boom Babies'

Financial Bust," *Journal of Political Economy* 87, no. 5 (October 1979), pp. S65–S97.

3. Easterlin, *Birth and Fortune*, p. 1.
4. James Q. Wilson and Richard Hernstein, *Crime and Human Nature* (New York: Simon and Schuster, 1985), p. 436.
5. Levy and Michel, "The Economic Future of the Baby Boom," p. 9.
6. In 1984 dollars.
7. Ibid., p. 17.
8. Ibid., pp. 17–18.
9. Quoted in the *Washington Post*, August 30, 1986, p. E1.
10. Russell, *The Baby Boom Generation*, p. 166.
11. Phillip Longman, "The Mortgaged Generation: Why the Young Can't Afford a House," *The Washington Monthly* 18, no. 3 (April 1986), p. 17; Longman makes a similar argument regarding Medicare, hinting that the elderly would be doing baby boomers a favor if they wouldn't linger on quite so long at the end of life.
12. Ibid., p. 19.
13. Ibid., p. 15.
14. Joseph C. Goulden, *The Best Years: 1945–1950* (New York: Atheneum, 1976), pp. 139–41.
15. Quoted in Eric Kingson, Barbara Hirshorn, and John Cornman, *The Ties That Bind: The Interdependence of Generations* (Washington: Seven Locks Press, 1986), p. 25.
16. B. Rollins and R. Galligan, "The Developing Child and Marital Satisfaction of Parents," in R.M. Lerner and G.B. Spanier, eds., *Child Influence on Marital and Family Interaction* (New York: Academic Press, 1978), p. 83.
17. Quoted in the *New York Times*, March 6, 1986.
18. These figures are drawn from a joint study by the Consumer Research Center of the Conference Board, a private research organization, and the U.S. Bureau of the Census, titled *A Marketer's Guide to Discretionary Income* (New York: The Conference Board, December 1985).
19. Samuel H. Preston, "Children and the Elderly: Divergent Paths for America's Dependents," *Demography* 21, no. 4 (November 1984), p. 436.
20. Ibid., p. 452.
21. Gary M. Nelson, "Tax Expenditures for the Elderly," *The Gerontologist* 21, no. 5 (October 1983), p. 474.
22. Edward Schneider and Jacob Brody, "Aging, Natural Death, and the Compression of Morbidity: Another View," *New England Journal of Medicine* 309, no. 14 (October 6, 1983), p. 854.
23. Anthony Pellechio and Gordon Goodfellow, "Individual Gains and Losses from Social Security Before and After the 1983 Amendments," *Cato Journal* 3, no. 2 (Fall 1983), p. 442.
24. Phillip Longman, "Justice Between Generations," *The Atlantic Monthly* (June 1985), p. 78.

25. I served on the AGE Advisory Board in 1985–86 in large part because I felt the organization was asking important questions about the long-term impacts of the budget deficit, not because I endorsed the call for intergenerational accounting.

26. Kingson, et al, *The Ties That Bind*, p. 161.

27. Center for Political Studies, 1984 National Election Study (Ann Arbor, Michigan: Inter-University Consortium for Political and Social Research, 1985), variables 302 and 425.

28. ABC News/*Money* Poll, April 1986.

29. Daniel Yankelovich, *New Rules: Searching for Self-Fulfillment in a World Turned Upside Down* (New York: Random House, 1981), p. 139.

30. American Council of Life Insurance, *The Baby Boom Generation*, p. 32.

31. These are all figures for those who said parents owed their children a "great deal of responsibility."

32. CBS News/*New York Times* Poll, January, 1986; thanks to Barbara Farrah for her assistance in breaking the data into age groups.

33. *The Business Week/*Harris Poll, July 2, 1984.

34. The Roper Poll, reported in *American Demographics* 9, no. 4 (April 1987), pp. 56, 61.

35. See "Investment Risk," Market Facts, Inc., undated report.

3. A Generation Divided

1. CBS News/*New York Times* Poll, January 1986.

2. Kermit Baker and H. James Brown, *Home Ownership and Housing Affordability in the United States: 1963–1984* (Cambridge, MA: Joint Center for Housing Studies, 1985), p. 14; more recent reports by the Joint Center confirm the continuing trend.

3. Quoted in *Psychology Today* (February 1986), p. 48; the original article is well worth reviewing, and was authored by Zajonc and Gregory B. Markus, "Birth Order and Intellectual Development," *Psychological Review* 82, no. 1 (Winter 1975), pp. 74–88.

4. See William Altus, "Birth Order and Its Sequelae," *Science* (January 1966), pp. 44–49, for a list of studies linking birth order to achievement, starting with a study of British "men of greatness" published in 1874!

5. Susie Orbach, *Hunger Strike: The Anorectic's Struggle as a Metaphor for Our Age* (New York: W. W. Norton, 1986), p. 40.

6. Elinor Waters and Vaughn Crandall, "Social Class and Observed Maternal Behavior from 1940 to 1960," *Child Development* 35, no. 4 (1964), pp. 1021–32.

7. James Gilbert, *A Cycle of Outrage: America's Reaction to the Juvenile Delinquent in the 1950s* (New York: Oxford University Press, 1986), p. 77.

8. Benjamin Spock, *The Common Sense Book of Baby and Child Care*, 3rd ed. (New York: Duell, Sloan and Pearce, 1957), pp. 1–2.

9. Sandra L. Hofferth, "Updating Children's Life Course," *Journal of Marriage and the Family* 47, no. 1 (February 1985), p. 99; figures are the proportion of

white children in families composed of two natural parents, both married once.

10. David Leavitt, "The New Lost Generation," *Esquire* (May 1985), p. 88.

11. Ethel Klein, "The Gender Gap: Different Issues, Different Answers," *The Brookings Review* 3, no. 1 (Winter 1985), p. 35.

12. See Ronald Rapport, "Sex Differences in Attitude Expression: A Generational Explanation," *Public Opinion Quarterly* p 46, no. 2 (Spring 1982), pp. 86–96, for a discussion of the 1972 data.

13. Klein, "The Gender Gap," p. 37; see also Klein, *Gender Politics* (Cambridge: Harvard University Press, 1984), for further background on her argument.

14. Klein, "The Gender Gap," p. 37.

15. Here, as elsewhere, the baby boom is defined as those respondents born from 1946 to 1964.

16. 1984 National Election Study, variables 313, 317, 320, 323, 330, 424, 443–44, and 553; party identification figures include those who said they were either strong or weak Democrats, but not those who said they were independents who leaned toward the Democratic Party.

17. Nikki Heidepriem, Carol Tucker Foreman, Celinda Lake, and Elizabeth Cox, *The Women's Vote Analysis* (Washington, D.C.: The Women's Vote Project, 1986), pp. iv–vii.

18. Celinda Lake, "Guns, Butter, and Equality: The Women's Vote in 1980" (Paper delivered at the Midwest Political Science Association Meetings, Chicago, April 28–May 1, 1982), p. 7.

19. Heidepriem et al., *The Women's Vote Analysis*, pp. 13–14.

20. Charles Brody, "Differences by Sex in Support for Nuclear Power," *Social Forces* 63, no. 3 (September 1984), p. 227.

21. Carol Gilligan, *In a Different Voice: Psychological Theory and Women's Development* (Cambridge: Harvard University Press, 1982), p. 42.

22. Orbach, *Hunger Strike*, p. 40.

23. See Catherin Favor, *Women in Transition: Career, Family, and Life Satisfaction in Three Cohorts* (New York: Praeger, 1984), for a study of changing channels for the expression of achievement motivation.

24. Klein, *Gender Politics*, p. 4.

25. Quoted in the *National Journal* (December 19, 1987), p. 3214.

26. 1984 National Election Study, variables cited in note 16, plus variable 437 on the difficulty of finding work.

27. 1984 National Election Study, variables 101, 106, 449–51, 453–54, 544–49, 707, 714, 720, 727, 733, 740, 746, 803, and 5829.

28. 1984 National Election Study, variables 402, 404, 449, 451, and 453.

29. David Gordon, "The New Class War," *Washington Post*, October 26, 1986, p. B1.

30. Robert Kuttner, "The Declining Middle," *The Atlantic Monthly* (July 1983), p. 60; see also Thomas Edsall, *The New Politics of Inequality* (New York: W. W. Norton, 1984).

31. Sar A. Levitan and Peter Carlson, "Middle-Class Shrinkage? Not to Worry

—It's Largely a Statistical Illusion," *Across the Board* 21, no. 10 (October 1984), pp. 55–59.

32. Barbara Ehrenreich, "Is the Middle Class Doomed?" *New York Times Magazine* (September 7, 1986), pp. 44, 50.

33. Ibid., p. 50.

34. Stanley Greenberg, "Plain Speaking: Democrats State Their Minds," *Public Opinion* 9, no. 4 (Summer 1986), p. 44.

35. M. Kent Jennings and Richard Niemi, *Generations and Politics: A Panel Study of Young Adults and Their Parents* (Princeton: Princeton University Press, 1981), pp. 368–69.

36. Jennings, "Residues of a Movement," p. 378.

37. MacPherson, *Long Time Passing*, p. 7.

38. Jennings and Niemi, *Generations and Politics*, pp. 378–79.

39. Testimony by John Wilson before the United States Senate Committee on Veterans Affairs, quoted in MacPherson, *Long Time Passing*, pp. 221–22.

40. Norman Hearst, Thomas Newman, and Stephen Hulley, "Delayed Effects of the Military Draft on Mortality," *New England Journal of Medicine* 314, no. 10 (March 6, 1986), p. 620; veterans were "65 percent and 49 percent more likely to die from suicide and motor-vehicle accidents, respectively [than non-veterans]."

41. Louis Harris and Associates, Inc., "Survey of Aging Veterans," Study conducted for the Veterans Administration, December 1983.

42. See Evans Witt, "What Republicans Have Learned About Women," *Public Opinion* 8, no. 6 (October/November 1985), pp. 49–52.

43. William Schneider, "The New Shape of American Politics," *The Atlantic Monthly* (January 1987), p. 44.

44. Barbara Farrah and Helmut Norpoth, "Trends in Partisan Realignment, 1976–1986: A Decade of Waiting" (Paper delivered at the Annual Meeting of the American Political Science Association, Washington, D.C., August 27–31, 1986), p. 9.

45. I.A. Lewis and William Schneider, "Black Voting, Bloc Voting, and the Democrats," *Public Opinion* 6, no. 6 (October/November 1983), p. 10.

46. Charles Franklin, "Party Identification and Party Realignment" (Paper delivered at the Annual Meeting of the American Political Science Association, Washington, D.C., August 27–31, 1986), p. 10; Franklin's work is central to the overall argument made later in this book regarding the baby boom's potential for performance-based voting. If blacks became more Democratic because of how Johnson performed in office in the mid 1960s, why can't other voters respond to performance in the 1990s and beyond?

4. A Generation United

1. Goulden, *The Best Years*, pp. 136–37.

2. Ronald Inglehart, "The Silent Revolution in Europe: Intergenerational

Change in Post-Industrial Societies," *American Political Science Review* 65, no. 4 (December 1971), pp. 991–1017.

3. Ronald Inglehart, "Post-Materialists in an Environment of Insecurity," *American Political Science Review* 75, no. 4 (December 1981), p. 895.

4. Ibid., p. 992.

5. Yankelovich, Skelly and White, "Summary Part A" (New York: The Yankelovich Monitor, 1985), p. 11.

6. Benjamin Ginsberg and Martin Shefter, "A Critical Realignment? The New Politics, the Reconstituted Right, and the Election of 1984," in M. Nelson, ed., *The Elections of 1984* (Washington, D.C.: Congressional Quarterly Press, 1985), p. 5.

7. Ibid., p. 6.

8. Quoted in "American Values: Change and Stability, A Conversation with Daniel Yankelovich," *Public Opinion* 6, no. 1 (December/January 1984), p. 6; see also Yankelovich, *New Rules.*

9. American Council of Life Insurance, *The Baby Boom Generation*, pp. 25–26.

10. 1984 National Election Study, variables 407, 454, and 447.

11. Cheryl Merser, *Grown-Ups: A Generation in Search of Adulthood* (New York: Putnam, 1987), p. 214.

12. Joseph Veroff, Elizabeth Douvan, and Richard Kulka, *The Inner American: A Self-Portrait from 1957–1976* (New York: Basic Books, 1981), pp. 17–18; see also the excellent analysis of individualism in Robert Bellah, Richard Madsen, William Sullivan, Ann Swidler, and Steven Tipton, *Habits of the Heart: Individualism and Commitment in American Life* (Berkeley: University of California Press, 1985).

13. Veroff et al., *The Inner American*, p. 18.

14. Ibid., p. 141.

15. Ibid., p. 19.

16. Jones, *Great Expectations*, p. 1.

17. See Paul Light, *Artful Work: The Politics of Social Security Reform* (New York: Random House, 1985), for an assessment of how the changing economic performance affected Social Security.

18. Christopher Lasch, *The Culture of Narcissism: American Life in an Age of Diminishing Expectations* (New York: W. W. Norton, 1979, Warner Edition, p. 137).

19. Jones, *Great Expectations*, p. 43.

20. Russell Belk and Richard Pollay, "Images of Ourselves: The Good Life in Twentieth Century Advertising," *Journal of Consumer Research* 11, no. 1 (March 1985), p. 894.

21. Ibid., pp. 894–95; the percentages sum to more than 100 percent because some ads contained multiple imagery.

22. David Tyack and Elizabeth Hansot, "Hard Times, Then and Now: Public Schools in the 1930s and 1980s," *Harvard Educational Review* 54, no. 1 (February 1984), p. 40; see also their book, *Public Schools in Hard Times: The Great Depression and Recent Years* (Cambridge: Harvard University Press, 1984).

23. Alan Binkley, "All Things to All People: Fifty Years of American Schools," essay review of *The Troubled Crusade*, by Diane Ravitch, and *Public Schools in Hard Times*, by David Tyack, Robert Lowe, and Elizabeth Hansot, *Harvard Educational Review* 54, no. 4 (November 1984), pp. 67–68.

24. Diane Ravitch, *The Troubled Crusade: American Education, 1945–1980* (New York: Basic Books, 1983), p. 15.

25. Ibid., p. 45.

26. Jones, *Great Expectations*, p. 60.

27. Tom Shales, "The Re Decade," *Esquire* (march 1986), p. 67.

28. Bellah et al., *Habits of the Heart*, p. 280.

29. Wilbur Schramm, Jack Lyle, and Edwin Parker, *Television in the Lives of Our Children* (Stanford, CA: Stanford University Press, 1961), p. 27.

30. Ibid., p. 58.

31. Ibid., p. 156.

32. Eugene Glynn, "Television and the American Character—A Psychiatrist Looks at Television," in W. Elliot, ed., *Television's Impact on American Culture* (East Lansing: Michigan State University Press, 1956), p. 181.

33. Quoted in James Baughman, *Television's Guardians* (Knoxville: University of Tennessee Press, 1985), p. 61.

34. Joseph Dominick and Millard Pearce, "Trends in Network Prime-Time Programming, 1953–74," *Journal of Communication* 26, no. 1 (Winter 1976), pp. 70–80. Thanks to Robert Katzmann for insights on this issue.

35. Ibid., p. 79.

36. Schramm et al., *Television in the Lives*, pp. 139–40.

37. Wilson and Hernstein, *Crime and Human Nature*, p. 352.

38. Ibid., p. 354.

39. Jones, *Great Expectations*, pp. 124–25.

40. David Clark and William Blankenburg, "Trends in Violent Content in Selected Mass Media," in G. Comstock and E. Rubinstein, eds., *Television and Social Behavior*, vol. 1 (Washington, D.C.: U.S. Government Printing Office, 1972), p. 197.

41. George Gerbner, "Violence in Television Drama: Trends and Symbolic Functions," in Comstock and Rubinstein, eds., *Television and Social Behavior*, p. 48.

42. Ibid., p. 61.

43. See Thomas Exter and Frederick Barber, "What Men and Women Think," *American Demographics* 9, no. 8 (August 1987), p. 35.

44. Jonathan Freedman, *Crowding and Behavior* (San Francisco: W.H. Freedman, 1975), p. 1.

45. Quoted in *Psychology Today* (January 1985), p. 50.

46. C.R. Creekmore, "Cities Won't Drive You Crazy," *Psychology Today* (January 1985), pp. 46–53.

47. Stanley Milgram, "The Experience of Living in Cities," *Science* (March 13, 1970), pp. 1461–68.

48. See Mark Baldassare, *Residential Crowding in Urban America* (Berkely: University of California Press, 1979), pp. 3–35, for a summary of the field.

49. Walter Gove, Michael Hughes, and Omer Galle, "Overcrowding in the Home: An Empirical Investigation of its Possible Pathological Consequences," *American Sociological Review* 44, no. 1 (February 1979), pp. 77–78.

50. Russell, *The Baby Boom Generation*, pp. 24–25.

51. Ibid., p. 30.

52. Ravitch, *The Troubled Crusade*, p. 327.

53. Gene Glass, Leonard Cahen, Mary Lee Smith, and Nikola Filby, *School Class Size: Research and Policy* (Beverly Hills: Sage, 1982).

54. Leonard Bird, "Big School, Small School: A Critical Examination of the Hypothesis," *Journal of Educational Psychology* 60, no. 3 (August 1969), pp. 253–60.

55. Allan M. Winkler, "A 40-Year History of Civil Defense," *Bulletin of the Atomic Scientists* 40, no. 6 (June/July 1984), p. 20.

56. Robert Musil, "Growing Up Nuclear," *Bulletin of the Atomic Scientists* 38, no. 1 (January 1982), p. 19.

57. Albert Furtwangler, "Growing Up Nuclear," *Bulletin of the Atomic Scientists* 37, no. 1 (January 1981), p. 44.

58. See Winkler, "A 40-Year History," pp. 16–22, for these and other examples of the early 1950s.

59. Paul Boyer, "From Activism to Apathy: America and the Nuclear Issue," *Bulletin of the Atomic Scientists* 40, no. 7 (August/September 1984), p. 15; see also Boyer's book *By the Bomb's Early Light* (New York: Pantheon, 1985).

60. William Carey, "Psychological Fallout," *Bulletin of the Atomic Scientists* 38, no. 1 (January 1982), pp. 20–24.

61. Sybille Escalona, "Children and the Threat of Nuclear War," in M. Schwebel, ed., *Behavioral Science and Human Survival* (Palo Alto, CA: Science and Behavioral Books, 1965), pp. 203–6.

62. Milton Schwebel, "Nuclear Cold War: Student Opinions and Professional Responsibility," in Schwebel, *Behavioral Science*, p. 217.

63. Boyer, "From Activism to Apathy," p. 18.

64. See William Beardslee and John Mack, "Adolescents and the Threat of Nuclear War: The Evolution of a Perspective," *The Yale Journal of Biology and Medicine* 56, no. 1 (January 1983), pp. 79–91, for a summary and critique of the literature through 1983.

65. J. Bachman, "American High School Seniors View the Military," figures quoted in Beardslee and Mack, "Adolescents and the Threat of Nuclear War," p. 99.

66. Beardslee and Mack, "Adolescents and the Threat of Nuclear War," pp. 81–82; see also Robert Coles, *The Moral Life of Children* (Boston: Atlantic Monthly Press, 1986), chapter 7, for his thoughts on children and the nuclear bomb.

67. See the CBS News/*New York Times* Poll, January 1, 1986, for an example; one third of the under-40 age group said arms control was the nation's most important problem, compared to 20 percent of the 40–64 age groups and 20 percent of the 65-and-over age group; the same pattern shows up in the Gallup Poll for January 25–28, 1985, and October 11–14, 1985.
68. Lawrence Langer, *The Age of Atrocity* (Boston: Beacon Press, 1978), p. 2.

5. A Portrait of Separation I

1. Veroff et al., *The Inner American*, p. 239.
2. Ibid., p. 192.
3. Arthur Norton and Jeanne Moorman, "Marriage and Divorce Patterns of U.S. Women in the 1980s" (Paper delivered at the Annual Meeting of the Population Association of America, April 3–5, 1986).
4. Cheryl Russell, "Sitting Ducks," *American Demographics* 8, no. 8 (August 1986), p. 7.
5. Veroff et al., *The Inner American*, p. 239.
6. Thomas Espenshade, *Investing in Children: New Estimates of Parental Expenditures* (Washington, D.C.: The Urban Institute, 1984), p. 6.
7. W. Pratt, W. Mosher, C. Bachrach, and M. Horn, "Understanding U.S. Fertility: Findings from the National Survey of Family Growth, Cycle III," *Population Bulletin* 39, no. 5 (1984).
8. Veroff et al., *The Inner American*, pp. 239–240.
9. Jane Mencken, "Age and Fertility: How Late Can You Wait?" *Demography* 22, no. 11 (November 1985), pp. 469–83.
10. Ibid., p. 480.
11. Michael Maccoby, *Why Work?* (New York: Simon & Schuster, 1988), p. 7.
12. Ibid.
13. Ibid., p. 119.
14. Robert Bellah et al., *Habits of the Heart*, p. 69.
15. Maccoby, *Why Work?*, p. 119.
16. Barbara Ehrenreich, "Strategies of Corporate Women," *The New Republic*, January 27, 1986, p. 29.
17. Yankelovich, Skelly, and White, "Management Summary: The Overall Social Climate" (New York: The Yankelovich Monitor, 1985), p. 3.
18. Ibid., p. 21.
19. Ibid., p. 22.
20. Quoted in Barbara Lippert, "A Man for '87—Joe Isuzu," *Washington Post*, December 28, 1986, p. D1.
21. Thomas Exter, "Looking for Brand Loyalty," *American Demographics* 8, no. 4 (April 1986), p. 33.
22. Schneider, "The New Shape of American Politics," p. 50.
23. Seymour Martin Lipset and William Schnedier, *The Confidence Gap* (New York: The Free Press, 1983), p. 3.

24. Patrick Caddell, "Crisis of Confidence: Trapped in a Downward Spiral," *Public Opinion* 2, no. 6 (October/November 1979), p. 58.

25. 1984 National Election Study, variables 544–45.

26. The percentages are for 18- to 29-year-olds, from the Harris Poll, November 1–4, 1985.

27. Most comparisons involve the under-30 versus the over-50 age groups, the Gallup Poll, March 17–20, 1985.

28. See Lipset and Schneider, *The Confidence Gap*, pp. 296–98.

29. Schneider, "The New Shape of American Politics," p. 52.

30. *Washington Post/*ABC News Poll, reported in the *Washington Post,* December 19, 1987.

31. Free Greenstein, "The Benevolent Leader: Children's Images of Political Authority," *American Political Science Review* 54, no. 4 (December 1960), p. 940.

32. Robert Hess and David Easton, "The Child's Changing Image of the President," *Public Opinion Quarterly* 24, no 1 (Winter 1960), pp. 632–44.

33. David Easton and Jack Dennis, "The Child's Acquisition of Regime Norms: Political Efficacy," *American Political Science Review* 61, no. 1 (March 1967), p. 38.

34. David Easton and Jack Dennis, "The Child's Image of Government," *Annals of the American Academy of Political and Social Science* 361, no. 3 (September 1965), pp. 40–57.

35. Daniel Yankelovich, "Farewell to 'President Knows Best,' " *Foreign Affairs* 57, no. 2 (Spring 1979), p. 670.

36. David O. Sears, "Political Socialization," in F. Greenstein and N. Polsby, eds., *The Handbook of Political Science,* vol. 2 (Reading, MA: Addison-Wesley, 1975), p. 105.

37. Roberta Sigel, "Image of a President: Some Insights into the Political Views of School Children," *American Political Science Review* 62, no. 2 (March 1968), pp. 216–26.

38. Ibid., p. 226.

39. Paul Sheatsley and Jacob Feldman, "The Assassination of President Kennedy," *Public Opinion Quarterly* 28, no. 4 (Summer 1964), p. 199.

40. See Karen Orren and Paul Peterson, "Presidential Assassination: A Case Study in the Dynamics of Political Socialization," *Journal of Politics* 29, no. 2 (May 1967), pp. 388–404.

41. Martha Wolfenstein, 'Death of a Parent and Death of a President: Children's Reactions to Two Kinds of Loss," in M. Wolfenstein and G. Liman, eds., *Children and the Death of a President* (Garden City, NY: Doubleday, 1965), p. 76.

42. Ibid., pp. 78–79.

43. Ibid., p. 87.

44. Robert Sigel, "An Exploration into Some Aspects of Political Socialization: School Children's Reactions to the Death of a President," in Wolfenstein and Kliman, *Children,* p. 34.

45. James Sundquist, *Dynamics of the Party System: Alignment and Realignment of Political Parties in the United States* (Washington, D.C.: The Brookings Institution, revised edition, 1983), pp. 400–401.

46. Juan Williams, *Eyes on the Prize: America's Civil Rights Years, 1954–1965* (New York: Viking, 1987), p. 287.

47. Doris Kearns, *Lyndon Johnson and the American Dream* (New York: Harper and Row, 1976), pp. 251–52.

48. Jerold Bachman and Elizabeth Van Duinen, *Youth Look at National Problems* (Ann Arbor, MI: Institute for Social Research, 1971).

49. Howard Tolley, Jr., *Children and War: Political Socialization to International Conflict* (New York: Teachers College Press, 1973), p. 71.

50. Christopher Arterton, "The Impact of Watergate on Children's Attitudes Toward Political Authority," *Political Science Quarterly* 89, no. 2 (June 1974), p. 286.

51. Bachman and Van Duinen, *Youth Look at National Problems*, p. 34.

52. 1984 National Election Study, variables 5902–5904.

53. Arthur Miller, "Is Confidence Rebounding?" *Public Opinion* 6, no. 4 (June/July 1983), pp. 16, 20.

54. These figures are from Miller, "Is Confidence Rebounding?" and the 1984 National Election Study, variables 548 and 5903.

55. William Schneider, "Political Pulse: A Victim of Law of Unintended Consequences," *National Journal*, (February 7, 1987), p. 325.

56. U.S. Congress, Office of Technology Assessment, *New Developments in Biotechnology—Background Paper: Public Perceptions of Biotechnology*, OTA-BP-BA-45, Washington, D.C., U.S. Government Printing Office, May 1987.

57. Ibid.

6. A Portrait of Separation II

1. *Times Mirror* Poll, November 1987.

2. Helmut Norpoth and Jerrold Rusk, "Partisan Dealignment in the American Electorate: Itemizing the Deductions since 1964," *American Political Science Review* 76, no. 3 (September 1982), pp. 535–36.

3. Paul R. Abramson, "Generational Change and the Decline of Party Identification in America: 1952–1974," *American Political Science Review* 70, no. 2 (June 1976), pp. 469–78.

4. Norpoth and Rusk, "Partisan Dealignment," p. 536.

5. Abramson, "Generational Change," p. 475.

6. M. Kent Jennings and Richard Niemi, "The Transmission of Political Values from Parent to Child," *American Political Science Review* 62, no. 1 (March 1968), p. 174.

7. Ibid., p. 183.

8. These data are drawn from Jennings and Niemi, *Generations and Politics*.

9. Gregory Markus, "The Political Environment and the Dynamics of Public

Attitudes: A Panel Study," *American Journal of Political Science* 23, no. 2 (May 1979), p. 354.

10. Farrah and Norpoth, "Trends in Partisan Realignment," p. 14.

11. See Morris Fiorina, *Retrospective Voting in American National Elections* (New Haven, CT: Yale University Press 1981).

12. See Stephen Craig and Michael Martinez, "Not a Dime's Worth of Difference: Perceived Choice and Partisanship in the United States, 1964–1984" (Paper delivered at the Annual Meeting of the American Political Science Association, August 27–31, 1986).

13. Veroff et al., *The Inner American*, p. 474.

14. 1984 National Election Study, variables 5311 and 5320.

15. Fiorina, *Retrospective Voting*, pp. 203–204.

16. David Broder, *The Party's Over* (New York: Harper and Row, 1972).

17. The negativity hypothesis was articulated by Stephen C. Craig in "The Decline of Partisanship in the United States," *Political Behavior* 7, no. 8 (1985), pp. 57–78.

18. The neutrality hypothesis was articulated by Martin Wattenberg, *The Decline of American Political Parties, 1952–1980,* (Cambridge: Harvard University Press, 1980); the quote is at pp. 126–27.

19. Samuel Popkin, John W. Gorman, Charles Phillips, and Jeffrey Smith, "Comment: What Have You Done for Me Lately? Toward an Investment Theory of Voting," *American Political Science Review* 70, no. 3 (September 1976), p. 804.

20. Ibid., pp. 799–800.

21. Charles Franklin and John Jackson, "The Dynamics of Party Identification," *American Political Science Review* 77, no. 4 (December 1983), p. 968.

22. Charles Franklin, "Issue Preferences, Socialization, and the Evolution of Party Identification," *American Journal of Political Science* 28, no. 3 (August 1984), pp. 473–74.

23. Linda Bennett and Stephen Bennett, "Questions about the Power of the Central Government, 1964–1984." (Paper delivered at the Annual Meeting of the American Political Science Association, Washington, D.C., August 27–31, 1986).

24. 1984 National Election Study, variables 401, 403, 405, 450, and 452.

25. Paul Sniderman and Richard Brody, "Coping: The Ethic of Self-Reliance," *American Journal of Political Science* 21, no. 3 (August 1977), p. 505.

26. Bellah et al., *Habits of the Heart*, p. 55.

27. Maccoby, *Why Work?*, p. 103.

28. 1984 National Election Study, variables 449 and 453.

29. The Gallup Poll, March 7–10, 1986.

30. American Council of Life Insurance, *The Baby Boom Generation*, p. 41.

31. 1984 National Election Study, variable 320.

32. Veroff et al., *The Inner American*, p. 59.

33. Yankelovich, Skelly and White, *A Fifty-Year Report Card on the Social Security*

System: The Attitudes of the American Public (New York: Yankelovich, Skelly and White, August 1985).

34. Veroff et al., *The Inner American*, p. 89.

35. Ibid., pp. 132–33.

36. Ibid., pp. 529, 531.

37. Ibid., pp. 530–31.

38. Paul Starr, "The Meaning of Privatization" (Washington, D.C.: Project on the Federal Social Role, Working Paper 6, 1985), p. 3.

39. American Council of Life Insurance, *The Baby Boom Generation*, p. 44.

40. Veroff et al., *The Inner American*, p. 135.

41. Albert O. Hirschman, *Shifting Involvements: Private Interest and Public Action* (Princeton: Princeton University Press, 1982), p. 10.

42. Ibid., p. 100.

43. Arnold Mitchell, *The Nine American Lifestyles: Who We Are and Where We Are Going* (New York: Warner Books, 1983), p. vii.

44. See Bickley Townsend, "Psychographic Glitter and Gold," *American Demographics* 7, no. 8 (November 1985), for an introduction to psychographics.

45. James Atlas, "Beyond Demographics," *The Atlantic Monthly* (October 1984), p. 56.

46. Greenberg, "Plain Speaking," p. 44.

47. Times Mirror Corporation, *The People, Press, & Politics* (New York: Times Mirror Corporation, 1987).

48. See Leo Bogart and Charles Lehman, "The Case of the 30-Second Commercial," *Journal of Advertising Research* 23, no. 2 (February/March 1983), for the complete statistics; it is important to note that the authors of the study were employed by the Newspaper Research Bureau, an organization which was inclined by nature to find fault with television advertising.

49. Kenneth R. Hey, "We Are Experiencing Network Difficulties," *American Demographics* 9, no. 10 (October 1987), p. 40.

50. Bogart and Lehman, "The Case of the 30-Second Commercial," p. 14.

51. Leo Bogart, "War of the Words: Advertising in the Year 2010," *Across the Board* 22, no. 1 (January 1985), pp. 21–28.

52. Carrie Heeter and Bradley Greenberg, "Profiling the Zappers," *Journal of Advertising Research* 25, no. 3 (April/May 1985), pp. 16–17.

53. Joseph A. Campana, vice president of marketing, quoted in "Chrysler Takes a Sharp Marketing Curve," *Marketing and Media Decisions* 20, no. 1 (January 1985), p. 38.

7. The Baby-Boom Agenda

1. Charles Reich, *The Greening of America: How the Youth Revolution Is Trying to Make America Livable* (New York: Random House, 1970), p. 226.

2. See William Maddox and Stuart Lilie, *Beyond Liberal and Conservative: Reassessing the Political Spectrum* (Washington, D.C.: Cato Institute, 1984).

3. See the exchange between Boaz, Atwater, and Caddell, in D. Boaz, ed., *Left*,

Right, and Baby Boom: America's New Politics (Washington, D.C.: Cato Institute, 1986).

4. Jenning, "Residues of a Movement," pp. 380–81.

5. Ibid., p. 381.

6. Barry Sussman, "Of Polls and Porcupines," *Washington Post*, August 5, 1985, p. B5.

7. James Sundquist, "Has America Lost Its Social Conscience—and How Will It Get It Back?" *Political Science Quarterly* 101, no. 3 (1986).

8. James Davis, "Conservative Weather in a Liberalizing Climate: Change in Selected NORC General Social Survey Items, 1972–78," *Social Forces* 58, no. 3 (June 1980), p. 1137.

9. These figures are from John Robinson, "The Ups and Downs and Ins and Outs of Ideology," *Public Opinion* 7, no. 2 (February/March 1984), pp. 12–15.

10. Davis, "Conservative Weather," p. 1149.

11. Thomas Exter and Frederick Barber, "The Age of Conservativism," *American Demographics* 8, no. 11 (November 1986), pp. 30–37; it is unclear why the article is so strongly titled when the data contained within supports a more tentative conclusion.

12. Sundquist, "Has America Lost Its Social Conscience?" p. 526.

13. 1984 National Election Study, variables 707, 714, 133, 727, and 746.

14. Ibid., variables 448 and 452.

15. Thomas Ferguson and Joel Rogers, "The Myth of America's Turn to the Right," *The Atlantic Monthly* (May 1986), p. 44.

16. Jennings, "Residues of a Movement," p. 378.

17. Schneider, "The New Shape of American Politics," p. 53.

18. 1984 National Election Study, variables 803, 5912, 5829, and 5849.

19. Ibid., variables 425, 439, and 442.

20. CBS News/*New York Times* Poll, January 1, 1986.

21. *Business Week*/Harris Poll, July 2, 1984.

22. *Los Angeles Times* Poll, July 9–14, 1986.

23. Helen Axel, *Corporations and Families: Changing Practices and Perspectives* (New York: The Conference Board, 1985), p. 51.

24. CBS News/*New York Times* Poll, January 1, 1986.

25. Gallup Poll, April 17–18, 1986.

26. *Los Angeles Times* Poll, November 1–7, 1985.

27. Yankelovich et al., *Fifty-Year Report Card.*

28. Ibid., p. 13.

29. Robert Binstock, "The Oldest Old: A Fresh Perspective or Compassionate Ageism Revisited," *Milbank Memorial Fund Quarterly* 63, no. 2 (Spring 1985), p. 445.

30. Yankelovich, Skelly, and White, "Trend Reference Book" (New York: Yankelovich Monitor, 1985), p. 26.

31. American Council of Life Insurance, *The Baby Boom Generation*, p. 30.

32. Gallup Poll, August 13–15 and October 11–14, 1985, and March 7–10, 1986.

33. Ferguson and Rogers, "The Myth of America's Turn," p. 53.

34. Erasmus Kloman, "Competing for a Future in Space," unpublished draft, February 1988, p. 37.
35. Sundquist, *Dynamics of the Party System,* pp. 441–42.
36. Ibid.
37. V.O. Key, Jr., with Milton C. Cummings, Jr., *The Responsible Electorate: Rationality in Presidential Voting* 1936–1960 (Cambridge: Harvard University Press, 1966), pp. 1–8.

8. The Golden Days

1. Peter Marin, "The New Narcissism," *Harper's,* October 1975, pp. 45–56.
2. Tom Wolfe, "The 'Me' Decade and the Third Great Awakening," *New York,* August 23, 1976.
3. Veroff et al., *The Inner American,* p. 16.
4. Paul Wachtel, "The Politics of Narcissism," *The Nation,* January 3, 1981, pp. 13–15.
5. Bellah et al., *Habits of the Heart,* p. 76.
6. Arch Patton, "The Coming Promotion Slowdown," *Harvard Business Review* 59, no. 2 (March/April 1981), p. 46.
7. Anthony Carnevale, "Retaining and Retraining Older Employees" (Paper delivered at the Travelers Symposium on America's Aging Workforce, February 26–28, 1986).
8. Janet Near, "The Career Plateau: Causes and Effects," *Business Horizons* 23, no. 10 (October 1980), pp. 53–57.
9. See Douglas Hall and Lynn Isabella, "Downward Movement and Career Development," *Organizational Dynamics* 14, no. 1 (January 1985), pp. 5–23.
10. James Wolf, "Career Plateauing in the Public Service: Baby Boom and Employment Bust," *Public Administration Review* 43, no. 2 (March/April 1983), p. 62.
11. Pat Choate and Susan Walter, *America in Ruins: The Decaying Infrastructure* (Durham, NC: Duke University Press, 1981), p. 1.
12. National Infrastructure Advisory Committee to the Joint Economic Committee of Congress, *Hard Choices: A Summary Report of the National Infrastructure Study* (Washington, D.C.: National Infrastructure Advisory Committee, February 1984).
13. Donald Bartlett and James Steele, *Forevermore: Nuclear Waste in America* (New York: W.W. Norton, 1985), p. 21.
14. Alan Otten, "The Oldest Old: Ever More Americans Live into 80s and 90s, Causing Big Problems," *The Wall Street Journal,* July 3, 1984, p. 1.
15. Menken, "Age and Fertility."
16. Robyn Stone, Gail Cafferata, and Judith Sangl, "Caregivers of the Frail Elderly: A National Profile," National Center for Health Services Research, U.S. Department of Health and Human Services (Washington, D.C.: Government Printing Office, 1986), pp. 11–12.

17. Pamela Doty, "Family Care of the Elderly: The Role of Public Policy," *Milbank Memorial Fund Quarterly* 64, no. 1 (Winter, 1986), pp. 48–49.

18. Harold Richman and Matthew Stagner, "Children in an Aging Society: Treasured Resource or Forgotten Minority?" *Daedelus* 115, no. 1 (Winter 1986), p. 171.

19. Alan Pifer, "The Public Policy Response to Population Aging," *Daedelus* 115, no. 1 (Winter 1986), p. 377.

20. Ibid., p. 379.

9. 2016

1. Kingson et al., *The Ties That Bind*, p. 143.

2. See Ben Wattenberg and Karl Zinsmeister, "The Birth Dearth: The Geopolitical Consequences," *Public Opinion* 8, no. 1 (December/January 1986), pp. 6–13.

3. See Ann Cooper, "Population Promoter," *National Journal* (February 22, 1986), p. 447.

4. The figures are from Jacob S. Siegel and Cynthia M. Taeuber, "Demographic Dimensions of an Aging Population," in A. Pifer and L. Bronte, eds., *Our Aging Society* (New York: W. W. Norton, 1986).

5. Pifer, "The Public Policy Response to Population Aging," p. 379.

6. Ibid, p. 383.

7. Matilda White Riley and John W. Riley, Jr., "Longevity and Social Structure: The Added Years," *Daedelus* 115, no. 1 (Winter 1986), p. 53.

8. Ibid., p. 75.

9. James Fries, "Aging, Natural Death, and the Compression of Morbidity," *The New England Journal of Medicine* 303, no. 3 (July 17, 1980), p. 135.

10. The actuaries struggle against an uncertain world in drawing scenarios of the future; they are individuals of integrity and deserve credit for their efforts to anticipate crisis; see my review of the increasing politics of the assumption-building process in "Social Security and the Politics of Assumptions," *Public Administration Review* 45, no. 3 (May/June 1985), pp. 363–71, for an examination of some of the problems in forecasting the future. See also the exchange between former Social Security chief actuary Robert Meyers and myself for needed corrections and clarifications in *Public Administration Review* 46, no. 3 (May/June 1986), pp. 256–66, and a final postscript by another former chief actuary, Robert Bartlett in *Public Administration Review* 46, no. 6 (October/November 1986), pp. 682–83. Meyers was correct to defend the integrity of the Social Security actuaries. However, I remain convinced that the forecasting process for Social Security—indeed for many federal, state and local programs—has been politicized. Those who control the forecasts of the future wield great political power, for they can make problems appear and disappear at will with the flick of a computer key.

11. Peter A. Morrison, "Changing Family Structure: Who Cares For America's Dependents?" Document No. N-2518-NICHD (December 1986), The Rand Corporation, Santa Monica, CA, pp. 14-15.
12. Siegel and Taeuber, "Demographic Perspectives on the Long-Lived Society," in Pifer and Bronte, eds., *Our Aging Society*, pp. 113–14.
13. John Palmer and Stephanie Gould, "The Economic Consequences of an Aging Society," *Daedelus* 115, no 1 (Winter 1986), p. 314.

A Note on the Data

MUCH OF THIS BOOK is based on public opinion surveys. Because surveys use very small numbers of people—usually around 1,500—to represent the views of millions, the average survey carries a sampling error of approximately three percent one way or the other on any given question. Because of sampling and other potential measurement errors, surveys are best viewed as rough measures of what people think, not as absolute measures of opinion. They can show the baby boom's movement over time and comparisons with other age groups.

Moreover, most surveys do not break the baby boomers away from other age groups as cleanly as one might wish. Survey researchers use a standard set of age breakdowns to divide most survey data—for example, 18–24, 25–34, 35–44, 45–54, 55–64, and 65–plus. Unfortunately, in 1984, the baby boomers were between 20 and 39. Short of revising hundreds of surveys at a prohibitive cost, one can only use such data to give general approximations of where the baby boomers fall compared to older Americans.

Caveats given, surveys are a valuable tool for tracking public opinion. When surveys are done exceptionally well, as at the

University of Michigan's Institute for Social Research, the Gallup Poll, the Roper Poll, the Harris Poll, the *New York Times, Washington Post, Wall Street Journal,* ABC, CBS, NBC, and so on, they can yield a harvest of data on what Americans think.

Index

Iacoca, Lee, 158, 209
ideologies of baby boomers,
224–28
income inequality in America,
95–96
incomes of baby boomers, 20–21
individualism of baby boomers,
131
inflation, 46–47
infrastructure problems, 261–62
Inglehart, Ronald, 112–13
The Inner-American (book), 149,
199, 201
Inner-Directed people, 206,
207–8
intergenerational equity, 55–56
attitudes toward, 71, 73
economic power of the elderly,
59–61
historical perspective on, 58–59
homeownership and, 55–57
national debt crisis and, 62
political activities regarding,
67–68
as short-term political issue,
268–69
Social Security system and,
63–67
interstate highway system,
261–62
introspectiveness of baby
boomers, 200–204, 253–57
Iran-contra scandal, 176
Isabella, Lynn, 259

Jackson, Jesse, 99
Jackson, John, 193
Jennings, M. Kent, 37, 100, 101,
186, 227
job plateaus problem, 257–61
Johnson, Haynes, 72
Johnson, Lyndon B., 169–70,
171, 185
Jones, Landon, 27, 54, 70, 80,
118, 119, 123, 129

Kearns, Doris, 171
Keaton, Diane, 42
Kemp, Jack, 226
Kennedy, Edward, 94, 210
Kennedy, Jacqueline, 165
Kennedy, John F., 43, 137, 138,
209, 210
assassination of, 165–69
Kennedy, Robert, 29, 144
Key, V. O., 251
Khrushchev, Nikita, 137
Kim, Peter, 61, 234
Kimmich, Madeleine, 268
King, Martin Luther, Jr., 209,
210
Kingson, Eric, 68–69, 273–74
kitchens in 1950s, 111
Klein, Ethel, 84, 86, 90–91
Kloman, Erasmus, 247–48
Kubrick, Stanley, 139
Kulka, Richard, 116, 117–18,
147, 148, 149, 150, 189, 199,
201, 203, 254–55
Kuttner, Robert, 48–49, 96
Kutza, Elizabeth, 264

Ladd, Everett Carll, 191
Lake, Celinda, 88, 91
Lamm, Richard, 61
Langer, Lawrence, 142–43
Lasch, Christopher, 119, 224
learning abilities of baby
boomers, 80
Leavitt, David, 83–84
Leisure Technology, Inc., 61
Levitan, Sar, 97
Levy, Frank, 48, 51, 52, 74
Lewis, I. A., 107
liar commercials, 157
liberalism among baby boomers,
224, 230–37
libertarianism among baby
boomers, 225–26
Libya, U.S. bombing of (1986),